*The* **Guardian**

# Guide to the
# internet

For George McClellan 1929–1988

# *The* Guardian

# Guide to the internet

## by Jim McClellan

FOURTH ESTATE • London

First published in Great Britain in 1999 by
Fourth Estate Limited
6 Salem Road
London W2 4BU

A catalogue record for this book is available from the British Library.

ISBN 1-84115-236-6

Designed and typeset by Blackjacks, London.

Printed in Great Britain by
Cox & Wyman Ltd, Reading, Berkshire.

# CONTENTS

●●●●●●●●●●●●●●●●●●●●●●●●●●●●●●●●

## SECTION 3
## GETTING TO GRIPS WITH THE NET

## Acknowledgements

Thanks to Ian Katz for getting me started on these books. I would never have managed to finish this particular effort without the advice, support and patience of my editor Mathew Clayton. Thanks to my agent Cat Ledger for sorting things out as usual. Thanks also to Apple for the loan of the iMac and to Gateway 2000 for the loan of a PC.

In places, I re-worked bits of the journalism I've cranked out over the years. So thanks to the numerous editors who have (a) made my copy much better with their various suggestions and (b) put up with my hopeless deadline surfing. Thanks in particular to Matthew Collin, John Godfrey, Sheryl Garratt, Charles Gant, Vic Keegan, Jack Schofield and Simon Waldman.

Over the years, various people have pointed me in the right direction – thanks and big ups to Ekow Eshun, Peter Howarth, Amy Raphael, Tom Hodgkinson, Lindsay Baker, Joe McGee, Simon Rogers, Hari Kunzru, Jim Flint, Avril Mair, Dylan Jones, Nick Logan, Terry Jones, Bill O'Neill, Dave Winder, Ivan Pope, Dave Green, Kodwo Eshun, Steve Beard and Steve Bode – apologies if I've forgotten anyone.

Big shouts to friends and family who were roped into long conversations about this book – George and Janet, Graham and Moira, Sheryl and Mark, Nicki and Russell, Andy and Sonia, John and Corinne, Pat and Geoff and my brothers Jon and Rob and my mum Helen. I owe a serious debt of gratitude to Phill, Graham, Jonathan and Lydia for coming to my aid one weekend. Thanks also to Peter Sutherby for his constant support and hospitality. Finally, thanks to my kids, Lee and Cameron for putting up with me while I did this and, most of all, thanks once again to Kim – I definitely couldn't have done this one without you.

# INTRODUCTION

• • • • • • • • • • • • • • • • • • • • • • • • • • •

The aim of this book is to help you make use of the net. The idea is to get you online and reaping the benefit as quickly and easily as possible. At the same time, I suspect that you'll want to know a little bit more about the net than just the straight 'how to' advice. Most net guides effect what you might call a 'dummy-ing' down of their readers. You agree to identify yourself as an 'Idiot' and then are led very slowly, step by step, through the confusing world of the net and the software you need to use it.

I agree with the need for clear and simple instructions on how to do things but I don't think people are dumb just because they don't know how to work a web browser. And I don't think that you need to switch off the bulk of your brain when you sit down to read a net manual. Some cultural/historical information can make it easier to grasp certain aspects of the net. My hope is that, by the end of this book, as well as knowing how to use certain programs, you'll have accumulated a measure of what we could call net literacy, or perhaps 'net savvy', a more general knowledge of the online world which ought to help your dealings there run more smoothly.

< 13 >

Unlike most net manuals, this guide is not written from an American perspective. Obviously, part of the hype about the net is that it's a global thing, but geography still matters. Many American manuals are written for people who pay a flat rate for their local telephone calls and hence can, after a certain point, afford to spend the whole day online without too much worry. Lots of people here are campaigning for that kind of flat rate pricing in the UK. It may happen one day. But for the moment, for the most part, we still pay through the nose for our local calls. Consequently people here use the internet very differently. They go online quickly, grab the stuff they need, log off and read it offline. This guide will take that sort of thing into account. It will recognise the cultural and technical differences between UK and US net culture and will look at sites of UK interest as well as some of the impressive American efforts.

Unlike many other net manuals, this one won't be mindlessly gung-ho about the net. I am pretty enthusiastic about the online world. But there are plenty of things online I don't find that convincing as yet (internet telephony – making long distance telephone calls over the net) and plenty of activities I don't personally devote that much time to (online chat, for example). It may be that the stuff that I don't like will be the stuff that particularly draws you in. That is one of the good points about the net. Whatever some techno-gurus might suggest, getting online is not like signing up for some monolithic crusade. You don't have to buy into the whole program. You can pick and choose.

This book is aimed primarily at absolute beginners. My aim is to help you progress – or should that be regress – from upstanding healthy

< 14 >

examples of Homo Erectus to stoop-shouldered, screen-eyed, mouse-clutching versions of that lesser known but quickly growing species – Homo Connectus. That said, I hope there will be useful information in here even for those who are comfortably navigating the web.

**Section 1 – Before You Get Connected** gives you some general advice about getting your bearings online. It also takes apart some of the things people have said about the net over the years. If you're in a hurry to get online, you could skip the latter and save it for later.

**Section 2 – Getting Connected** gives advice on the hardware and software you need, getting an internet connection and connecting for the first time.

If you already have a computer, modem and net connection, go straight to **Section 3 – Getting to Grips with the Net**, which offers detailed advice on how to get the most of out the main net activities:

## The World Wide Web

The web is usually the thing people immediately 'get' when they go online. The multimedia part of the net, the web is made up of sites (or pages) put up by everyone from multinational media corporations to charities, pressure groups and, yes, ordinary people like you. On the web, you can read online magazines which feature text and graphics, or you can watch videos, download music, buy books and CDs, book flights and holidays, even play games. You can move between sites by clicking

< 15 >

on hypertext links, wandering far from the pages you originally accessed. This section will tell you how to find your way round the web and how to work with your browser (the software program you use to move around the web) so that your time online is more productive.

## Searching the Web

One of the hardest things online is finding your way to the information you're interested in. That's where you need search sites – online resources which keep track of what's out there and point you in the right direction, usually. This section will tell you how to use search engines, online directories and other search sites. There are also a few tips about using the web as a general research tool.

## Electronic Mail

Email is one of the things people immediately latch on to when they first get online. The attractions of being able to communicate with friends around the world for the cost of a local telephone call are pretty obvious. This section tells you how to send and receive email, looks at web-based mail and mailing lists and concludes with some advice on how to get the best out of email without it ruining your life.

## Usenet newsgroups

Like the web, Usenet is just one part of the net proper, a collection of thousands of 'newsgroups', online forums where people discuss a variety of subjects. You post your thoughts on something, someone else reads

< 16 >

them and posts a response and gradually over time you build up a kind of conversation (or 'thread', as the online jargon has it). This section will tell you how to select and use the newsgroups you're interested in, how to cope with the huge amount of information that appears there everyday and how to survive in one of the wilder, more raucous parts of the net.

## Downloading files and software

The internet is packed with interesting files and useful bits of software. Using your web browser (or FTP software – FTP is a bit of compuspeak which stands for File Transfer Protocol), you can find files and software you're interested in and download them on to your own computer. You can also upload files and software of your own. This section will give you the basics on downloading and offer some general advice on keeping track of material you get from the net.

## Online chat

For many people, chat is one of the most compelling parts of the net. You can talk, or rather type, to people in real time online, in special chat rooms. Yes, people often talk dirty, creating private rooms where they can indulge in collaborative one-handed typing. But they also talk about much else, swapping news and ideas. This section will point you to the best places to chat online, tell you the software you need and offer advice on how not to let online chat take over your life (or your telephone bill).

I've put the web and email at the beginning of this section because they seem to be the most popular online activities. However, it may be

< 17 >

that chat will be the thing for you. In other words, feel free to read this section in any order. Strictly speaking, it might even be sensible to start off with the section on downloading software online. It's up to you. In this section I've concentrated on giving detailed advice about the latest versions of the two most popular browsers – version 4.6 of Netscape Navigator (which is part of the Communicator package of net tools) and version 5.0 of Microsoft's Internet Explorer. If you sign up with one of the major internet service providers, you'll probably get one of these (or be offered a choice if you're lucky). By the time you read this, version 5 of Navigator may have been released, in which case you might get that. But if you're using something older or newer, don't worry. Browsers don't change that much and you should still be able to follow the advice.

You can use your browser to handle email and newsgroups and to download files, so I've also concentrated on these in the relevant chapters. However, I've also included pointers to alternative standalone programs you could use instead. So don't feel you have to use the browser for everything. This section goes into things in a fair amount of detail. The idea is to help you to minimise hassles when you're just getting started. The later sections are less detailed – the assumption being that by then you will be more comfortable with the net.

**Section 4 – Taking the Web to the Next Level** deals with web multimedia and shopping on the web. It also includes a list of 100 indispensable website.

< 18 >

**Section 5 – Looking After Yourself Online** offers advice on protecting yourself and your kids online. It covers privacy, censorship, junk email, legal issues and features some general survival tips.

**Section 6 – Doing It Yourself** is for those of you who decide to get really serious about the net. There's advice on starting mailing lists and newsgroups and putting up your own web page. Finally, at the back of the book you'll find information about UK internet service providers.

Throughout the book you will see various captions boxed-off from the main text, featuring useful bits of information – look out for:

## Read About It Online

The net is often the best place to find out about the net, especially the latest developments. So every now and then, I'll include details of sites on the net where you can find more information on a particular topic. If you're just starting out, these might look a bit confusing at first, but once you're familiar with the web you can always come back and check them out.

## Jargon File

Brave new worlds require brave new words. The net and its related technologies come with all manner of slanguage, jargon and puzzling technical terminology. Some of it is amusing, some of it is irritating. Check these boxes to find out what it all means.

< 19 >

## Tips

These feature bits of advice I've found useful, tricks of the trade, rules of thumb and all that. Perhaps we should kick off with a sort of all-purpose tip, which is: if you feel a little nervous about getting online, don't worry. Self-induced technophobia is often the biggest problem people face when dealing with computers. It's true that connecting to the net is still a lot harder than it should be but it's nowhere near as hard as it used to be. If you know how to use a PC running Windows or an Apple Mac, you will crack the net.

As proof, I cite myself. I've never studied computers or computer science. I've got a vague idea how they work, but no deep technical knowledge. In fact, I got interested in computer culture and the net via literature. In 1986, I read *Neuromancer*, the novel in which SF writer William Gibson first developed his vision of cyberspace, and became interested in computer networks. I read more about the net, made some geeky friends and shoulder-surfed a bit in the early nineties, eventually getting online properly at the start of 1994.

This may not be what you want to hear from the author of a net guide on which you've spent good money. But the point is, if I managed to figure out the net, so can you. I did it in part by flicking through the odd manual, although there weren't that many when I started and most read as if they were compiled by malfunctioning artificial intelligence programs. But mostly I just tried things out, messed about with software, clicked buttons and pulled down menus to see what would happen.

< 20 >

With some net pursuits, you do need to learn some technical text commands (some chat programs for example), but most online software is pretty intuitive. Tinkering is the way to learn. People who aren't familiar with computers are often worried that they will 'break' them if they press the wrong button. Once again, it's true that computers are not as robust and reliable as they should be, but they're not that feeble. And there are always support lines and guarantees to fall back on. So get stuck in and you'll soon be hooked.

Once you find your telephone bills going through the roof and your social life in ruins, if you're looking for someone to blame, feel free to drop me a line – **jim.mcclellan@guardian.co.uk**. Though I've done my best, there are bound to be a few errors in the book you're about to read – if only because things are constantly changing on the net. Companies merge or go out of business. New bits of software, new ideas or new sites appear and take the net by storm. At a more basic level, web sites just go offline or change addresses.

So if you find something that's wrong – an address that doesn't seem to work, for example – just drop me a line and I'll do my best to point you in the right direction. Mistakes aside, if you just feel like telling me what you think of the book, it would be great to hear from you. Lots of people did just that after reading the first edition of this book and their thoughts and ideas were a great help when it came to doing this update. Thanks to everyone who wrote in. I did my best to reply to everything, but the mail did pile up. If I failed to get back to you, please accept my apologies here. I'll try to do better this time round.

< 21 >

Finally if you get the chance, drop in at this book's website **http://www. guardianunlimited.co.uk**. ▲

< 22 >

# 1 BEFORE YOU GET CONNECTED

• • • • • • • • • • • • • • • • • • • • • • • • • • • • • • • • •

## Get your online bearings

Some net guides and manuals start with lengthy histories of the development of the internet and even detailed technical descriptions of how it all works. This can be pretty interesting. Really. And it can help you use the net in a more productive way. However, I'm not sure it's the best idea in the world to force beginners to bone up on the history of US Cold War research institutions and the intricacies of packet-switching before they've even had a chance to look around online.

To get started online, to orientate yourself on the net, you only need to know a few basics. You don't need a detailed knowledge of the net, but it helps to have some sort of mental picture of it. One way of thinking of the internet is as a network of networks. This gets across the fact that the net isn't one coherent, unified entity, it's a multiplicity. It's always good to remember this when people try to boil the net's variety down into one thing, and tell you that, for example, the net is naturally libertarian in its political outlook.

< 23 >

## Jargon file – Packet-Switching

When messages are sent via a network, they are broken up into individual packets of bits that are then sent separately. Packets contain details of the place they came from, and the address they're going to, amongst other things. ▲

At a very basic level, a computer network is a collection of computers – say in an office – connected in such a way that they can communicate with each other and share information. The net takes this to a global scale. It's a kind of global network that has emerged as more and more local and national networks hook up with each other. To connect to and communicate with each other, computers rely on shared standard languages, or, to use the technical term, protocols.

When you're online, you'll encounter different sorts of protocol. For example, there's FTP, aka File Transfer Protocol, which allows you to upload or download files to and from the net. The World Wide Web, the multimedia part of the net, relies on something called HTTP – Hyper Text Transfer Protocol. The basic protocol which enables the net to work by letting computers round the world communicate with each other is TCP/IP – aka Transmission Control Protocol/Internet Protocol. All these letters may look like the leftovers from a game of Scrabble, but after a while you will get used to them and will use them without thinking.

Another way to think about the net is as a many-to-many network. This is shorthand for the fact that, when online, everyone can send as

< 24 >

## Jargon file – Top Down, Bottom Up

Two related terms you hear a lot online. The former refers to
authoritarian/hierarchical structures in which order (and other things)
are imposed by the people at the top. The latter refers to more open
grass-roots structures in which order (and other things) emerge from
the actions of ordinary users and trickle up. ▲

well as receive messages. In contrast, broadcast TV is often characterised
as a one-to-many network – meaning one node or station sends messages
and all the rest of us can do is consume those messages. Some businesses
are attempting to bring the top-down, one-to-many model of TV to the
net (the theory being that this will bring ordinary users online). But never
forget – the net lets you send messages, publish your own ideas, and
upload your own videos.

### Net addresses

So how do you and your information know where you are and where
you're going on this wonderfully various many-to-many network of
networks? Thankfully, the net, like the real world, has a system of
addresses. All computers that are connected to the internet have a unique
IP (as in Internet Protocol) address. This is a collection of four sets of
numbers, separated by full stops/periods (e.g. 123.45.56.891).
Incidentally, there are plans afoot to extend and expand this system, since
there are worries that shortly the net will run out of available addresses.

< 25 >

Obviously large groups of numbers are not the easiest things to remember (or type). So, as well as the IP addresses there is also something called the Domain Name System which translates all those numbers into words. Along with an IP address, each computer connected to the net has its own unique domain name. These may look just as forbidding as IP numbers at first but you will soon get used to them.

Take the address for the Guardian's web site –
**http://www.guardianunlimited.co.uk.**

The first part – **http://** – refers to the protocol used to access this address, in this case Hyper Text Transfer Protocol

The second part – **www** – indicates which part of the net we're talking about – in this case, the World Wide Web.

The third part – **.guardianunlimited** – is the name of the institution or people running the site/the computer it's stored on.

The fourth part of the address – **.co** – is known as a 'top level domain'. It tells you what sort of institution is behind the site. So **.co** indicates that it's a commercial/business site. A variety of other identifiers could appear here:

**.ac**    indicates a college, university or other sort of academic establishment

< 26 >

**.edu**   also indicates academic establishments, used mainly in the States
**.gov**   a government-run site
**.mil**   a site run by the military
**.org**   used by non-profit organisations
**.com**   the non-country specific version of **.co**, this is used by companies
that want to look like global businesses
**.net**   used mainly by internet service providers

There are plans to add a variety of new top-level domains in the near future – things like **.firm** and **.store** – but at the time of writing, these still haven't been finalised.

---

**Read about it online – .tv nation**

Last year, it was reported that the Polynesian island Tuvalu was hoping (via a deal with a Canadian marketing company) to make millions of dollars from selling the rights to use its **.tv** domain to TV stations around the world. Sadly, it seems that the island's nine thousand inhabitants will not become domain millionaires – though they will make some money. Other desirable domains include **.to** – short for Tonga, which means you can have addresses like **http://www.ready.to/rock**. For an interesting story from the webzine Salon about these 'domain names from paradise', go to **http://www.salon.com/tech/feature/1999/05/17/tonga/index.html**. ▲

---

< 27 >

Finally the fifth part of the address – **.uk** – tells you in which country the site is located. These are generally pretty easy to figure out – **.jp** is Japan, **.de** is Germany as in Deutschland and so on. for the most part, American sites (or site that use **.com** or **.net** domains) can get away without indicating which country they're in.

The addresses for electronic mail work in the same way, with the name/nickname of the person (or department) you want to contact appearing before the basic domain name, as in **jim.mcclellan@guardian.co.uk**.

Once you get used to it, the domain name system is pretty easy to use. And that's what most people do – just get on with things without giving it a second thought. However, domain names and the things people do with them are a source of endless fascination, or irritation, for some net users. The result is a kind of net name subculture, which encompasses blaggers, politicians and artists. For example, some people took advantage of the mainstream business world's failure to get the net and, in a practice known as domain squatting, bought up famous domain names e.g. **www.bootsthechemist.co.uk**. Their hope was that the company in question would cough up serious money to get its name back. Some did, but most now call their lawyers.

Some net users have advanced conspiracy theories about the CIA connections of one of the organisations that makes a fat profit from running the domain name system (Network Solutions Inc.). Everyone from artists to gamey entrepreneurs have attempted to set up alternative domain name systems. Once you get online, you'll be able to read a lot more about all this. In fact, a keen interest in net addresses is

< 28 >

**Read about it online - sex.com**

Some domains are desirable for obvious reasons and people will do anything to get hold of them - for a fascinating story about the ownership of the lucrative name sex.com, go to Wired News at **http://www.wired.com/news/news/business/story/19140.html**. ▲

probably one of the key signs that you're well on the way to becoming a screen-obsessed Homo Connectus.

One key sign is when you start using Network Solutions' WHOIS database to find out who has registered certain domain names **http://www.networksolutions.com/cgi-bin/whois/whois**. This might not sound like much fun, but it has become a useful investigative tool for

**Read about it online - Domain Names**

To find out more about domain names on the net – how to register them, how to sell them, who runs them and much else – try Internet Goldrush – **http://www.igoldrush.com**. A non-profit corporation called ICANN (as in the Internet Corporation for Assigned Names and Numbers) has been set up to deal with the technical management of the domain name system. Many net activists are worried that it will overstep its brief and allow governments a way of exerting some control over the net – for more on this, go to ICANN Watch **http://www.icannwatch.org**. ▲

< 29 >

journalists and others. Last year *Star Wars* fans kept watch on the domain names George Lucas was registering whilst he was making *The Phantom Menace* and were able to conclude from this that the film, which was shrouded in secrecy, was going to feature something called a pod race. (Lucas Films had apparently registered **podracer.com**).

## Mapping the net

Addresses only go so far when it comes to finding your way around online. It's also helpful to construct a kind of mental map of the net. By this, I don't just mean something as practical and accurate as an A-Z – although there's some fascinating work being done at the moment on producing workable maps for the net. It's more a question of conceptual images or the metaphors you use when you think and talk about the net.

If you use a standard computer with a graphic interface (i.e. a screen full of little cartoon icons) and a mouse, you'll be used to what computer types call the desktop metaphor. This means all the images of folders, files and trash cans you see on your screen. By making your PC seem familiar, these symbols help you to interact with your computer. Much net software continues the desktop metaphor, even when it doesn't seem that good a fit – for example, though awash in travel imagery, the Navigator browser lets you 'bookmark' your favourite web sites.

However, some net theorists have argued that at a higher level we use a few general metaphors when using the internet and that these metaphors make this strange new technology seem more accessible. Hence, we think of the net as being like a huge global library, or a community meeting

< 30 >

**Read about it online – Mapping**

If you want to have a look at some recent efforts to provide visual maps of cyberspace, go to **http://www.cybergeography.org/**. ▲

place, or a souped-up shopping mall. We think of it as a new frontier, or even as a kind of prototype interactive TV delivering something approaching video (or rather thirty-second video clips) on demand.

You could argue that the first example of a net metaphor is to think of it as a space in the first place, to think that, to rework Gertrude Stein, there is a 'there' there. In a way, that awful cliché of the early nineties – the information superhighway – was also a kind of net metaphor (the net as digital motorway). It was used by American Vice President Al Gore when he needed to sell the American public the more intangible (not to say dry) idea of a National Information Infrastructure. The contagious spread of I-way imagery back then showed that we do need concrete, familiar images to help us get a handle on the immaterial realm that crackles into life over the wires. Metaphors like the net as library or community help us first grasp the online world, then get things done.

Some critics (e.g. Mark Stefik in his book, *Internet Dreams*, published back in 1996 by MIT Press) argue that we need to choose our net metaphors carefully, because they will determine what sort of net we end up building. You can see what he means. As mentioned above, many big media companies have invested heavily in the mainstream-friendly

< 31 >

## Jargon file – Interactive TV

Much hyped in the early nineties before the net came along. This was supposed to be a TV set you could use to order pizza and videos and generally control when you saw certain TV shows. Some people think the net killed off interactive TV, but it remains the holy grail for certain big tech companies such as Sky Digital and Microsoft. ▲

idea that the net might be 'like television' and have pushed development in that area (e.g. in sending real-time video over the net). Whilst it's true that some areas of the net are a bit like television, overall the net as television metaphor offers a drastically diminished, rather passive idea of what the online world is and might be in the future.

Perhaps the best thing here is to be flexible. No single metaphor tells the whole story about the net. And all of them can apply at the same time. You can shift between them, depending on what seems useful at the time – whatever gets you through the net, as it were.

## Try before you buy

After getting a little conceptual, perhaps we should end by coming back down to earth. If you haven't actually been online before, the only sensible thing to do is to try the net before you spend any real money. You need to get an idea of what it's really like. It may be that you'll discover that the net isn't really for you. It's more than likely that this won't be the case. But it isn't guaranteed. So be sensible and try before you buy.

< 32 >

The easiest option is to go round to a friend who's already online and blag a few hours on his or her computer. People often suggest you persuade a wired-up buddy to give you a guided tour. I've done a few of these site-seeing sessions and people always start looking slightly glazed midway through – usually somewhere between the online bookstore amazon.com and Need to Know, the UK zine/mail-out that serves up a weekly shot of hip geek tech news, wind-ups and gossip. It may be my choice of sites. Then again, the net is not something you watch other people doing. The point is that you find your way around. You connect to the information and people you choose. So if you do head round to your net-literate friend, take a copy of their favourite video and a six-pack with you. Ask them to show you round for a while. Then sit them down with the video and beers. They will be there if you get stuck but will leave you alone for a couple of hours and let you get on with things.

If the computers at work are hooked up to the net, you could try it out there. Remember, though, that your boss is paying and is more than likely using a piece of software (sometimes called spyware) to check on what the employees do online.

### Jargon file – Cybercafe

A cafe complete with a few terminals where you can buy coffee and access the net for an hour or so. Very popular a few years ago, cybercafes will need to develop if they are to survive over the next ten years. ▲

< 33 >

**Read about it online – easyEverything**

The company behind easyJet has launched a new chain of cheap cybercafes. Called easyEverything, these charge £1 for an hour online and are open twenty four hours a day. The first easyEverything opened just round the corner from Victoria BR station in London – the perfect spot to get all those foreign backpackers who want to check their email and send messages to their parents/friends. For more details, try **http://www.easyeverything.com**. ▲

There are other places where you could go for a test run in cyberspace. Your local library may have a few PCs hooked up to the net. Alternatively, try your local cybercafe. Most towns and cities now have one. In general, these can be rather expensive – rates of around £6 for an hour online are not unknown.

Cybercafes can be a little confusing if you've never been online, but there should be help on hand to get you started (alternatively, you could take this book along and cut to the later sections). The better places also tend to have reasonably quick connections and the latest software. If you're not sure where your local is, there are plenty of online lists of UK cybercafes (admittedly, if you're not connected, they're not going to be that much use). For more info, try Internet Magazine's list **http://www.internet-magazine.com/resources/caffs.htm** or the list at **http://www.cyberiacafe.net/cyberia/guide/ccafe_uk.htm**. Alternatively look for the Internet Cafes section on the UK Yahoo **http://www.yahoo.co.uk.**

< 34 >

## Net myths deconstructed

People have said a lot of apparently sensible, vaguely contentious, mildly dubious or just plain daft things about the net over the last few years. Before we go any further, it might be helpful to clear your head of some of what's been said. Think of this chapter as a quick debriefing session, a Pass Notes for cyber babble.

*Everyone talks about the net being a worldwide phenomenon but really it's just an American thing*

Americans remain the most sizeable national presence on the net and they often act as if they own the thing, setting 'global standards' without bothering to consult the rest of the world (though perhaps we should be understanding about this since they did invent it). It's also clear that claims for the net's global reach are overstated. Most of the Southern hemisphere

---

### Read about it online – Europe Online

If you want to find out what's online in Europe (and there's plenty) try Euroferret, a European search engine **http://www.euroferret.com** or Europages **http://www.europages.com**, a European business directory. Alternatively, try The European Directory aka TED at **http://www3.ukshops.co.uk** for a more general directory of sites up and running across the channel. ▲

< 35 >

**Read about it online – Net Surveys**

If you want to read the latest surveys of the net population and
what they get up to, go to the site maintained by the Irish net
consultancy Nua **http://www.nua.ie/surveys/**, which features details
of, and links to, most recent net surveys. ▲

isn't connected. Even in the West, most people are not online. That said,
more and more non-English-language web sites are coming online.

*The net is a sort of digital locker room, a toy for the boys*

There are still more men online than women, though some areas are
more balanced – AOL recently claimed that over 50 per cent of its users
were women. According to some surveys, young women in their teens are
outpacing young men when it comes to the net. Unfortunately, many
men already online do behave exceedingly badly, especially the
troglodytes in some online chat rooms. But things are changing. Just

**Jargon file – Chat Room**

An online space where you can chat (i.e. exchange text messages in
real time) with a group of users. ▲

< 36 >

## Read about it online – Silver Surfers

There are lots of American web sites aimed at older users – try Third Age **http://www.thirdage.com**. For something similar in the UK, have a look at I Don't Feel 50 **http://www.idf50.com**. Alternatively, check out Hairnet **http://www.hairnet.org**, the UK's first internet training scheme for the over-50s.  ▲

remember that there's nothing inherently male about the net. The theory that it is 'a guy thing' often seems like something dreamt up by boys who don't want to share.

*The net is a youth thing. If you're over forty you won't get it*

It's no surprise that older people are vaguely net-phobic. Many don't have any experience of computers or the net. Some techno-gurus get paid a lot to tell them they wouldn't understand it all anyway. But think of the benefits of getting online: staying in touch with family and friends, accessing useful information (e.g. on health, holidays and finance), shopping without leaving home. Older people could get as much out of these as the young. And many have the time and the money for the net. Indeed some of the smarter net companies are now planning to target the so-called 'silver surfers'. So if you are an older reader, forget the prevailing wisdom and have a go.

< 37 >

*The net is packed with geeks and nerds. So it can be of little use to ordinary, well-adjusted people like me*

The media don't seem to like geeks. Perhaps journalists are subconsciously afraid of them. After all, geeks understand the computers that journalists rely on (but are largely clueless about). Really we should be grateful to the computer geeks who were obsessive enough to get something like the net up and running, though that doesn't mean you have to spend hours talking to them about rebel operating systems. Obviously there are lots of geek-oriented resources online. But the net is now a mainstream thing as well. There's plenty to interest people who don't spend their lives pondering continuity errors in *Star Trek*.

*Most of the information on the net is rubbish – just not worth bothering with*

There's an awful lot of witless stupidity on the net. But before you use that as a reason to stay offline, wander into your nearest bookshop. What do you see? Jeffrey Archer novels, ghosted autobiographies by B-list sportsmen, shelves of *Men are from Mars, Women are from Venus* claptrap. Milton, Blake, Joyce and Jane Austen don't usually take up the bulk of the display space. The net is just like TV, radio and print. There is a lot of rubbish but there's good stuff too, if you look.

< 38 >

*The net lets you find out what ordinary people really think*

Get online and you can indeed read web pages in which ordinary folk talk about their hopes, fears, dreams, favourite breakfast cereals and sad fixation with 'Star Wars'. The problem here is that journalists take all this a little too much at face value. Show them a couple of sites enthusing about how cool an upcoming film is going to be and they write a piece about the massive grassroots buzz surrounding the new hot movie. Show them a review on Ain't It Cool News **http://www.aint-it-cool-news.com** that says advance screening audiences think the new Will Smith effort stinks and they report it as gospel. Those sites and that advance gossip might be bona fide. But the sites might also have been faked up by clever marketing types and the gossip might come from a rival film company keen to spike the competition. The truth is, the net is media now, like everything else. It's still an open form of media that ordinary people can use, which is great. But it can also be abused and manipulated by all the usual suspects. Just remember this when you go online.

This collapse of trust online doesn't just affect entertainment trivia. During the Kosova conflict, there was much talk about how the net gave ordinary people on both sides a way of talking about their experiences. It did. Lots of powerful email messages were circulated online. But the soldiers and politicians on both sides quickly got wise and began to use the net as part of their info-war effort. The end result was that, because it was hard to tell real stories from propaganda, people began to distrust all the first person accounts of the war that circulated on the net.

< 39 >

## Read about it online – Illegal material

Under pressure from the police and the government, the UK net industry has made attempts to deal with the problems posed by child pornography. If users find child porn (or other illegal material online), they are encouraged to report it to The Internet Watch Foundation, who will then attempt to take some sort of action. Read more about what they're up to at **http://www.iwf.org.uk/**. ▲

*Log on to the net and you will immediately be assaulted by pornographic images, perverts and paedophiles*

There is a lot of porn online – some of it foul stuff. Generally it doesn't leap out at you when you log on. You're more in danger of being 'assaulted' by the images peering down from the top shelf in your local newsagent. You usually have to go looking for porn online (though not always – for more on this, go to page 379). A hormonal teenager would have no problem finding it. Of course, in pre-net days, hormonal teens generally found ways to get hold of pornographic images. It is one of the standard male adolescent pursuits. Still the net does make it easy – the barriers that exist in the real world – the top shelf, shop assistants willing to enforce the over-eighteen rule – aren't there yet. However, there are plenty of things parents can do to protect their children and further frustrate their teenage sons. As for paedophiles, they use the net, just as they use telephones and the mail. They go online to swap pornographic

< 40 >

imagery and there is also evidence that some hang out in chat rooms popular with teenagers and children. However, paedophiles are not online in anything like the numbers some alarmists claim. Parents should ignore the panicmongers but take sensible precautions – as they would with the real world. This whole area is covered in more depth on page 379.

### *The government should do something to protect our children from the horrors of the net*

Where material online is clearly illegal, as with child porn, action is already being taken by many UK internet service providers who choose to block access to newsgroups that circulate it. Most people can agree on the need to do something about child porn, but other areas (hardcore porn for the over-eighteens, political 'hate speech') remain more contentious. Protecting children without ruining all the good things about the net remains a difficult problem. It won't be solved by rushing in some new kind of law. A better way forward might be to let individual users control what their computers can access via online ratings systems and filterware, but this certainly isn't the problem-free solution some claim. Again, there's more on this on page 379.

### *If you give out your credit card details online, hackers will get hold of them and use your account to subsidise their crack habits*

Online security still isn't quite what it could be, but many of the

< 41 >

## Jargon file – Filterware

A software package designed to block access to certain sites: either those the maker of the program deems unacceptable or sites specified by the user. ▲

worries about using credit cards online have more to do with technological novelty than with a sensible appreciation of the risks involved. You don't usually worry about giving out your credit card number over the telephone, but do you know where the card number you handed over will be stored? Hackers tell stories of swapping stolen card numbers, but they often get them by breaking into poorly protected computers at companies who collected them in normal ways (via mail and the telephone).

*If you connect your PC to the net, it will soon be awash with strange computer viruses*

Viruses don't jump down the telephone line and deliberately seek out your PC like some malevolent killer bug. If you get a piece of email entitled "!!! This is a Virus – Your Machine is already infected !!!", it's a wind-up. The only thing in danger of being infected is your mind – with groundless worries. However, you should be careful about software you download from the net. Always run a virus check on it. And you should be careful

< 42 >

with email that arrives with attached Microsoft Word documents. These can carry viruses. If you open them, you will get infected. That was how the Melissa virus spread. The solution is not to be suspicious of Word attachments in general and don't open those that just arrive out of the blue from people you don't know. There's more on this on page 421.

*On the net no one knows you're a dog*

The punch line from a famous cartoon showing two dogs in front of a computer. The net does let you communicate in relative anonymity. In an online chat room, people know as much about you as you choose to tell them. Hence, one of the great male online pursuits – going to a chat room and pretending to be a woman. All harmless fun – usually – but the anonymity afforded by the net can be abused and some of the most enduring spaces on the net are those where people give their real names and take responsibility for their words. That said, the net is not as anonymous as it might seem. Everywhere you go in cyberspace, you leave trails that can be followed fairly easily. There's more on this on page 396.

*Using the net will turn your children into deranged homicidal maniacs*

In the aftermath of the terrible shootings at Columbine High School in Littleton, Colorado, the US media looked around for someone to blame and, in some cases, came up with computer games and the net. The killers played violent video games, it was reported, and one of them had

< 43 >

put up a web site that featured bloodthirsty imagery. Case closed. The internet did it really. Some critics even seemed to suggest that the net is so powerfully intense that, as it brings a wide, wild world into the home, it can't help but corrupt children and take them over the edge. In other words, let them spend some time online and before you know it, they'll be doing dodgy things with bags of fertiliser.

That's not the case. That said, a disturbed, depressed child will find material online that may do them harm online. But happy, well-adjusted children aren't one click away from turning into gun-toting psychopaths. It's true – we do need to develop barriers online that keep unsuitable material from children (something that won't be simple). And parents should take an interest in what their kids do online. There's more on this on page 389. But don't think that attempting to censor the net is going to solve society's problems or bring an end to school massacres. If Americans want to pass some laws that might help with that, how about gun control?

### *The net is a functioning anarchy – no one's in charge and that's why it works so well*

One of the great net clichés, and true, up to a point. A Cold War invention, the net was conceived as a decentralised communications network. The idea was that without an obvious centre through which all messages passed, it would be less vulnerable to enemy attack. OK, so there is no central command. And the committee of boffins – the Internet

< 44 >

Engineering Task Force **http://www.ietf.org** – that sets the technical standards that keep the net running is a very open and democratic structure. However, there is a central organisation in charge of administering the system of net addresses. And whilst the government doesn't control the net, if you keep posting reports on your web pages about what MI5/MI6 are really up to, you may receive an unwelcome dawn wake-up call.

*If we wire our schools, our education worries will be over*

Obviously children need to be taught about computer networks. And the net can be a wonderful educational resource. But on its own, it won't solve the problems our schools have. In fact, much of the money being lavished on the 'national grid for learning' might be better spent elsewhere – on decent textbooks, repairing facilities and paying teachers enough to enable them to regain some sense of self-worth and purpose.

*If you don't get online now, right now, you'll be left behind, you'll be toast, roadkill on the superhighway*

A variation on standard computer industry ad hype – that if you don't buy a PC now, you'll never catch up, you'll be history. And if you do buy a computer now, you'll need to buy another one in two years' time or you'll be history again. Taking cyber-hypesters at their word, net critics often ask about those who will be left behind because they can't afford the net, suggesting that a two-tier society of information-haves and infor-

< 45 >

mation-have-nots will be created. The cyber-hypesters generally reply that no one will really be left behind, that there won't be information-have-nots, just information-have-laters. In fact, they suggest, we should all be grateful to the info-have-nows because they're testing out bug-ridden products, paying through the nose for things that will eventually be sold much more cheaply to the mainstream when they actually work. This is pretty glib. Access to the net for those who are less well off remains a problem. As for the claims that you have to get online or risk being info-highway roadkill, there are now lots of good reasons for getting online. Worrying that you'll be 'left behind' if you don't is not one of them. ▲

< 46 >

# 2 GETTING CONNECTED

• • • • • • • • • • • • • • • • • • • • • • • • • • • • • •

So you're ready to get online. You want that twenty-first-century, information-at-your-fingertips cyber-blast and you want it now. Unfortunately, before you surf anywhere, you will have to spend some money, especially if you don't already have a computer. Even if you do already have a PC of some sort, you may need to buy a modem. You'll also have to fork out for a connection to the net. The good news is that, what with free ISPs, free off peak telephone calls and even free PCs, the cost of getting online has been coming down. The bad news is that, despite all those mentions of the 'f' word, the net still doesn't really come cheap. Handing over wads of money to salespeople, especially computer salespeople, is never a happy or painless process. However, in the next section we'll help you to find a reasonable deal when it comes to kitting yourself out for the internet.

## Hardware

You can now use all sorts of things to access the net – natty digital personal organisers (for example Psions and Palm Pilots), cutting-edge

< 47 >

mobile phones, TVs fitted with special set-top boxes. At the moment, many of these gizmos are best left to specialists, business people and gadget boys. The net-friendly mobile phones and personal organisers are extremely useful for business people who are on the road a lot and need to access their email. But you certainly wouldn't want to have one of these as your first choice for accessing the net.

The various set top boxes that let you access the net via your TV have been hyped as perfect for non-computer types and are being promoted energetically by various big media companies. At the moment, though, I'm still not sold on the idea of checking out the net as it stands – i.e. web pages and email – via some sort of smart TV. The problem isn't just that TV monitors still aren't best suited to delivering legible text (and there's still an awful lot of text online). It's more that accessing the web via the TV set raises the wrong sort of expectations. The web isn't really like TV yet – for most of us online, video is still scratchy and very small screen. And watching TV and wandering round the net are two very different

## Read about it online – Web TV

The big player, when it comes to accessing the web via TVs and set-top boxes, is the American company Web TV (owned by Microsoft). They try to sell themselves as not so much an internet thing, more a way to make TV more interesting. There's more information on their web page **http://www.webtv.net**. ▲

< 48 >

experiences. The former is more passive; the latter is more active. You need to be up close to the screen, figuring out what to do and where to go next. And it's not easy writing email perched on the couch pecking away at a cross between a TV remote control and a miniature keyboard.

It's worth keeping tabs on set top boxes though, especially as super fast 'broadband' connections to the net become more available. Broadband will make it possible to deliver material over the net that looks OK on TV screens – for example, video on demand. As broadband spreads, the TV will probably become more intelligent, will merge with the computer in some way and you will use this new piece of kit to access some part of the net. Too many people with a lot of money want it to happen. But it won't be the net as we know it today. It will probably be some sort of extension of the services currently being tested by British Interactive Broadcasting on Open, its interactive TV network.

Perhaps you've read about these. If your TV is already hooked up to a BIB Digital Satellite set top box, you should now be able sort out your bank account via the small screen TV (if you have an account with the right bank). You can also change camera angles and call up statistics during a football match. During the same match, you can send email via your TV to a friend – presumably to wind them up if their team is losing. You can order pizza online. If you see a music video online that you like, you can buy the CD immediately, via one of the big name retailers Open has signed up.

At the moment, it's unclear which of these services people really want (the shopping seems likely to appeal, but all that changing camera angles

< 49 >

stuff sounds like a dud). And it will be a while before they work really well. If you've already signed up for digital TV, you might as well have a look at what's on offer. But what's on offer isn't the net. It's closer to a televisual version of the old online services, where you didn't go out on to the net but just stayed on their little network. Apparently, Cable and Wireless and TeleWest are planning more genuinely open interactive TV services that do use the net. For a look at an American company working in developing just that, try B3TV **http://www.b3tv.com**.

When these new smart connected TVs become functional and affordable, people will probably use them as well the more basic PC hooked up to the net. Indeed, in the future, we'll more than likely have all sorts of information appliances that are all connected to the net in some way. We'll use each one to do something different. But that's a way off yet. For the moment, ignore the hype around set top boxes. If you're starting out, your best bet if you want to get online is still a home computer.

---

## Read about it online – Open for business

If you want to see what kinds of interactive services Open is currently delivering to your TV and what's on the way, check out the web page at **http://www.open-here.co.uk**. The company has a good line-up of high street retailers ready to offer TV shopping – partners include WH Smith, Next, Argos, Summerfield, Woolworths and The Carphone Warehouse. ▲

< 50 >

### The Computer - Mac or PC?

Perhaps we should address the Mac versus PC thing first. When it comes to buying a home computer to access the net, you have a choice between an Apple Macintosh or an IBM-compatible PC running Microsoft Windows. (Of course you could go for one of the other machines – Acorns, Amigas and the rest – which are fine, but less well supplied when it comes to net software.) Though some people pursue it with religious intensity (mainly Mac owners – most PC owners don't love their machines enough), the Mac/PC debate is one of the more boring things about computer culture. Actually the choice is pretty simple. If you want to be able to swap files and other bits and pieces with friends and work colleagues, you should buy the same sort of computer as them, which will usually mean a computer running Windows (Microsoft has 90 per cent of the PC market). If you want something easy to use, some sort of Apple Mac is still usually the best bet, despite the advances made by Microsoft. The Mac is also still the choice of many creative professionals – artists, journalists, designers, publishers. If that's what you do (or hope to do in the future), the Mac is probably what you want.

Perhaps the real difference between what we might call Macolytes and PC clones is that the latter accept that they're buying a fallible piece of machinery. They expect it to break down and malfunction. People who buy Macs know that they are buying more than a machine. They are buying into a kind of cult based around a piece of technology that once promised to change the world, a cult obsessed with the superiority

< 51 >

**Read about it online – Open for business**

The net may be dominated by PC clones but there are plenty of sites that specialise in news about Apple Macs and iMacs in particular. For general news try MacCentral **http://www.maccentral.com**. For specific iMac news and views and loads of links to similar sites, try the iMac Channel **http://lowendmac.com/imac/index.shtml**. ▲

of its icons and interface, that religiously reads all those articles in the technology press headlined 'Rotten to the Core – Will Apple Fall?'

Macolytes have had a big boost over the last year with the arrival of the iMac, which has re-established Apple's reputation for consumer-friendly design (and did a lot for its bank balance in the process). Having used one whilst writing this book, I can confirm that iMacs are very nice looking computers. They're affordable. They're easy to set up. They have everything you need to connect to the net. They also make connecting relatively easy (something that previous Macs didn't always do, for all their much-vaunted user-friendliness). However, new PCs do all this as well. OK, you can't pick one that matches your curtains, though whatever PC you do buy, it will have a floppy drive, something iMacs seem too cool for.

The truth is, it's as easy to set up a new PC as it is an iMac. It's also easy to find an ISP that's happy dealing with PCs. That isn't quite the case with Macs. You have to hunt around a bit. The iMac's ad campaign

< 52 >

described it as 'the internet for the rest of us', which is a great line. Unfortunately, on the net, the rest of us are using PCs. The net is a very PC-centric place. At the moment the bulk of new net software comes out first for the PC. Some of it never comes out in a Mac version.

That said, the iMac has tried to make things easier. Its **Internet Setup Assistant** does have come with pre-installed connection packages for several of the big ISPs – some free (Virgin, Line One), some subscription-based (Demon Internet, Direct Connection, BT Internet). However, given its sale pitch for the iMac, it seems strange that Apple didn't go the whole hog and also set up its own free ISP (as the likes of Gateway and Dell have done) and bundle it with their new machine. There are rumours that the company is planning something along these lines, though nothing definite has been announced at the time of writing. Given the loyalty that Apple inspires in its customers, you can imagine most Mac users switching to a free ISP set up by the company.

## Modems

A computer isn't the only piece of hardware you need to get online. You also need a modem, which will convert the digital information your computer works with into audio signals that can then be sent down a standard telephone line. (The name's a compression of the technical term Modulator Demodulator, by the way). Virtually all new PCs and Macs now come with internal modems as standard. However, if your computer doesn't already have something suitable installed inside its beige casing, you can buy an external modem.

< 53 >

## Read about it online - Open for business

There's lots of useful advice online about modems. Try 56k.com **http://www.56k.com** or Modem Help at **http://www.modemhelp.com**. ▲

You connect this to your computer via one of the serial ports at the back of your machine and it sits on your desk, next to your phone. External modems need to be plugged into the mains (at the moment) but they are generally easier to install and easier to replace if they go wrong or you buy something newer and faster. You can also watch their status lights flashing on and off and kid yourself you know exactly what's going on. Of course, you can always buy an internal modem and open up your machine and install it yourself. They don't require an extra power source, which may be an issue if you're short of sockets at home. They also save on cable spaghetti.

If your computer doesn't already have a modem pre-installed, you can spend anything up to £200 on a top-of-the-range item, which these days is a multi-purpose beast which doubles as a speaker phone and does your

## Tips - Modem Speed

Is it that important? Yes, but . . . Sometimes things are just slow online and it's nothing to do with your connection. Whatever you get, you'll wish you had something faster. ▲

< 54 >

voice mail and faxes. However, the first thing you should think about when buying a modem isn't that snazzy voice mail feature but the speed at which it can send information, measured in bps (or bits per second). The higher the speed, the faster data gets sent back and forth between you and whatever you're accessing online. So in this case, speed is good.

The minimum modem speed you should put up with is 28.8 Kbps (which means data gets sent at 28,800 bits per second). Nowadays 56.6 Kbps modems are standard. For various technical reasons, they receive data at 56.6 Kbps but send it back at 36.6 Kbps. In addition, only in ideal conditions will they receive data at 56.6 Kbps. Most of the time they'll chug along at something between 40 and 50 Kbps. There are other modems on the way that promise even faster connections but at the

---

### Tips - Serial Ports

If you are going to use an older machine to get online, you need to check that it can cope with modern modems. Look in the manual and check that the serial port you are going to hook your modem up to (usually COM2) has something called a 16550 UART. Alternatively, if you've got a PC, go to the DOS prompt and run msd.exe, which should tell you what you need to know. If you don't have a 16550 UART, you'll need to upgrade your serial port – possibly not something you want to get into if you're not that comfortable with computers. ▲

< 55 >

moment, 56.6 Kbps is probably the easiest option if you want something vaguely speedy and you don't want to break the bank.

## How Much Power Do You Need?

So long as you don't expect the multimedia animations and video feeds, so long as you're happy with reading and writing text and don't want pretty pictures, you can actually get by online with a very low tech, low spec computer – an old 486 DX PC that runs Windows 3.x and has 8 Mb of RAM and a couple of hundred Mb of hard disk space or an old Mac from two or three years ago. But I really wouldn't advise it. Struggling along with this will be very tiresome. If you want to see a bit more of what's on offer online, the minimum requirements are:

**RAM** You can just about get by with 16 Mb but you're better off with 32Mb (64 Mb if possible). It will make the latest web browsers run a lot quicker.

**Hard Disk** Browsers and other bits of software are getting ever more bloated and once online you might find yourself amassing a sizeable collection of software. Realistically you'll need at least a 1 gigabyte hard disk – though something bigger would be preferable. Most new machines come with much more.

**Multimedia** If you want to listen to music or watch video clips online, you need a decent soundcard and speakers, a video card with a megabyte

< 56 >

or two of video RAM and graphics accelerators. Most new computers now carry this kind of thing as standard. If you want to telephone people via the net, you might find a microphone useful.

**Processor Speed** This isn't as much of an issue as some make out, but a reasonable Pentium won't hurt. Even if you buy second-hand these days, you're likely to get something like that.

**Monitors** Size is up to you, though there's something slightly domineering about some of the huge computer monitors now appearing on the market. More important, if you're going to use a creaky old PC or buy second-hand, check that your monitor has at least 256 colours. If you're buying new, don't worry about this.

**Operating Systems** Though you can, in theory, get by with a computer that runs an old operating system (i.e. Windows 3.x), everything becomes that bit more fiddly. You have to get separate bits of software for different tasks. Windows 95/98 and NT have the programs you need to get online already built into them. The same goes for Macs from System 7.5 on.

**CD ROM Drive** This has been a standard on new PCs for years now. In fact many new PCs now have DVD ROM drives. However, if you are running an older computer which doesn't have a CD ROM drive, getting software on old 3.5 floppy discs is going to be a real problem.

< 57 >

**Modem** As mentioned above, you can get by with a 28.8K modem but something that runs at 56.6K will make your life online a lot easier. 14.4K modems are probably much too slow for the web these days.

If all you're planning to do online is send email and check out the web, if you don't intend to wander through any 3D online environments and you don't mind if the video you see online is a little jerky, you'll be fine with an entry-level home/multimedia PC. Prices and specs change month by month in the computer business. But as this book was going to press, even entry level PCs (priced between £600-800) had at least: a speedy Pentium III processor, 64 Mb of RAM, a 6-8 Gigabyte hard disk, 32-speed CD ROM drive, 8 Mb 3D video card, 15 inch monitor, sound card, speakers and 56.6k fax modem, plus software. For £779, you could get an iMac with a 333MHz Power PC G3 processor, 6GB hard disk,

---

### Tips – Buying a Computer

Before you buy, think about what else you plan to do with your computer. If all you're going to do, aside from going online, is word processing, you don't need a screamingly fast processor and gigabytes of disk space. On the other hand, if you want to play computer games (especially the latest generation of 3D efforts), then a faster machine with a lot of memory and special graphics cards is a big help. ▲

---

< 58 >

56K modem, 32Mb RAM and the colour scheme of your choice. Both of these are more than adequate.

## Laptops

If you move around a lot and need to take your PC with you, you could go for a laptop. It's pretty easy to find something that fits most of the above requirements (though you might have to take a drop on processor speed if you're on a budget). You'll need a PCMCIA modem, which is about the size of a credit card and slots into the back of your machine. These cost more than standard PC modems. The same goes for laptops in general. Mobility costs. To complement the iMac, Apple just launched its new laptop the iBook, which looks just as swish and has some useful net features. For example, you can set up its AirPort feature, which works in a similar way to a cordless telephone and lets you dial in to the net without having to be sat near your telephone socket.

## Future Proofing

When it comes to buying new computers, computer magazines sometimes tell you to look at something mid-range, which tends to mean shelling out anything from £1000 to £1,500, plus VAT. Apparently you should do this to ensure a bit of future proofing. Put simply, this means spending money to ensure that, in the eyes of the industry at least, your shiny new PC doesn't become a worthless piece of junk the day after you buy it. In the computer business, obsolescence doesn't have to be deliberately planned. It's the way of the world. Chip speeds increase and the

< 59 >

cost of memory falls almost month by month. Matching this, software developers continually increase the size of their products to take advantage of these gains, resulting in what cynics refer to as 'bloatware'. So whilst everything seems to be changing, everything also seems to be standing still. What all this apparently means for the ordinary punter is that you need to buy mid-range if you want your machine to have enough power to handle the new software programs that come out the year after you buy it – hence future proofing.

Actually many people make do with the software bundled with the computer when they bought it. They don't always go out the next year and buy the new version of Microsoft Office or whatever. That said, it is nice

## Read about it online – Moore's Law

Why does your PC feel like a worthless piece of junk a year after you bought it? Blame Moore's Law, the principle first laid down in 1965 by Gordon Moore, co-founder of the chip company Intel, who suggested that the number of transistors you can pack on to a single chip will double every eighteen months. Actually he didn't quite say that, but that's what people decided he said, and he went along with them. Moore's Law is the reason that computers that cost the same get faster and faster each year. Tech journalists often claim that Moore's Law no longer applies or is about to, in the jargon, 'hit a wall'. For the record, Gordon Moore thinks it's good 'til 2012. Read his thoughts on Intel's site **http://developer.intel.com/solutions/archive/issue2/feature.htm**. ▲

< 60 >

to feel that the machine you bought a few months ago hasn't already been dismissed as an antique by the industry. If you do have the money to 'future proof', the thing is go for first is extra RAM – you can never have enough of that stuff. Then go for a big hard disk. Processor speed isn't that important unless you're going to play lots of computer games – in which case, the faster the better. If you don't want to buy a completely new computer, you can upgrade your existing model. If you're reasonably handy, you can do this yourself. Inserting extra chunks of RAM into a PC is actually pretty easy. As ever, it's easier still for Mac owners. However, if you are a computer innocent, the idea of fiddling with computer innards will undoubtedly seem a little daunting. You can get people to upgrade for you, though by the time you've paid for them and the extra components, you might find you could have bought a new machine for the same money.

## Buying a computer

Be sensible – do a bit of research before you buy. Read the consumer computer magazines. Scope out the prices and specifications on different brands and models. Think a bit about what you want. Once you've done this, you can either go to a shop or buy direct from one of the big manufacturers. This is a matter of taste. Some people like to play around with something before they pay. I've always bought direct and had no problems. More and more, you can specify exactly what you want.

As mentioned above, the new machines from some computer manufacturers (e.g. Dell, Gateway) now come with the software needed to connect to the net via their own free ISPs. This is undoubtedly very

< 61 >

convenient. But it's not hard to find the software you need to connect to one of the free ISPs (especially if you use a PC). Discs are given away by banks, high street stores and newspapers. So, on its own, this shouldn't be a reason to buy from one of these companies.

You may see all sorts of brilliant deals advertised in the computer magazines. But before you bite, think a bit about the companies behind them. You want reliability from your PC. You want to be able to take it back to the manufacturers if problems occur (or at least give them a call). Some of the companies offering those great prices look like they might not be around that long.

Should you buy a second-hand computer? Obviously this will save you a lot of money, though it can be a minefield for beginners, worse than second-hand car dealing. If you are going to buy an old machine, take along a computer-literate friend so you don't get conned. That said, this could be worth investigating. The computer world is full of speed

## Tips - Guarantees

Wherever you buy your computer, it's worth spending money on extending guarantees or service warranties. Computers remain unreliable machines. It shouldn't be that way. They should be as reliable and robust as the average TV set. But at the moment, they still aren't – another irritating thing about the computer business – so it's a good idea to cover yourself. ▲

< 62 >

junkies who sell off perfectly good machines so they can get the latest, fastest thing. So you may find a real bargain.

## Free PCs?

One idea currently all the rage in America is the 'Free PC'. Some companies will now give you a free computer so you can access the net. If you think this sounds too good to be true, you're right. You have to give something back. In some cases you have to provide detailed information about where you go and what you do on the net. In others, you have to sign up with a particular telecommunications provider and make a certain amount of calls per month. In others, you have to use the ISP run by the company giving away the machine and pay several years subscription in advance.

So there is no such thing as a completely free lunch. Nevertheless, in America, the idea has caught on. Free PC **http://www.free-pc.com**, the company that started it all, has been joined by several competitors, including Free Mac **http://www.freemac.com**, who, as you might have guessed, aim to give away free iMacs. AOL, the massive online service/ISP, has also joined in. In the States, it plans to give away PCs made by E-Machines to customers who agree to sign up to its Compuserve service for three years. Similarly, Microsoft is planning a similar giveaway to people who sign up for three years to its MSN service in America. All this is a sign of how important market share is to net companies these days. They will do anything to get hold of (and keep) users. Their hope is that, if they get a good deal now, these users will

< 63 >

stick with them and will turn into lucrative customers in the future.

Some UK companies have tried out the free PC idea. Both Tiny Computers **http://www.tiny.com** and Time Computers **http://www. timecomputers.co.uk** dabbled with the idea over the summer but now seem to be playing it down. Tiny Computers were offering a computer with a 300 MHz processor, a 3.2 GB hard disk and 32 Mb RAM. A monitor wasn't included in the package but you did get an adaptor so you could hook the computer up to your TV. To qualify, you had to sign up to the company's telephone service for twelve months and make over £25 worth of calls a month. But in August, the company dropped the idea saying that most of its would be customers had preferred a different offer, which gave them £200 off a higher spec Pentium III machine if they signed up with Tiny's telephone service.

For Tiny, the free PC offer was clearly first and foremost a clever publicity stunt that succeeded in generating lots of interest in its products in general. So it seems more than likely that someone else will have a go. Keep an eye on the ads in the newspapers' computer supplements (e.g. The Guardian's Online, which comes out on Thursdays). Alternatively, try the specialist computer/net magazines. These offers always come with strings attached, but they may be worthwhile.

## Your connection

You have your computer and modem. The next thing you need is a connection to the net. The best bet for the beginner is the telephone line. It's simple and just about everyone's got one. If you do get keen on the

< 64 >

net, you may want to move on to something faster. In the next few years, various companies plan to offer us high-speed wireless, cable and satellite connections to the net. For the moment, one option that might be appropriate for home users with a bit of money is an ISDN line (the letters stand for Integrated Services Digital Network).

Over the last year, BT has been trying hard to sell ISDN to ordinary users. Basically, ISDN is a digital telephone line that offers faster connection times than current modems – up to 128 Kbps, with some jigging about. ISDN also lets you do two things at once; you can be connected to the net and talking on the telephone at the same time, all via the same line. However, you will need to get various bits of hardware and software to connect. Though BT have cut the prices, rental and call charges are a lot higher than normal telephone lines. So I'd think hard before you sign up for this.

It might be worth waiting to see what happens with another new BT service – ADSL (the letters stand for Asymmetric Digital Subscriber Line). The important thing about this is that it uses the normal copper telephone

### Read about it online – Fast Net Access

Find out more about BT's ADSL plans at **http://www.bt.com/ADSL**. You can see a preview of some of the special services BT hopes to provide over high-speed connections at **http://www.btinteractive.com**. For more about Home Highway ISDN, try **http://www.homehighway.bt.com**. ▲

< 65 >

lines to deliver a high speed connection to the net – speeds on offer go up
to 2 Mb a second – that's around 40 times faster than a 56K modem. You
pay a flat monthly fee and get a connection to the net that is 'always on'.
Unfortunately, at the moment, BT is pricing the service rather high and
clearly wants to target it at small businesses. But it's worth keeping an eye
on the price, which seems likely to fall over the next year or so.

All this is a bit academic. If you're starting out, you should use your
telephone line while you get your bearings. Remember to disable call
waiting if you have it. Otherwise it may break into your net calls and cut
you off. You may also experience problems if you've set your telephone
up to withhold Caller Line Identification (CLI), information that is
forwarded with calls made from BT residential lines (it helps the 1471
function work). You can remove this on a call-by-call basis, though it is
a bit fiddly. Basically, you need to get your net dial-up software to add
1470 at the start of your net account number. Whilst we're on the subject

---

### Tips – Family and Friends

Look at the latest pricing offers from BT, if you get your telephone
service from them. It's probably a good idea to put the number of
your internet service provider on your Family and Friends list or make
it your Best Friend number. You will save a bit of money. Not much,
admittedly, but every bit helps. If you do become a serious user,
check out their Premier Line deal. ▲

< 66 >

of BT services, Call Minder can be useful. This takes voice messages while your line is engaged, then calls you afterwards to tell you that you have voice mail. However, if you become a heavy net user, it's probably worth getting an extra line. That way, you can also keep track of exactly how much you are spending on the net.

## Internet Service Providers

Your computer is hooked up to your modem, which is plugged into your phone line. Next you need to dial up someone who can provide you with a connection to the internet. A couple of years ago, you were faced with a choice between the internet service providers and the online services. The former provided you with a connection to the net and the software you needed to get about. The latter gave you access to the net and to their own private networks of services – databases of information, online editions of well-known magazines and newspapers, cinema listings, travel information, shopping, user forums, live chat rooms, online celebrity chats and much else. You paid for both.

All that's changed now. In truth, the distinction between online services and internet service providers often seemed a bit blurred. Some of the companies that described themselves as ISPs offered the same sorts of things as the online services. But now, there are hardly any classic online services remaining. The only companies that really fit the bill are AOL, Compuserve (which is owned by AOL) and Microsoft's MSN. That said, when it comes to choosing a form of net access, you still have two basic options. However, now the choice is between companies that

< 67 >

**Read about it online – Fast Net Access**

This certainly isn't a reason not to choose AOL, but you should be aware that AOL users are still the subject of significant prejudice and occasional abuse online. The hardcore geek elite assume all AOL users are incompetent and accuse the company of delivering a bad service and of being anti-net and pro-censorship. If you want to know why some older members of the online population thinks that 'AOL sucks', try **http://www.aolsucks.org/**. ▲

charge you some sort of monthly fee for accessing the net and those that don't. It's between AOL and the subscription-based ISPs like Demon, UUNet Pipex Dial, Global Internet, CIX and Easynet or free ISPs like Freeserve, where you only pay for your telephone call charges.

## The Free ISP Revolution

'Revolution' is a term that gets bandied about rather a lot in connection with the Internet. Whilst those jumping on the rhetorical barricades are usually indulging in empty hype, the word is actually justified when applied to the UK's free ISPs. Though free net service was actually pioneered in the UK by The X-Stream Network, the electronics retailers Dixons, with its Freeserve service, has, yes, revolutionised the ISP business over the last year or so. At the time of writing, Freeserve claims to have around 1.5 million registered users – a figure that makes it far and

< 68 >

away the UK's biggest ISP, free or otherwise – not bad for a company that only got started in the autumn of 1998. It's also become the first British internet company to be successfully floated on the stock market.

In retrospect, the success is easy to understand. By removing the price barrier of monthly subscription fees, Freeserve made trying the net out a virtually risk-free option for mainstream punters who had computers but hadn't yet made the leap online. Its business model may seem confusing at first sight. If it doesn't charge anything, how does it stay afloat? Thanks to the way telecommunications pricing is currently structured in this country, the free ISPs take a cut of the charges collected on the calls made to connect to their services. That said, Freeserve in particular now has enough users to start making money from advertising and e commerce.

Given Freeserve's success, it's no surprise that it's been joined by scores of other competitors also offering free access. ISPs that used to charge have now gone free (e.g. Virgin, LineOne, Tesco and UK Online). Famous names from other fields have entered the market. WH Smith, Waterstones, The Sun (via CurrantBun.com), The Mirror Group (via

---

### Jargon File - E Commerce

A catch-all term for business of all kinds that's done online. The e commerce that the big free ISPs are interested in is net shopping. They have agreements set up to allow them to take a cut of sales made from net shops via links on their homepages. ▲

< 69 >

ic24.com), Barclays Bank, The BBC (with its Free Beeb service), Arsenal and Manchester United are all now free ISPs, as are technology-based businesses like the games company Eidos and PC manufacturers Gateway and Dell. According to some analysts, there are now at least 200 businesses offering free net access. They're attempting to service an increasingly large net population in the UK. Some estimates now suggest that over 10 million adults here are now online and 10,000 new users are joining them every day. In particular, the free ISPs have brought a new sort of mainstream, non-techie user onto the net.

With the free ISP market now so crowded, companies are having to work harder to attract (and hold on to) users. Some try to do it via content (on their home pages) and special services (e.g. a telephone

### Read about it online - Free ISP listings

By the time you read this, it's likely that loads more companies will have jumped onto the free ISP bandwagon. The net is one of the best places to keep track on the new companies that have entered the market. Try the listing at Yahoo **http://www.yahoo.co.uk**. The quickest way to get what you need is to do a search on "Free ISPs" on the front page. Rich Clickings **http://www.richclickings.co.uk** has a useful list of free ISPs, helpfully split up into 'brand names' and 'no names'. Alternatively, for a listing of all the ISPs (free or fee) in the UK, try **http://thelist.internet.com/countrycode/44/**. ▲

< 70 >

number you can use to pick up voicemail, email and pager messages). Some attempt to target particular sectors of the market, presenting themselves as family-friendly services. An increasing number of free ISPs offer shares to users (e.g. The Mutual.net **http://www.themutual.net**, Totalise **http://www.totalise.net** and Blue Carrots **http://www.bluecarrots.com**). The idea is that the more you use the service, the more your shares will increase in value – in theory. One company is even offering users money in return for the time they spend online. Sign up with 4thenet **http://www.4thenet.co.uk** and you collect points for each minute you're online. Amass enough points (and you need a lot) and you'll get some money back.

Some are offering free telephone calls at off peak times (i.e. the evenings and the weekends) so that your net surfing then really is free of charge. The pioneers were Screaming.net **http://www.screaming.net**, an ISP set up by the electronics retail chain Tempo and the Surrey-based telecommunications provider LocalTel. Here, if you dial into the net at weekends or after six in the evening, you pay nothing at all. However, you do have to sign up with LocalTel. You also need to find a Screaming.net disc. These are only available through branches of Tempo, and, when it started out, the company sensibly chose to ration their distribution. Even so, it experienced serious problems when it first got started, with the service very slow during the 'free' periods. But at the time of writing, it seems to have sorted things out and now runs just fine.

Other companies also attempting to offer completely free time online include Freedom I – the ISP run by Freedom Telecom **http://www.**

< 71 >

**freedomi.com**. Freedom currently offers advertising-funded free telephone calls to its customers. Every five minutes during a call you get a thirty-second ad break. Its net service will offer users sixty minutes of charge-free call time per day. Apparently, this will be funded by focused advertising targeted at individual users.

The subscription-based ISPs have responded with their own offers of free telephone calls. For example Clara.net **http://www.clara.net** now offers a variety of pricing packages, each one with a different amount of charge free telephone call time – usually at weekends and in the evening. Knocked off the top ISP spot by Freeserve, AOL has responded by launching its own free ISP, Netscape Online **http://www.netscapeonline.co.uk**. It also announced trials of a pricing model in which users pay a flat monthly fee and get unlimited calls to a freephone number. If you use the net a lot, this would end up being cheaper than the free ISPs.

Indeed it's close to the American model for pricing telephone calls, where you pay a flat rate for unlimited free local calls and a flat monthly

## Read about it online – CUT

An organisation has been set up to campaign for American-style pricing of local telephone calls here in the UK. It's called the Campaign for Unmetered Telecommunications (as CUT) and its website is a good place to go to keep up with developments in the area **http://www.unmetered.org.uk**. ▲

< 72 >

rate for your net access. Many hard core net users here say they would prefer the 'unmetered' American model. It's clear that AOL would also prefer things to be structured that way in the UK. It has complained that the free ISP business is based on a kink in the way telecommunications pricing is structured here. Certainly, if that kink were ironed out, many free ISPs would struggle. But at the moment, Oftel, the telecoms regulator, seems happy to let things stay as they are. Indeed, give that so many people now connect via free ISPs, changing the way they work will be difficult.

## Which ISP?

The boom in free net access really has benefited ordinary users. Not only has it made getting online cheap. It's made it easy too. Getting hold of the software is not a problem. Of course, it never was, as far as the online services were concerned. AOL in particular flooded the market with its free monthly trial discs. It was hard at one point to pick up a magazine that didn't have one gummed to the front. They're still easy to find – just buy a computer/net magazine. Alternatively go to page 444, where you'll find contact numbers for AOL and the other remaining online services. You'll also find numbers there for the subscription-based ISPs and the free ISPs. Calling up is the best way to get connection discs from the former. Many of the bigger subscription-based ISPs now offer the same sorts of free monthly trials made popular by the online services. And their software has become similarly easy to use.

If you want to get hold of some free ISP discs, you could try the numbers given on page 444. But a walk down your local high street will

< 73 >

**Read about it online – ISPA**

UK ISPs now have their own trade organisation, the Internet Service Providers Association (aka ISPA UK) which was set up to counter misrepresentation of the net and lay down a code of practice for ISPs in Britain. For a peek at their idea of acceptable ISP behaviour (with respect to user privacy and the like), go to **http://www.ispa.org.uk**. ▲

also suffice. Freeserve discs are given away at branches of Dixons. You can get Tesco's discs at Tesco supermarkets, obviously. Asda is giving away the CurrantBun.com discs. You can get the WH Smith software from any of its local branches, though you do have to pay 50p (it goes to charity, apparently). Once you're online, you can also download connection packages from free ISP web sites, which makes it easy to switch to new companies, if your first choice isn't performing that well.

Not only are ISPs queuing up to give you software. They're desperately trying to make it as user-friendly as possible. Nowadays, if an ISP's installation software isn't simple to use, if it doesn't offer a standard package of services, it might as well pack up and go home. It's a long way from the old days when companies gave you a connection and expected you to get your own software.

That said, choosing between the different ISPs, free and subscription-based, can be rather confusing, if only because there's so many, all offering different things. If you ask me, it's not as bad as sorting out a

< 74 >

---

### Jargon File - TCP/IP

As mentioned before, TCP stands for Transmission Control Protocol. IP stands for Internet Protocol. Both 'protocols' (think of them as networking languages) allow your computer to communicate with the internet. ▲

---

mobile phone, but there are lots of different offers. You do need to think a bit about what you want to use the net for, when you're going to connect and how much time you're going to spend online. All ISPs now let you connect via an 0845/0645 local call rate number. All of them give you access to the web and the software you need, which means a web browser and nothing else. More often than not, you're offered Microsoft's Internet Explorer, though some ISPs do give you a choice between Explorer and Netscape Navigator.

If you are using an ancient machine – a PC running Windows 3.x or a pre system 7.5 Mac, you'll also need a TCP/IP stack. A TCP/IP stack is several bits of software in one – TCP/IP software, packet driver software and sockets software – each of which is needed in order to send and receive data across the net. It's highly unlikely that the free ISPs will be able to help you here. They're geared to a post Windows-95 world. So you might have to go with one of the subscription-based ISPs.

In general, ISPs offer you variations on a standard package of services. Here's a few of the things you should look out for.

< 75 >

**Email** Most ISPs give you your own email account, usually a POP3 mail account – though the odd free ISP suggests you make do with a free web email service. Most, but not all, will also give you unlimited email addresses on the same account. This can be useful for families, since it means each family member can have their own personal address.

**Newsgroups** Some free ISPs don't bother with the newsgroups, figuring perhaps that they belong to the old geeky net. They may be right. On the other hand, newsgroups may be the part of the online world that does it for you. And, whilst you can access them via the web, it's not as convenient as doing it via an ISPs news server. If Usenet sounds like your thing, check on which newsgroups an ISP carries and whether they'll get certain groups if you ask.

**Web space** Virtually all ISPs, free or otherwise, offer you space online where you can put up your own web pages. The amount of space varies

---

### Jargon File - POP3

POP3, as in POP3 mail, stands for Post Office Protocol, version 3. This is the protocol that is used when it comes to receiving email. SMTP (aka Simple Mail Transfer Protocol) is used to send email. POP3 is pretty much the standard and helps you pick up your mail while you're travelling. ▲

< 76 >

### Jargon File – Client/Server

Two bits of technical jargon for the price of one: you can't have one without the other. Servers are central computers on which data is stored. Clients are the software programs that access data stored on a server. In a more general sense, client often means any bit of software that accesses information via a network. ▲

– anything up to 20 Mbs). Most assume that if you do get into this, you'll treat it as a bit of fun. If you get serious, you may find yourself having to pay the ISP for hosting your pages. This is perhaps looking a little far ahead but if you do put up a page and it becomes 'too popular', your ISP can cut it off. You might want to check their policy on this.

**Content** Most ISPs offer their users some sort of 'content', usually in the form of a homepage which features news, community areas where you can chat and post messages, shopping services, search engines and much else. Usually you don't have to sign up with a service to access their home page. You don't need to be Freeserf to use the Freeserve homepage, for example. There are exceptions. You do need to sign up to AOL (and hand over some money) to access its chat rooms and information services. At the moment, you also need to sign up with the free ISP CurrantBun.com before you can access its homepage and the various services and content on it. Net pundits often say that the content similar

< 77 >

to the stuff you pay for on certain services is available for free on the net. Often true, but if information you're particularly interested in is available only via a certain provider, it's as good a reason as any to sign up (provided their basic net access provision is up to scratch).

**Support** Telephone support used to be one of the big differences between the free ISPs and the companies that charge subscriptions. On the latter, customer support calls are generally charged at local rates (though in some cases they are free). Free ISPs used to charge around £1 a minute for calls made to their support lines. Charges have gone down now. It's generally something between 50 and 25 pence per minute. Some ISPs offer free calls while you're getting started. A few now offer free technical support all the time. All of them put very detailed technical advice up on their sites. It is possible to get too hung up on the need for technical support. Many free ISPs have made connecting so easy that you often don't need much help.

**Mac Support** As mentioned before, PC users are the dominant population online and many ISPs are generally much happier dealing with them rather than Mac users. Some don't even supply Mac software. However, some ISPs make a point of being Mac friendly. At least it narrows down the field if you're a Mac user. Of the subscription-based ISPs, Direct Connection is supposed to be Mac-friendly. When it comes to free ISPs, Mac users should try Tesco.net, CurrantBun.com, Virgin or UK Online.

< 78 >

**Pricing** Subscription-based ISPs usually have a variety of differently priced access packages on offer. If you know you're only going to use the net for a certain amount of time, you can get a lower monthly rate. Or you can pay a certain fee and get a number of free off peak telephone calls thrown in. Some subscription-based companies now have schemes that give the cut of the telephone charges that the free ISPs rely on back to the ordinary user. Several free ISPs now offer free calls at off peak times. If they can also offer decent service at these times, these offers can definitely be worth it.

**Connections** When you start out, you're probably going to be connecting via a standard telephone line and a modem. But you may want to upgrade to something quicker – an ISDN line, for example. So you should check that your ISP can handle it.

**Loyalty Schemes** Several free ISPs now have loyalty schemes in place which reward users with shares in the company and sometimes even money. In part, this is a sign of how much free ISPs worry about customer loyalty. In theory, there's not much stopping users from flitting from one free ISP account to another. However, the offers of free shares seem as much about generating publicity as they are about encouraging loyalty. Look at them closely and they often don't add up to much.

**User Names and Domain Names** Some ISPs let you pick your own user name. Some don't. If that's the case, find out the kind of thing you're

< 79 >

## Tips – Old 56K modems

If you're using an older computer or one you bought second hand, you may just encounter some problems with older 56K modems. When these were first introduced there were two competing standards – x2 and K56flex. The dispute was resolved, a standard was agreed (called V.90) and now all 56K modems work the same way. But back then, not all the ISPs supported both types of 56K modem. If you have an older machine with a 56K modem, find out what sort it is, then check with your ISP that everything will be OK. More than likely it will be. ▲

likely to be stuck with. If you're planning to use your net connection for business purposes, some ISPs will help you with registering the appropriate domain name (i.e. something like **daves-hot-pies.co.uk**), though it may cost you quite a bit. It may be useful to find out what's on offer.

**Extra Services** In a bid to position itself as a family-friendly service, WH Smith offers free use of the Cyber Patrol filterware package for a year – this will stop your kids accessing 'unsuitable' sites, though it's not without problems. There's more on this on page 391. In an attempt to attract business people, other ISPs offer things like unified message services – i.e. a telephone number you can use to pick up voicemail, email and pager messages. Some subscription-based ISPs offer free virus-

< 80 >

## Jargon File - Spam

Net slang for unsolicited email sent in bulk to thousands of users at once, i.e. electronic junk mail. It's also a verb – you can spam someone as well as receive spam. The name comes from the Monty Python sketch and is supposed to refer to the way it keeps on coming. ▲

checking programs and extras like Real Audio feeds, so you can add music to your website. If you get more serious about the net, it's particularly worth seeing what the subscription services are offering.

**Spam** Some ISPs take action to try to stop it before it gets to your mailbox. Others will offer advice and, in some cases, spam-filtering software.

**Advertising** Some critics suggest that the free services are clogged with ads. This can be overstated. True, the X Stream Network does pump ads at you while you surf. And Freedom I plans more of the same. But the others just deliver the banner ads you find on the commercial web. More irritating, in a subliminal way, is WH Smith's version of Internet Explorer, which features little company logos all over the borders of the browser frame.

< 81 >

You could also look into the background and history of the ISP you're thinking of using. Don't immediately assume that a well-known high street name will be any better at providing net access than someone you've never heard of. It all depends on who that famous name is working with. It can also help to ask around among friends who are online and find out which ISP they use and what they think of them. Then again, perhaps that's not such a good idea. Moaning about your ISP is default behaviour among net users.

If you want to get really serious about all this, try looking at the ISP performance surveys in the specialist net magazines. For example, Internet Magazine regularly rates all the major ISPs, using a series of tests that check how easy it is to connect and how fast those connections are. Results are given for last month's performance. But there's also a chart showing performance over the last half year, which is useful. New ISPs

## Tips - Net Magazines

Both of the leading UK net magazines – Emap's *Internet Magazine* and Future Publishing's *.net* are pretty good places to keep up with ISP performance, new developments online and new net software. Both regularly feature cover discs with demo versions of net programs and copies of the major web browsers. .net is a more consumer-oriented title and Internet probably aims more for the business market, but both are worth checking. ▲

< 82 >

can often start well, then slip down the charts as they become overwhelmed with traffic.

If all this sounds a bit confusing, it shouldn't be. Here's a few questions and answers that may help you make a decision.

## Why use AOL and the other online services?

If you're particularly nervous about getting online, AOL and MSN offer both ease of use and cheap technical support if you do encounter problems. They're family-oriented and their conferences and chat rooms are moderated. In other words, in theory, there's someone around to deal with the pests that pop up occasionally in the online world. They also let parents set up controls that protect their children from some of the dodgier things online. There is some good content on AOL in particular. The shopping area is good and the chat rooms are, um...always interesting.

They are both local and global in scope. Though AOL is an American company, it has worked hard to provide a lot of dedicated British content and services. In addition, it claims that it's one of the more balanced spaces online – women apparently comprise over 50 per cent of its users. If you sign up with an online service, you will also be able to travel round the world (ok, the Western world) and still access the net and pick up your mail. In the past, Compuserve (which targets professionals and business people) has been particularly strong on this. The bad things about the online services (aside from the charges) are the things that might attract some people. They are very modern-mainstream, very commercial – the corporate towns of cyberspace.

< 83 >

## Why sign up with a subscription-based ISP?

In contrast to the likes of AOL, they offer a freer, less controlled, less censored experience. You're encouraged to get out on the net rather than hang around on the services' own private network. Again, you get ease of use and cheap technical support. Though in the past, some flat-fee ISPs were terrible at customer service, they've realised that if they're going to survive they need to get a lot better. That said, in terms of basic connectivity and services, there's often not much difference between them and the free ISPs – besides the fact that you're paying for the former. Certainly, the subscription ISPs have seen their growth slow drastically in the last year. They've responded by concentrating more on business users. Certainly, if you do get serious about the net and want to use it for business purposes, you should probably go with the subscription ISPs. You'll then have a right to demand the reliable service you'll need. You're paying, after all. You'll also be able to get advice and useful extra services.

## Why sign up with a free ISP?

Why not? Free ISPs have made it so easy to find and use their discs that you might as well give them a go. It can't hurt. In general, I think home users who are starting out on the net should probably go with a free ISP at first. They do offer a risk-free cheap way of checking out the net. Once you've been online for a while, you'll have more of an idea of what you want to use the net for. Then you can change to a different provider if necessary.

< 84 >

## Tips - Free Trials

In theory, there's nothing to stop you from using an AOL trial disc, taking advantage of the technical support, getting used to the net, then signing off at the end of the free period and signing up with a free ISP. But if you try it, you may find that it's not that easy to sign off quickly. You might end up paying for a month or so, which, some might say, would serve you right. ▲

## Why stick with a free ISP once you've signed up?

This is the real question as far as free ISPs are concerned. The answer is, you shouldn't if they don't deliver good basic connectivity and the standard services. Indeed, you shouldn't stick with AOL or any other net service provider if they're not performing. You should be able to connect easily at peak times and the service then shouldn't be too slow. You should get lots of email accounts, free web space and access to the newsgroups at the very least. If your free ISP doesn't provide all that, try someone else.

Some analysts have suggested that in future, people will have several free net accounts and will switch between them. I'm not sure if most ordinary net users can really be bothered. Analysts tend to underestimate the role inertia plays with many people online. Service has to get pretty bad before people change. That said, money is always a decisive factor. So the likes of Freeserve could be threatened by the services offering free tele-

< 85 >

phone calls as well as free net access. Certainly, it's worth keeping tabs on offers in this area. See the section on managing multiple ISP assounts.

If you do feel like chopping and changing, if you want to set up several free ISP accounts, so you've got an alternative if your main choice is down or particularly slow one evening, it's easily done. As mentioned before, you can download connection software from the web sites of most of the big free ISPs. Although you can download lots of ISP connection packages, only one can be your default – i.e. the one that starts up automatically when you launch your browser. If you don't want to use your default, locate the connection you want to use in **Dial-Up Networking**, and start it from there. If you're using Internet Explorer, it's also very easy to change the default connection. Select the **Tools** menu, then **Internet Options**, then click on the **Connections** tab. In the **Dial-up settings** box you'll see all the net accounts you've installed. Click on the one you want as the default, then click the **Set Default** button.

One thing to watch out for. Freeserve reconfigures your browser so that it uses a proxy server – a computer which stores copies of popular web pages and hence helps speed up access times. This will cause problems when you try to access via other net accounts. But it can easily be fixed.

▶ In Internet Explorer, select the **Tools** menu, then **Internet Options**, then click the **Connections** tab. Click on the Freeserve account in the **Dial-up settings** box, then click on **Settings**. In the dialog box that comes up, remove the tick in the box next to the line **Use a proxy server**.

▶ In Navigator, select the **Edit** menu, then **Preferences**, then click on the **Proxies** section in the **Category** box on the left (you'll find it in the

< 86 >

**Advanced** section). Put a tick in the box next to **Direct connection to the internet.**

Finally, if you do run several free ISP accounts, email can be confusing, unless you use a single free web mail address.

## Next Step
You have several discs from various free ISPs. Alternatively, you have something from AOL or one of the subscription-based companies. The next step is to put one of them in your computer and get online. Don't worry. You may have heard that connecting to the net is a deeply fraught experience. It used to be. It isn't any more.

## Connecting for the first time
Talk to anyone who started out on the net a few years ago and you will undoubtedly hear a few first-time-connection horror stories. An early subscriber to Demon, the UK's first ISP, apparently commented that setting up an account and connecting was 'a bit like giving birth – so difficult that afterwards, you can never quite remember how you did it'. (This comes from 'net.wars', Wendy Grossman's enjoyable book about net culture).

Back then, if you'd actually bought into all that techno-hype about how you had to get online right now or risk being left behind, experiencing difficulties connecting for the first time was deeply depressing, even vaguely humiliating. It was as if you'd bought a car but then

< 87 >

couldn't figure out how to get the key into the ignition. There you were, ready and willing to get with the program. All around you, people seemed to be moving effortlessly forward into the smart new digital future. But you just couldn't hack it.

The worst thing about all this was, nine times out of ten, it wasn't your fault. In the early days, internet service providers seemed to set out to make the whole process as difficult as possible. Their connection software often refused to connect to anything but still made a mess of your hard disk in the process. Their 'easy to follow' guides always seemed to be written by someone fluent in C++ but with only a passing acquaintance with English. When you did get through to their telephone support line, you discovered that it was manned by the CEO's idiot kid brother.

More generally, ISPs were so keen to talk up the net, they failed to tell first-timers that it still wasn't 100 per cent reliable, that sometimes you could do everything right and still not get online. The good news is that things are a lot easier now. Many ISPs have learnt from their mistakes and now go out of their way to help out nervous newcomers. Of course attempting anything for the first time is always a little disconcerting. But don't worry. This will be easy. The thing to remember about all those connection horror stories is that eventually people sorted out the problems and got online.

## Installing your modem

If you buy a new computer, it will more than likely come with a pre-installed modem. If you do need to install your own external modem, it

< 88 >

should be a problem-free process. Hook your modem up to your computer, turn it on, then turn on your machine. Often your computer will detect your new modem and then ask you to insert the special installation disc it came with. If that doesn't happen, if you're running Windows 95/98, it's pretty easy to set the installation process going yourself. Click the **Start** button, then select **Settings**, then **Control Panel**, then double-click on the **Modems** icon. You'll then be walked through the installation process and prompted to insert the disk. Then it's just a question of specifying the modem you're using from a list of possibles. Once that's done, if you need to, you can always click on the **Properties** button to change the settings. The only thing you really need to worry about here is connection speed. Always pick a speed well above that officially listed for your modem, preferably double.

## The Connection

Competition between ISPs is now so fierce that any company whose installation software isn't simple and easy to use is asking for trouble. Most ISPs now provide introductory packages that walk you through the installation and configuration process and make the first connection for you, setting up your account automatically. All you have to do is put one of their discs in your computer and follow the instructions. They all work slightly differently, but they're all roughly the same, if you see what I mean.

Typically, with a free ISP, once the disc has started, you may first have to enter some information about your system – whether you're using

< 89 >

Windows 95 or 98 or some version of the Mac OS. Then you click on a **Register** button and the disc will use your computer's internet connection package to dial up the ISP. You'll usually go to a registration form. To fill it out, just click in the relevant boxes. At this point, you'll pick a password and confirm it. You'll also be given the chance to choose your email name – i.e. the name that will go at the start of your mail address at the ISP (as in **jim@anotherfreeisp.net**). You'll probably also have to specify the speed your modem connects at.

Look out for something about the ISP sending you email and regular mail in the future about all their wonderful projects. It's up to you, but generally I prefer not to get too much of this kind of stuff. So make sure the relevant box is ticked or unticked as necessary. Once the form is sent, you usually get a message confirming the details you entered. Often you get something telling you that your nickname/email name has already gone and you have to come up with something else. From here you can click on your browser and you're ready to go.

Alternatively, sometimes, once the set up process is done, you'll be disconnected. You can then connect properly by starting your browser. That will also start up the connection file created on your disc by the ISP. Once your connection software is running, you'll hear the modem open the telephone line and tap out a number. If your ISP isn't engaged, you'll hear chirruping fax-like noises as your modem establishes a connection. Onscreen, you'll see a dialog box that tells you what's happening – when your computer is dialling, when it's verifying your password. Once you're connected, a dialog box will appear telling you you're online. This

< 90 >

usually has a **Disconnnect** button you can use to log off. It also keeps tabs on how long you spend online, which can be very useful. As you'll discover, it's easy to lose track of time online. Your browser will then load its homepage. It will usually be something put up by your ISP. Congratulations. You're online. Now it's just a matter of deciding where you want to go or what you want to do.

You don't have to click on your browser to connect to the net. These days, most ISP installation packages create a little icon that sits on your desktop. Click on this and it will start the whole connection process and launch your browser. You could also manually start up the connection file yourself. For example, with Windows 95/98, open the **Dial-Up Networking** folder (You'll find it in the **My Computer** folder on your desktop). In here you'll see the connection file your ISP's installation software created. Click/double-click on this and you'll connect to the net.

---

### Tips – Try another disc

If you use a free ISP disc and it doesn't make connecting easy – if it crashes your machine or if it isn't easy to understand, bin it and get something else. Don't get on the phone to the ISP to ask for help. They'll charge you and they don't deserve your money if their installation package isn't easy to use. Instead, call another ISP and get their disc sent over. There are plenty to choose from. For some contact numbers, go to page 444. ▲

< 91 >

If you're using a free trial disc for AOL or one of the subscription-based ISPs, it should work in roughly the same way. Each trial disc usually has a number on it. You'll be asked to enter this at some point. You'll also be asked for your credit card details. Don't worry about this – it's one part of the general security procedures to make sure that you don't keep trying to log on for free with trial discs. You won't be charged. At least you shouldn't be, unless you decide to sign up at the end of the trial period. However, some companies have had problems with what you might call general billing anomalies. So if you decide after the trial that you don't want to subscribe, check your next credit-card bill just to make sure there haven't been any mix-ups.

When you connect to an online service like AOL, you do get a chance to pick your own name, though this can be frustrating. They have such huge numbers of subscribers that you can pretty much guarantee that someone will already have your preferred nickname. If you want to use your real name, you may have to resign yourself to being JimMcClel9687 or JaneMcClel5271. This may not seem too much of an indignity but for some it's a symbol of the corporate, impersonal nature of the services like AOL. Once you've connected properly, you'll see AOL's homepage. You aren't on the net, not yet, not quite. You're accessing information from AOL's own network. If you want to explore the internet proper, look around for a big button marked **Internet**. Click on that and you will be taken to the Internet Gateway.

< 92 >

## Connecting with pre-installed ISP software

If you've bought a new PC or an iMac, you won't necessarily need to get hold of a free disc to connect to the net. Most new computers now come with software from several ISPs already installed. As mentioned before, iMacs come with several ISP connection packages. To use one, start up the **Internet Setup Assistant** (you'll find it in the **Assistants** folder – alternatively, select the **Apple** menu, then **Internet Access**, then **Internet Setup Assistant**). This walks you through setting up an account, prompting you for details of the modem and telephone connection. Then it asks whether you want to register with an ISP. If you indicate that you do, you're asked to pick your country, then you're offered a choice of various ISPs. You're given some information (about charges or the lack of them) to help you make your choice. Once you're satisfied with your choice, the **Internet Setup Assistant** will dial up the ISP and start your browser. Then you'll go to the ISPs registration page. You then fill out the form and choose your password. Then, usually, **Internet Setup Assistant** will kick back in and remind you of the details you entered. You may then be disconnected. If you are, you can then get back online and browsing by double-clicking on your browser icon or on the **Browse the Internet** icon.

New PCs tend to come with free trial accounts for both AOL and MSN. You can also use the **Internet Connection Wizard** to sort out an account. On some new PCs, you sometimes see an icon on the desktop for this. If you don't you can start the **ICW** by clicking the **Start** button, then **Programs**, then **Accessories**, then **Communications**. Select the

< 93 >

**Internet Connection Wizard.** You call up a screen that offers you various choices. Choose to sign up for a new internet account. The program will then dial up a page that has information about various ISPs, some free, some subscription-based. If any takes your fancy, you can set up an account with one of them.

## Connecting with an older computer

Connecting is usually not too much of a problem these days. However, if you are using an older computer, there's altogether more potential for hassle. To connect to the net, you need something called a TCP/IP stack. As mentioned before, if your computer runs Windows 95/98, Windows NT or Macintosh System 7.5 (and anything after that), then you already have something suitable. Your ISP's introductory package will work with the TCP/IP stack already on your machine. When you install it, it will create a connection file that it will then use each time you call up your ISP. However, if you're running Windows 3.x, you will need to install a TCP/IP stack. Your ISP should have sent you what you need – probably

---

### Tips - Dodgy discs

Without wishing to name any names, more than a few of the free ISPs that claim to support Macs seriously under-perform. The discs they supply can be buggy and harder to use than is necessary. So, if you've got an iMac, it may be easier to use the pre-installed accounts. ▲

---

< 94 >

a version of Trumpet Winsock. If you have an older Macintosh, you'll need MacTCP/MacPPP. Talk to your ISP about this.

## Manually configuring your connection

If you are running Windows 3.x and using something like Trumpet Winsock, you will have to manually configure your TCP/IP stack. Usually, you can kick the process of by selecting the **File** menu, then **Setup.** You'll then have to enter various bits of information – a list follows shortly. If you're running a more modern computer, you may still have to manually configure your own TCP/IP stack. Alternatively, you may want to change the details on an account you've already installed.

Windows 95/98 features an **Internet Setup Wizard** that makes the whole process easy. Set it going by clicking the **Start** button, then selecting **Programs**, then **Accessories**, then **Internet Tools**, then **Internet Setup Wizard**. The choose the 'set up an internet connection manually' option. Alternatively, click/double-click on the **My Computer** icon, then **Dial-Up Networking**. Click/double-click on **Make a New Connection**, then follow the directions. By the end, you will have created a connection file for your ISP. When you want to connect, just click/double-click on that icon. The Mac **Internet Setup Assistant** will also walk you through the process of making a new connection or re-configuring an existing one.

In both cases, you will need some technical information, addresses and telephone numbers about your ISP. They should send you what you need. Alternatively, look for **Readme** text file on the disc they send. This

< 95 >

should have the information you need. As you go along, you may need to enter some of the following:

**Domain Name** This is your ISP's domain name – something like **yourserviceprovider.net**

**Domain Name Server/IP Address** Four numbers separated by full stops. This is the computer version of the domain name

**Dial Up Telephone Number** The number you use to connect to your ISP

**Username and Password** The name and password you chose or were assigned when you subscribed

**Email Address** Your own personal Email address – as in **yourname@yourserviceprovider.co.uk**

**Email Account Username and Password** Relevant if you have a POP3 mail account – and you probably will

**Mail Server** This is the address of the computer that handles mail at your ISP – something like **mail.yourserviceprovider.net**

**News Server** The address of the computer at your ISP that handles Usenet newsgroups – usually something like **news.yourserviceprovider.net**.

This shouldn't be too confusing, but if you do have problems or if the basic information your ISP sent you seems unclear, then call them. It's in their interest to get you online as quickly as possible.

In the past, if you'd been connecting via an online service and then tried to install and use an ISP's connection software, especially something like Trumpet Winsock for Windows 3.x, you could occasionally

< 96 >

encounter problems. These were caused by competing versions of the same connection software getting tangled up. As far as I can tell, this isn't a problem with Windows 95/98 and the online services have sorted out the problem. But if you are using an ancient machine and plan to run accounts with an online service and an ISP at the same time, there's an outside chance you might have a problem. The safest bet is to call both just to check that there isn't going to be a problem.

## Troubleshooting

ISPs now make connecting pretty easy. But despite everyone's best intentions, things don't always go smoothly. Here's a few problems you might encounter.

### The dial-up number your ISP gave you is engaged

This is more likely to happen if you're calling during peak time – in the early evening, between seven o'clock and ten o'clock. If they encounter a busy line, many connection software packages will automatically try again a few times. If this doesn't work, wait a while and then have another go. If you find it happening a lot, you may want to call your ISP to ask what's going on. The first time someone showed me round the net, in 1993, we had to wait around twenty minutes to get through to his service provider. Things have got a lot better since then. According to recent surveys done by the specialist net magazines, around nine out of ten calls to ISPs get through the first time. If your ISP falls below that standard, try someone else.

< 97 >

### You connect but it all seems incredibly slow

Welcome to the net. Unfortunately, that's sometimes the way things are online. No doubt you've heard the gags about the World Wide Wait. Sometimes problems are caused because your provider just has too many subscribers online and hasn't upgraded bandwidth to cope. An efficient ISP should be able to keep things running smoothly as they grow. If things seem persistently slow, call your ISP and ask if they've been experiencing problems. They will probably say it isn't their fault. Often it's hard to disagree. There may just be heavy traffic online across the net in general, in which case there's nothing you can do about it.

Many UK net users claim that everything works just fine until the mid afternoon, when 'America wakes up, gets into the office and logs on' and everything online seizes up. You can see why this might be the case. But then again, the East Coast and the West Coast get up at different times, plus students, heavy users in the US, get up later than everybody else and stay up later than the average working stiff. So you do wonder if it's actually some sort of net myth. That said, things often do seem to get very slow online at around 3 or 4 o'clock in the afternoon.

If speed is a problem and you can be flexible, try different times of the day (and night). Alternatively, if you are connecting from home, you could try the weekend. Recent surveys have suggested that the bulk of UK users connect from the office so logically there ought to be a fall-off in UK-based traffic on Saturday. However, thanks to BT's new cheap weekend rates, these are becoming increasingly busy. Indeed, according to some sources, the busiest time online in the UK is Sunday afternoon and evening.

< 98 >

## Jargon File – Bandwidth

Network capacity, i.e. the amount of data that can be sent over a net connection. Bandwidth is the scarce resource of the digital age. We have plenty of information, but not enough space on the wires we send it down. Hence insults which refer to online incompetents as 'a waste of bandwidth', organisations like the Bandwidth Preservation Society and geek slang in which people who say a lot in a short space are 'high bandwidth' individuals. In the future, bandwidth will be plentiful, say the techno-Utopians – but don't believe it. Networks might be like roads – traffic will always expand to fill the available space. ▲

**The modem makes all the right noises and you seem to connect fine but when you try to start up your web browser, you can't get anywhere**

It may be that you haven't actually established a proper IP connection. Your connection software will usually tell you if that is the case. But if you're really keen, you can check the connection yourself with a program called Ping. Your ISP may give you this as part of the start-up kit. Some versions of Windows 95/98 come with Ping included. You can access it via the **Start** button. Select **Run** then use the **Browse** button to look for the Ping program. Start Ping up and type in a domain name (e.g. **www.guardianunlimited.co.uk**). If you have established a proper connection, this should be converted into an IP address, i.e. a group of four

< 99 >

## Read about it online – Net Traffic

Tracking traffic and conditions on the net – call it info-meteorology – is a growth area, especially in America. Texas-based outfit MIDS run a web page called The Internet Weather Report, which offers maps, graphs and even little animations detailing traffic hotspots and problems on the net round the world **http://www4.mids.org/weather**. One for the techies. ▲

numbers separated by full stops. If that doesn't happen, you have a problem. It could be that your software isn't configured properly. Alternatively, your ISP might be having trouble. Either way, have a look at your TCP/IP software and check the various addresses and names against the information sent by your ISP. Try connecting again. If you still have problems, call your ISP.

**Your modem dials up without any apparent hitch, you seem to get through fine, but then nothing happens**
This could be because your ISP's computers are down. This doesn't happen as often as it used to but is still not completely unknown. You could try telephoning customer support to find out what's going on but other frustrated users will probably be trying to do the same thing, so you might not get through. ▲

< 100 >

# 3 GETTING TO GRIPS WITH THE NET

●●●●●●●●●●●●●●●●●●●●●●●●●●●●●●●●●●●●●●

Before you start, a quick word about the way this section is organised. I've started with **The World Wide Web – The Basics**, because that seems to be the most popular part of the net. However, email comes a close second, so you could quite easily go to that part of the section first. If you do start with the Web, it would make sense to move on to **Searching the Web** next, then **Downloading Files From The Net**. If you start with the portion on email, then it might make sense to go next to **Usenet Newsgroups**, since once you've cracked mail the latter will be a doddle. After that, you will be well prepared to tackle **Online Chat**. In other words, read these sections in whatever order you like.

## The World Wide Web

The web is just one part of the internet. Of course, many people seem to think that the web is the net, end of story. And increasingly, they have a point. Many of the services you find elsewhere on the net – chat rooms, newsgroups, mailing lists – are now migrating on to the web (albeit in a slightly different form). But strictly speaking, the web is the

< 101 >

part of the net where you can not only read text, but look at pictures, both static and animated, watch video, listen to music, navigate 3D graphic worlds and much else. More to the point, it's the bit that comes with an easy-to-use GUI. For the most part, instead of typing in complicated commands, you can use the mouse to just point and click to wherever you want to go.

The writer David Hudson (the man behind the seemingly now dormant webzine Rewired – **http://www.rewired.com/**) has a nice line on the web. He describes it as a cross 'between a slick magazine and very slow television', which catches the web's hybrid nature and its ability to be both exciting and frustrating at the same time. Of course, for many would-be techno-business people, the web is simply 'where the action is'. Its graphic user-friendliness has led to it being embraced by entrepreneurs everywhere who think it might offer a quick route to riches. Web sites with good business ideas now routinely draw in millions of dollars of

### Jargon File – GUI

Graphical User Interface. Developed in the seventies at the Xerox PARC research lab, brought to ordinary punters in the eighties by Apple, the GUI made computers user-friendly by replacing text commands with a visual interface made up of icons, windows and the whole desktop metaphor. If you want to sound as if you know what you're talking about, pronounce it 'Gooey'. ▲

< 102 >

funding from investment bankers and go on to float for astronomical amounts on the stock market. As a result, some online old timers have written the web off as a transnational shopping mall. Certainly it's one of the places to go to see what the much-vaunted global economy actually looks like.

But the web isn't just a commercial thing. It also lets all sorts of ordinary individuals have their say. Seen from one angle, it is McLuhan's global village reconfigured as a virtual mall. But take another view and it looks like an international psychoburbia, a cacophony of competing voices in which the passions, obsessions and pathologies of those ordinary people who live next door to you are all out on show.

Like a lot of things online, the web had its beginnings in the world of academic research and is, believe it or not, a British invention. It was developed by British physicist Tim Berners-Lee, mainly as a way to help researchers at CERN (the European Particle Physics Laboratory in Geneva) access and share resources more efficiently. He came up with an extension of an old idea – hypertext. When you read a hypertext document, certain words or phrases are marked as links. Click on these and you go to another document with a connection to the first – an essay on a related subject or a table of statistics.

Hypertext links connect documents so you can easily move between them, following up specific ideas or trains of thought. Berners-Lee adapted this for computer networks. So a document stored on one computer (or server) could be linked via a network to another on a different computer. Berners-Lee first came up with the idea for the web

< 103 >

## Read about it online - Tim Berners-Lee

Tim Berners-Lee is currently working at the Massachusetts Institute of Technology and is also the director of the World Wide Web Consortium, an organisation set up to oversee the web's development and make sure that it retains common standards - amongst other things. The W3C site is a good place to go to catch up on new web developments – **http://www.w3.org/**. Berners-Lee's own page is at **http://www.w3.org/People/Berners-Lee/**. ▲

in 1989. Over the next two years or so, he developed HTML (HyperText Markup Language) which could be used to format and link text documents on a network and wrote the first web browser/editor, the first web server and most of the communications software.

Berners-Lee made his various innovations available online in 1991. Things really took off when the first graphic web browser was released in 1993 (something that angered Berners-Lee, who apparently thought images on web pages trivialised his original idea). Called Mosaic, it was developed at the National Centre for Supercomputing Applications at the University of Illinois (by, among others, Marc Andreessen – who went on to co-found Netscape).

The World Wide Web and Mosaic caught on for several reasons. The point-and-click interface made the net user-friendly. The web was also the first part of the net that looked sort of ok. In addition, it was

< 104 >

**Jargon File – Standard**

A format that is approved and accepted by the computer industry as a whole. Standards serve ordinary users because they mean that products – hardware and software – produced by different companies will work with each other. Ordinary users in the past have suffered because of competing standards (cf. Apple Macs vs. Windows). It was hoped that the web would offer a bright, new, universally compatible future. It hasn't quite turned out that way. ▲

available for free. If Berners-Lee and the programmers responsible for the first Mosaic had set out to make money, it's likely that other companies would have appeared with their browsers or 'new improved' versions of HTML that weren't compatible and everyone would have quickly found themselves bogged down in a battle over standards. By giving their ideas away, they helped establish a standard everyone could then work with. Faced with the web today, packed as it is with advertising sites, online shops and webzines put up by multi-national media conglomerates, it's easy to forget its beginnings in what some people refer to as the internet gift economy. But those roots are important and still exert an influence.

Another reason for the web's success is that HTML is relatively easy to use. After a couple of days of swotting, people could create their own web pages. When the web first got started, many people did just that, not

< 105 >

## Jargon File – Web Pages, Web Sites & Homepages

Let's get these straight before we go any further. A web page is a document, usually formatted in HTML, which might contain text, images, animations, sound and even video. A website is a collection of pages put up by an individual, institution or business. A homepage can be (a) the first page your browser shows when it starts; or (b) the first page of a website. But most non-geeky types now think of a homepage as a personal website put up by an ordinary net user to reflect their interests and obsessions. ▲

for profit but for fun or to get something off their chest. Personal homepages quickly became a sort of digital folk art. Some were the online equivalent of the slide shows you inflict on neighbours you don't really like – chock full of pictures of kids looking cute. But others were clever, thoughtful and passionate, like a good print magazine. Whilst big companies struggled to 'get' the web, many ordinary users just got on with it.

The rudimentary nature of the technology meant that someone in a bedroom in Brighton could create a website that was better than something done by a big company. The conventional wisdom is that, as the web has developed to incorporate multimedia, it's become a lot harder for ordinary users to compete with bigger companies. As a result, the argument goes, claims that the democratic nature of the web allowed ordinary people to become media producers now look a little overblown. However, it's still possible for someone with a good idea and the commit-

< 106 >

ment to see it through to make a splash on the web. Some well-chosen words can still beat flashy graphics and bouncy animations. Perhaps the attitudes or prejudices of web users (or rather, the journalists in the media who review web pages) is the real problem. As the web has become more slick and commercial, there has been a creeping tendency to see amateur sites and personal homepages as the preserve of cranks.

Sometimes it feels as if personal homepages have been drawn into the general commercialism of the web, with the baby pics taking a backseat to pages that aspire to being little more than digital business cards. Certainly, homepages have become big business for some. Companies like Geocities and Tripod have become successful by creating places where people can set up personal homepages.

So-called web community sites now host millions of homepages (and make their money via advertising). Users get help in creating their homepages (everything from advice to site templates they can follow) and can

### Read about it online - Home Page TV

American filmmaker Doug Block has made a documentary (called 'Home Page') about the early days of the web and some of the people behind some of the most popular homepages on the net. It was shown recently on HBO in the States and seems likely to turn up here late one night on BBC2 or C4. You can find out a bit more at Block's own page **http://www.d-word.com/**. ▲

< 107 >

put their site in online areas filled with like-minded users (everyone from science-fiction fans to family-values types can find their digital home).

These community sites are amongst the wilder, more chaotic areas of the web and have come under attack from various critics. Lots of people hate the intrusive pop-up and slide down ads on these sites. Many pundits have been sceptical about whether these spaces are real 'communities', suggesting that there isn't much interaction between users on these sites and that many of the pages are dead or dying. More specifically, Geocities was heavily criticised recently when it seemed to suggest that it 'owned' all the content on the pages on its site. It has now backed away from this. For a general look around, go to Geocities (or Yahoo Geocities, as it's known now) at **http://www.geocities.com**, Tripod at **http://www.tripod.com**, Angelfire **http://www.angelfire.com** or try the British competitor, Fortune City at **http://www.fortunecity.com**. Thanks to the web community sites, there are now more personal homepages than

---

### Read about it online – Small sites on top

For proof that small sites can still triumph online, go to Birds in a Cheshire Garden **http://www.abcissa.force9.co.uk/birds/**, a site put up by bird watcher Phil Barnett. Earlier this year (1999), it beat off various big name competitors to be named as 'Site of the Year' in the Yell UK Web Awards – there's more about these at **http://www.yell.co.uk/yell/yellawards/index.html**. ▲

< 108 >

**Read about it online – Net Diaries**

How personal are personal homepages? Very personal, it seems. Lots of people put their daily diaries – which cover everything from when they last had sex to the breakfast cereal they ate this morning – on the web for everyone to read. American critic Mark Dery once suggested that these net journals were both critiques of modern celebrity obsession and part of that obsession. Some net diarists are now online celebs thanks to their efforts. Take Justin Hall (who features in the 'Home Page' documentary mentioned above) **http://www.justin.org/vita/**. His monster site also has links to other diary pages. ▲

ever, and a lot of them are still worth a look. Sure, the commercial sites are exciting and useful, but in your rush to get the latest news, download some new music files by The Beastie Boys or buy the latest Alex Garland novel online, don't forget about the other side of the web.

## Portals

As you'll discover shortly, when you start up your browser, it loads what's known as a home page. A couple of years ago, various big companies decided that home pages were the way to make money online. Online services (AOL **http://www.aol.com**), software companies (Netscape **http://www.netscape.com**, Microsoft **http://www.microsoft.com**) search

< 109 >

sites and directories (Yahoo **http://www.yahoo.com**, Excite **http://www.excite.com**), big media companies (Disney **http://www.go.com**) and, over here, big ISPs like Freeserve (**http://www.freeserve.net**) all decided that there were serious advertising bucks in being the page you see when you start your browser. Consequently, they've created so-called 'portals', user-friendly sites which offer free email, search engines, online shopping, homepage areas, personalisation services that let you choose the news/information you want and much else. At first, the big portals were very successful at drawing online traffic. Recently, there have been signs that they aren't growing that quickly any more. Now the new fad is vertical portals (or, if you can believe it, vortals), portals which specialise in one area or interest. However, don't expect the big one-size-fits-all portals to disappear.

The theory behind portals is that they can 'supply all your net needs on one page'. In a way, they do. Unfortunately, they all do it in roughly the same way. And they all look and feel almost exactly the same. In a way, they take the modern mainstream feel of the old online services and impose it on the web. When you get online, give these sites a look. They can be very useful. But remember that though they're hyped as 'gateways to the net', the business plan behind them is built on the theory that they'll wind up as 'destinations'. The hope is that you won't go through the gateway that much but will stay on the site in question, be exposed to all the advertising and shop at the sites the portal has deals with (and hence earn them commissions). If you do stay, you'll also end up sampling a limited version of the net. When you're on a

< 110 >

portal, you can only access the news/shopping/search sites the portal has deals with. It's perfectly possible to assemble your own portal by putting together a list of your own favourite sites. If you find news/community/ shopping sites you like, you can 'bookmark' them (more on this shortly) and then you can get to them quickly without having to go to someone else's portal.

## Software

To access the web, you need a web browser. When browsers first appeared, they were, as the geeks put it, pretty 'cool'. But they were also pretty basic. In the last few years, browsers have grown into multimedia devices capable of handling sound, video and 3D graphics. They've also become multi-purpose net tools – the easy-to-use front end of what marketing types refer to as an integrated internet suite – i.e. a pile of related programs which you use to deal with your email, download software from FTP sites, read newsgroups and much else.

Getting a browser is pretty simple. There are two big players in the browser business – Microsoft and Netscape. Netscape's browser has always been called Navigator – except that now, somewhat confusingly, it's been swallowed up by Communicator, a 'suite of net tools'. Microsoft's browser is Internet Explorer. You can get this in the basic browser version or with all sorts of extra programs. Whilst I was writing this book, Navigator/ Communicator was on version 4.6 and Internet Explorer was on version 5.0. Throughout this book, the directions on specific tasks refer to these browsers.

< 111 >

Just to complicate things, the Mac version of Internet Explorer was only on 4.5. Version 5.0 is apparently on the way. In general, the Mac versions of the browsers are roughly the same as their Windows counterparts. Some menus have different names and some things that feature at toolbar buttons in the Windows browsers are accessed by little tabs at the side of the screen in the Mac equivalents. For the most part, Netscape does a better job than Microsoft when it comes to making its Mac and Windows browsers roughly the same. If there are differences that are confusing, I'll try to point them out as we go along.

Your ISP should supply you with one of big two browsers. The sensible thing to do is to try that out for a while. If you really don't like the browser your ISP gave you, go online (either to **http://www. microsoft.com** or **http://www.netscape.com**) and download the one you haven't got. (There's advice on how to do this on page 252.) Alternatively, look for the cover discs given away with the specialist net magazines. If you do decide to get a new browser, be prepared for a lengthy download (I can think of more amusing things to do when you first get online). When you get Communicator or Internet Explorer, you'll be offered various options. If you only want to use your browser for the web (and you don't have much disk space), go for the browser-only option. Otherwise, get the full versions, which come with all sorts of useful programs.

Both Microsoft and Netscape regularly pump out upgrades and new versions of their browsers. And both browsers have menu links that take you directly to pages where you can get new versions/upgrades. It's useful to check in at these pages every now and then, especially if you use

< 112 >

Internet Explorer – there are always lots of bug fixes and patches and security updates on the Microsoft page.

▶ In Internet Explorer, get online and select the **Tools** menu then **Windows Update**. You'll go to a page where you can download various Windows-related upgrades and extras.

▶ In Navigator, get online and select the **Help** menu, then **Software Updates**. You'll go to a page where you're walked through the upgrade process

Each new official release of the big two browsers now tends to come with roughly similar supposedly must-have cutting edge features. For example, the big idea in Version 4 of Communicator and Internet Explorer was 'push', a method of information delivery in which you signed up to web sites (or channels) which then pushed information at you at regular intervals. This was supposed to set the net alight but failed to sizzle even slightly and was quietly dropped for the next versions of both browsers. Since then, one of the big ideas has been something called 'smart browsing', which seems to be about helping users navigate the web and find good things quicker. For example, both browsers now use technology from a program called Alexa which lets users visit a site and call up a list of other pages which other users thought were similar. Netscape has also tied its browser more closely to its homepage/portal site, Netcenter. You can store personal details (for example, your Bookmarks list of favourite sites) so that you can access them whatever computer you're using. With Internet Explorer, Microsoft has begun to

< 113 >

concentrate more on snazzy media features – for example, there's now a special toolbar you can use if you want to use Explorer to listen to online radio stations (more on this on page 331).

When it comes to choosing browsers, factors beyond simple usability may influence your choice. If you despise Bill Gates and all his works, you may want to go with Netscape. Alternatively, even if you don't like Internet Explorer that much, you may want to stick with it because it works with all the other Microsoft software you have. Really, you should just make your decision, pick a browser, then forget about it and get on with the interesting stuff – i.e. wandering around the web.

According to some people, things aren't that easy. For them, picking a browser has become part of what net journalists used to call 'The Browser War' – as in the ongoing battle between Netscape and Microsoft to become the preferred way of accessing the web (and the net). It has to be said that this all feels somewhat less of an issue that it did a couple of years ago. When AOL bought Netscape in 1998, it made it clear that the browser wars were just a small skirmish in a much larger ongoing conflict. Over the next few years, AOL and Microsoft will clearly go head to head as both attempt to become the dominant force in the online world.

They've already started – take the recent clash between the two over Instant Messages, the small chat programs that let you 'page' friends when they come online and then chat with them. In the future, the big battles will be fought over cable and other forms of broadband access to the net. In that context, the browser war feels like just one campaign, not some huge all-encompassing battle. Actually, there was always some-

< 114 >

thing phoney about it. The war served mainly to pump up the image of the big two and to squeeze out alternatives. Since it has led to the arrival of incompatible standards – some web pages can't be accessed if you don't have Internet Explorer – it's also unclear whether it has actually benefited ordinary punters.

Recently, it was announced that Microsoft now had a slight lead in the browser war. That does represent a huge turnaround. Three years ago, Netscape was way out in front. It was the first company to realise the commercial potential of the web and the first version of its Navigator browser took over the net when it was released for free in 1994. Netscape had the market to itself then, because it took Microsoft a while to 'get' the net (i.e. realise that as computers became ever more connected, the browser might turn into an 'Operating System for the

---

**Read about it online – Non-Browser Specific WWW**

Once on the web, you might see signs on a site saying that it is 'best viewed with this or that browser'. This is the result of the likes of Microsoft and Netscape adding their own extensions to HTML rather than waiting for a standard to be approved. It irritates a lot of people and goes against the spirit of the web, which was supposed to be universal. Hence sites like the Campaign for a Non-Browser Specific WWW – not the catchiest title, but the website is worth a look – **http://www.anybrowser.org/campaign/**. ▲

< 115 >

net', capable of supplanting the ubiquitous Windows). It took Microsoft even longer to produce a reasonable version of its Internet Explorer browser. But by the time IE3 came out (1996), it was accepted that Microsoft had just about caught up, thus reinforcing the general perception that it takes the company three tries to get anything right.

Microsoft began to make up lost ground by giving IE away for free and has apparently pledged that it will continue to do so for ever (Netscape moved quite quickly to charging for Navigator, then changed its mind and started giving it away again). However, critics argued that the company was also trying to catch up by using its general dominance in computer software. The US government is currently taking action over claims that Microsoft unfairly used its operating system monopoly to win the browser war (for example, by pressurising computer manufacturers into including a copy of Internet Explorer in PCs that ran Windows). It's easy to understand the worries. Few users, particularly first-timers, will go to the trouble of downloading a copy of Navigator when Internet Explorer is there on their desktop.

Over the last two years, Microsoft's general strategy has been to integrate its browser and the Windows operating system ever more tightly, so that you move seamlessly between them. In other words, the operating system will be the browser (and/or vice versa). That was the big idea (sort of) behind Windows 98. Simplifying things slightly, this lets you put a browser-like interface on many of the files and apps on your computer. There are **Back/Forward** buttons and a location bar you can use to navigate your hard drive. Rather than clicking to select something and

< 116 >

### Read about it online – Anti-Microsoft Sites

The web is heaving with them – some silly and sophomoric, some very serious. In the latter category is the page on Microsoft and anti-trust issues maintained by the Consumer Project on Technology – **http://www.essential.org/antitrust/microsoft/**. Not everyone online hates Microsoft, though it sometimes seems that way. The Ayn Rand-ite magazine Capitalism has organised a campaign to stop the persecution of Microsoft and Bill Gates – it's at **http://www. moraldefense.com/microsoft/**. ▲

double-clicking to open it, you move the cursor over a file to select it and click once to open it – as you do on the web. Whatever you're working on your computer, it's easy to launch Explorer and move on to the web, then back to your desktop.

The conventional wisdom was that, in the end, this approach would inevitably win the war. As a result, the US government has attempted to intervene. There have been suggestions that Windows PCs should come with Navigator as well as Internet Explorer or that Microsoft should make it as easy to integrate rival browsers into its operating systems as Explorer. But step back for a minute and think. Do you really want the web 'seamlessly integrated' with the rest of your computer? Do you want it to be unclear when you move from your desktop to the web and back?

< 117 >

### Read about it online – Web Stalker

The digital art world is beginning to get involved in the browser wars. Take the Web Stalker, an alternative browser produced by I/O/D (a loose alliance of programmers and artists). It may not be the greatest piece of tech in the world but it does show you that there are different visions of the web. For a version of WebStalker and some interesting thoughts on the browser wars, go to **http://bak. spc.org/iod/**. There are plenty of other artists' browsers you can mess around with now – try Shredder **http://www.potatoland.org/shredder** or Netomat **http://www.netomat.net/**. The New York Times ran a good piece about all this (you will have to register with the site to access this) **http://www.nytimes.com/library/tech/99/06/cyber/artsatlarge/ 24artsatlarge.html**. ▲

Just before it was bought by AOL, Netscape pulled an interesting move. It tied itself to the Open Source movement and released the source code for Navigator 5.0 so that the programmers and geeks around the world could mess around with it and attempt to produce their own version of Netscape. Source code is seen by companies like Microsoft as their prime piece of intellectual property, something to be protected at all costs. In contrast, Open Source programmers argue that source code should be free (as in open to inspection). That way, users can work with it and collaborate to make it better. There was a great deal of idealistic

< 118 >

talk about Netscape's hook up with the Open Source movement. However, AOL's purchase of Netscape has slowed everything down. That said, various programmers are still working on the open source version of Netscape Navigator. It will definitely be worth checking out what they eventually come up with. For more information, go to Mozilla.org **http://www.mozilla.org**.

Have the browser wars benefited the ordinary punter? It's true that both big browsers are now available for free. But both have become rather bloated as each company adds new features and gimmicks in an attempt to get an edge. And because they rush them out too quickly, neither is as reliable as it ought to be (though they're getting better). And although both companies keeping adding new features that 'differentiate' their product, both big browsers are essentially the same. Certainly, they both push a fairly standard vision of what a browser could and should be. In the past some people expected you to take sides in the browser

---

### Tips – Browser Watch

There are several high-profile sites still tracking browser developments. MecklerMedia's Browserwatch is worth a look **http://browserwatch.internet.com/**. CNet's site **http://www.browsers.com** is good on links to what it calls 'rebel browsers' – translation – stuff not made by either Microsoft or Netscape. It does sound a bit more exciting than 'geek toys'. ▲

---

< 119 >

## Read about it online – Neo Planet

There's yet another new browser you might want to have a look at. Neoplanet claims to offer all the functionality of its competitors, but aims to also look a lot better. You can choose various sorts of 'skins' that sit on top of the basic browser – the choices on offer range from 'futuristic' to 'industrial' and 'nature' (if you fancy a browser with an on-screen wood finish. You can also create your own skins, if you're that way inclined. For more information, go to **http://www.neoplanet.com**. ▲

war. AOL's purchase of Netscape just underlined the fact that there wasn't much difference between the big two. Both are big companies keen to turn a profit. That said, Netscape's hook-up with the Open Source community did score them brownie points with geeks and people who work in the computer industry – who are understandably fed up with Microsoft's dominance.

However, ordinary punters often just want software that works and lets them share their work with friends and colleagues. And Internet Explorer has improved a lot. Perhaps the best thing to do is try them out and pick the one you like. If you have the disk space, keep copies of both and pick and choose. If you haven't got the space or memory to run either Microsoft or Netscape, there are smaller browsers you can try. It's perfectly possible to be a conscientious objector in the browser war. For

< 120 >

example, you could try Opera, a small but increasingly popular browser produced by a Norwegian software company. You have to pay for it, but it's fast, reliable, does virtually all the things the big browsers do and takes up less than 2 Mb of disk space. The makers say it will work fine with a 386 PC with 8 Mb of RAM. So if you're using an old PC, you know what to do. You can download a version from **http://www.opera.com**. An Opera for Macs is in development. In the meantime, Mac users might want to have a look at iCab **http://www.icab.de**.

## Surfing the web for the first time

You don't need to configure your browser before you can get moving – if all you want to do is go on the web. You will need to enter some information if you're planning to use it for email and Usenet newsgroups, but

---

### Read about it online – Surfing

It is one those bits of net slang everyone loves to hate. If you can't stand the term, blame Jean Armour Polly, who is officially accepted as the person who first came up with it – as the title for a piece she wrote about the joys of the net for a library journal back in 1992. Apparently, her inspiration came from a promotional mouse pad from the Apple Library which showed a surfer getting radical with a big tube (or something) and bore the legend 'Information Surfer'. Read all about it at **http://www.netmom.com/about/birth.htm**. ▲

---

< 121 >

### Tips – Non-Hypertext Links

There is an outside chance that you may click on something on the
page that isn't the standard hypertext link. Many web pages contain
email links, so that you can send feedback to the site easily. Click on
these and your mail program will start up in a separate window.
Obviously, we don't want to get into that, so close the window and
try another link. You may also click a link which causes some
software to download – if that happens, just hit the **Stop** button on
the toolbar and look for another link. ▲

otherwise you can get on the web without any hassle. So, get online, then
start your browser (i.e. click/double-click on its icon on your desktop).
When it loads, you'll most likely see either a Microsoft start page (if
you're using Explorer) or the Netscape homepage (if you're using
Navigator). Alternatively, your ISP may have configured the browser
they sent you so that you go to their site. (You can change your browser
so it goes first to a page of your choice but we'll get to that later.)

Whatever page loads first, you should see text, graphics, pictures and
little icons. To the right there will be a scroll bar that lets you move up
and down the page. You will see words either highlighted or underlined –
these are hypertext links. You may see a little animated icon, perhaps a
turning world, one of the great cliches of web design. As you move your
cursor over the highlighted words, the arrow will change to a pointing

< 122 >

finger, indicating a click-able link. If you click on this, you will move to another document or web page – either on the same computer or on another one on the other side of the world. On many corporate web sites, you'll also see colourful banner ads – usually featuring eye-catching animations. Click on these and you'll go to the site they're advertising.

Move the cursor over a link and click on it. If you haven't picked an email link, another page will load. Find a link on that and click on it. You'll go to another page. Find a link and click that and another page will come up. You could continue like this. Netheads call it 'surfing', though it's preferable to think of it as online rambling, a kind of serendipitous digital pottering-about which can take you to all sorts of unexpected places. The conventional wisdom is that people did this a lot in the old days of the web, but now they just find the sites they want and go there.

The buttons on the main toolbar are the easiest to use for basic navigation. If a page starts to appear that you don't like the look of, click the **Stop** button. That stops the page from loading. Click the **Back** button

---

**Read about it online – Surfers, not Netters**

Funnily enough, surfing seems to be the term net users prefer. The BBC recently conducted a poll and it came out on top as the preferred descriptive term, beating things like 'onliner' and 'netter'. For the full report, go to **http://news.bbc.co.uk/hi/english/uk/ newsid_407000/407022.stm**. ▲

< 123 >

and you'll move back to the page you were at previously. Click the **Forward** button and, surprise, surprise, you'll go forward to the page you just left. If you've followed a long set of links and just want to get back to your home/start page, click the **Home** button. As you go back through pages you've visited, you'll see that the links you clicked have changed colour. It's a simple way of helping you keep track.

How about going to a site you select for yourself? Let's try the Guardian's site. For this, you'll need the Guardian's URL (it stands for Uniform Resource Locator) or web address, which is **http://www.guardianunlimited.co.uk**. Web addresses are the sum of a few standard parts. First is the protocol **http**, it stands for HyperText Transfer Protocol and is used to send web pages across a network. Next comes the domain name of the computer that hosts the site **www.guardianunlimited.co.uk**. In this case, the computer is a web server – hence the **www** bit. The Guardian URL ends there, but URLs can specify a specific document (e.g. **document.html**) and the directories in which it's stored.

Click in the location bar at the top of your browser, just underneath the main tool bar, then delete the address that's there. Type in the Guardian URL, then hit **Enter/Return** or click on the little **Go** button at the right end of the location bar. Alternatively:

▶ In Internet Explorer, select the **File** menu, then **Open**, then write the URL in the text box and click **OK**.

▶ In Navigator, select the **File** menu, then **Open Page**, then write the URL in the text box. Check that the line **Open location or file in** has a tick next to the **Navigator** box. Then click **Open**.

< 124 >

▶ In Internet Explorer for the Mac, select the **File** menu, then **Open Location**, then write the URL in the text box and click **OK**. Alternatively, just write the URL in the location bar and click the **Go** button.

## Mouse Menus

Using the left mouse button to click on a link will bring up that link (or download a file or an image). You can also use the right mouse button to aid your web browsing. Right-click on something on a web page – a link, an image, the page background even – and a "mouse menu" will appear which offers you various options (saving the page, or 'creating a shortcut' – more on these later). As you attempt more complex operations online, you will find yourself right-clicking and using mouse menus a fair amount. Apple Mac users don't have a second mouse button, so they can't right-click. However, with newer Macs (and the newer browsers), you can call up mouse menus with a sort of delayed action click. Click on a link, but hold down the mouse button. Don't let it click. A mouse menu should appear. Choose the option you want all the while holding down the button. Then release the button, letting it click.

Here's a simple navigational trick that mouse menus make easy. At some point on the web you will inevitably find yourself waiting for a big page to load. You don't have to sit there twiddling your thumbs. You can open up a new browser window and check out another web page while you wait. In fact you can open several, though if you open too many you may end up slowing everything down. Using two or more browser

< 125 >

## Tips - Browsers

As mentioned before, your browser can do more than access the web.
You can use it to access newsgroups, send mail, download files via FTP
and much else. If you do, you have to enter addresses prefixed with
different protocols. So to access an FTP site, type **ftp://** before the
address. To go directly to a Usenet newsgroup, type **news.** before the
name of the group. More on this in the relevant sections. ▲

windows at once can be useful if you're looking at a page of useful links.
You can keep that page open and explore the links in new windows.

▶ In Internet Explorer, right-click on the link you're interested in, then
select **Open in a New Window**. Alternatively, select the File menu,
then **New**, then **Window**.

▶ In Navigator, select the File menu, then New, then **Navigator
Window**. Alternatively, right-click on the link you're interested in,
then select **Open in a New Window**.

## Frames, Image Maps and Forms

As you wander round the web, you'll come across pages with frames,
image maps and forms. Frames are used to create different sections within
a browser window. You might have a basic document in the main part of
the window, with an index to the website as a whole framed off on the left.
Frames came in with Navigator 2.0 (some older/low-tech browsers can't

< 126 >

cope with them) and they were misused by some web designers – let's call them frame spotters – who turned their pages into a mad patchwork of different boxes, some featuring text, some logos, some ads, some lists, some completely pointless graphic images. Things have improved (hyperactive webmasters have multimedia and animations to fiddle with now) and frames are now pretty easy to use. To use the example given above, clicking on a link in the index in the left frame will cause a new page to open in the large main frame. Frames can make general navigation a little more complex. For example, on a framed site, the **Back/Forward** buttons will sometimes take you back or forward within a frame.

Image maps are large graphic images, different portions of which are links to other documents. As you move the cursor over the image, you'll see the pointing finger appear, indicating the links. Image maps might seem more interesting than your standard list when it comes to presenting a set of links. But in the early days of the web they were often more trouble than they were worth. They took ages to load and it was

---

**Tips – Page Holder**

Internet Explorer 4.5 for the Mac has a very neat little feature that helps when you're using a page full of links. Using the **Page Holder** tab at the left of the browser, you can open a page of links in a browser bar. Then when you click the links, the pages they point to will open in the main window. ▲

---

< 127 >

often unclear what they were linking to. Things are generally better now, but if you get confused, move the cursor over the map and look for the URL/description that comes up in the bottom-left text box of your browser.

Forms are like forms in real life. Just click in the dialog box and type in the information required, then look for a **Send** button to click. You often have to refine the information you send via drop-down menus. Just click on the arrow pointing down to bring up a menu, select the relevant category, click then move on to the next question. Typically you use forms when you're using a search engine to look for something online, when you're buying something online or when you're trying to get into a site that requires you to register before they let you in. Before you send the information, your browser may flash up a warning about security. If you're not sending important information (e.g. credit card details), don't worry too much about this.

## More complex navigation

The **Back/Forward** buttons are useful enough if you're reading and moving between a few pages. If you build up a longer trail, then want to get back to an early page, you'll need something else.

▶ In Internet Explorer, look at the **Back/Forward** toolbar buttons. There's a little inverted triangle to the side of each. Move your cursor over it and it turns into a button. Click on it and a list of sites appears. Click on the one you want.

▶ In Navigator, you can pull the same trick with the **Back/Forward**

< 128 >

buttons. You can also select the **Go** menu and at the bottom, you'll see a list of sites previously visited. Select the one you want.

With both browsers, you can also pull down a list of the URLs you entered in the location bar by clicking on the pull-down menu at the right end of the box.

The above methods don't always work. Say you're on a site and you follow a set of links through it to a page you want, then use the **Back** button to come back to the front page, then follow a new set of links to a different document on the same site. The new trail of links will be recorded over the previous set, so that when you use the **Go** menu or the **Back/Forward** menus, you'll only see that latest trail. For a more comprehensive list of all the pages you've visited, you can use the **History** file, which will also let you get back to a site you visited right at the start of a long session.

Your browser keeps a **History** file of sites you've visited in this particular session (and over previous days). To access this:

▶ In Internet Explorer, click the **History** button on the toolbar (or the **History** tab if you're using the Mac version) and the history list will open in a separate frame (sometimes called a browser bar) on the left of your main browser window. Look for the site, click on it and it will come up in the main window. To remove the browser bar, click the **History** button again.

▶ In Navigator, select the **Communicator** menu, then **Tools**, then **History**. A separate window will open showing the sites you visited. Double-click on the one you want and it will open in the main window.

< 129 >

You can use the **History** file while you're online. But you can also go offline and use it to access sites you've previously visited – a rudimentary form of what's known as offline browsing. Both Navigator and Internet Explorer will let you go offline and then access pages you visited in your last session on the web. If your web use is confined to reading certain sites, the **History** file will definitely save you some money. Visit the sites you're interested in, make sure they've downloaded completely, then log off and read them offline via the **History** file. Internet Explorer is particularly slick here.

▶ In Internet Explorer, select the **File** menu then **Work Offline** (or **Offline Browsing** in the Mac version). Then click the **History** button. You'll then be able to move around as you wish within the history file, which is laid out by date and sites visited on each day.

▶ In Navigator, first set it up for work offline. Select the **Edit** menu, then **Preferences**, then **Offline**, then check the box next to **Offline Work Mode**. Then access the **History** file as normal.

You can specify how long you want your browser to keep details of pages in the History file.

▶ In Explorer, select the **Tools** menu, then **Internet Options**. Look for a section on **History** on the **General** dialog box, where you'll be able to change the number in the box next to the line **Days to keep pages in history**, then click **OK**.

▶ In Navigator, select the **Edit** menu then **Preferences**. In the **Navigator** dialog box, in the **History** section, change the number in the box next to **Pages in history expire after X days**, then click **OK**.

< 130 >

---

**Tips – Searching History**

Internet Explorer 5 will now let you search the **History** file to find a
particular page, something which can be useful if you've decided to
make it save a lot of entries. Click the **History** toolbar button, then
click the **Search** button at the top of the browser bar. You can also use
the **View** button to change the way your **History** list is ordered. ▲

---

▶ In the Mac version of Internet Explorer, select the **Edit** menu, then
**Preferences**. An **Internet Explorer Preferences** dialog box will appear.
In the category box on the left, select **Advanced** in the **Web Browser**
section. Then change the figure in the **History** section as required.

The thing to remember here is that the history file is a kind of interface for
documents stored in a file known as the cache. If you extend your history
file, but don't also allow more disk space for your browser's cache, you
won't be able to access some of the earlier entries (there's more on the cache
below). If you feel weighed down by the past, in both browsers there's a
**Clear History** button in the section where you specify the size of the history
file. Navigator now has a button here that also lets you clear the location
bar history, as in all the sites you've typed into the location bar.

### Getting to your favourite sites faster
As you get to know the web, you'll find yourself getting to like certain
sites. Browsers allow you to keep a list of your favourites, so that you

< 131 >

can access them a bit quicker. They let you do this in all sorts of ways.

▶ In Internet Explorer, if you're on the page you want to mark, click on the **Explorer document** icon in the location bar, hold down the button, then drag the icon across the screen and drop it on to the **Favourites** button. Alternatively, select the **Favourites** menu, then **Add to Favourites** or just right-click in an empty part of the page, then select **Add to Favourites** from the mouse menu. An **Add Favourite** dialog box will come up. Ignore all the stuff about subscribing to the site for the moment and tick the option to just add the page to your Favourites list, then **OK**. To use your **Favourites** list, click the **Favourites** button on the toolbar. It will open in a browser bar on the left of the main window. Click on the site you want to go to and (if you're online) it will load in the right-hand window. To remove the browser bar, click the **Favourites** button again. If you don't like the browser bar, you can use the **Favourites** menu to view your list.

▶ In Navigator, click on the **Page Proxy** icon (the funny little green thing next to the location bar) and, as above, drag and drop it onto the **Bookmark** button (on the toolbar to the left of the address text box). The **Bookmark** menu will open and you can drop the bookmark where you want. Alternatively, click the **Bookmark** button (which is to the left of the location bar), then select **Add Bookmark** or right-click on an empty space on the page and select **Add Bookmark** from the mouse menu. To access your bookmarks, click the **Bookmark** button and a list will come up. Click on the site you want to go to.

< 132 >

**Tips - CTheory**

As you use your browser you'll find that there are several different ways of doing the same thing. Don't worry about learning all of them. Just get comfortable with one and forget about the others. That way, you'll have some time to read 'The Technology of Uselessness', a reasonably pertinent essay about this kind of thing by the US art collective Critical Art Ensemble – at the webzine CTheory – **http://www.ctheory.com/a-technology_of_useless.html**. ▲

Both Navigator and Internet Explorer will let you bookmark sites without having to access them. Say you see a link on a page that looks good but you're too busy to get it now. Right-click on the link and **Add Bookmark/Add to Favourites**. Alternatively, click on the link in the normal way, hold down the mouse button and drag the link to the **Bookmarks/Favourites** toolbar button.

Navigator will also automatically check to see if your Bookmarks/ Favourites have changed since you last visited them.

▶ In Navigator, click the **Bookmarks** button then select **Edit Bookmarks**. When that window opens, select the **View** menu, then **Update Bookmarks**. You can then choose which sites you want to update.

< 133 >

There is little need to update **Bookmarks/Favourites**, though. Presumably you visit your favourite sites on a regular basis and get a feel for when they change. You don't need to tie up time online getting your browser to check for you. Still, give it a try if you like.

It's pretty easy to build up a big file of **Bookmarks/Favourites** after a while. So start organising and filing them into specific folders as soon as possible.

▶ In Internet Explorer, select the **Favourites** menu, then **Organise Favourites**.

▶ In Navigator, click the **Bookmarks** button then select **Edit Bookmarks**. Once you've put your bookmarks in folders, Navigator will let you put a particularly useful folder on the your **Personal** toolbar. Just right-click on it then select **Set as toolbar folder**.

If you build up a big **Favourites/Bookmarks** file, it can be time-consuming finding your way to the entry for the site you want. You can get round this by creating an **Internet Shortcut**. This is an icon on your desktop. Click/double-click on it and your browser will launch and load that site. The quickest way to create a **Shortcut** is first to access your chosen site. Then resize the browser window so you can see your desktop.

▶ In Internet Explorer, click on the **Internet Explorer document** icon and then drag and drop the icon on to your desktop.

▶ In Navigator click on the **Page Proxy** icon and then drag and drop it on to you desktop. Navigator will also let you create shortcuts to

< 134 >

links you haven't yet visited (though I'm not sure why you would want to) by right-clicking on the link, then selecting **Create Shortcut** from the mouse menu.

At the moment the Mac version of Internet Explorer is not that flexible as far as shortcuts are concerned. Navigator seems fine though. Shortcuts are useful, though they can clutter up your desktop. Instead you can put buttons on the toolbar for sites you access regularly. (Again, this is something the Mac IE doesn't really offer at the moment).

▶ In Internet Explorer, look for the word **Links** on the toolbar to the right of the address text box. There's a little ridge by the word. Click on this, hold down the button and slide it to the left to reveal the links bar (and hide the address box). Alternatively, move it down and the whole **Links** bar will be displayed below the location bar. You'll see various buttons that will take you quickly to various Microsoft sites (e.g. Best of the Web, Product News). Then go to your chosen site and drag and drop the **Internet Explorer document** icon on to the **Links** bar. A button will be created. Click on that in future and you'll go directly to that site.

▶ In Navigator, check that your **Personal Toolbar** is visible (via the **View** menu). This is a toolbar of quick links to Netscape pages listing new or cool sites. To add buttons for sites of your choice, access the site, then drag and drop the **Page Proxy** icon on to the **Personal Toolbar**.

< 135 >

Once you've mastered **Favourites/Bookmarks,** shortcuts and all the rest
of it, typing in web addresses may seem like an awful lot of hard work.
Actually, you don't have to type in the full **http** version to get where you
want to go. You can drop that. For example, if you want to go to the
Guardian site, just type **www.guardianunlimited.co.uk** into the location
bar. Internet Explorer has a function called AutoComplete which
watches while you type in URLs, guesses what they are, based on sites
and pages previously accessed, then tries to fill them in before you. This
could be useful if you have to type in particularly lengthy URLs, but it's
potentially irritating too. You can disable it by selecting the **Tools** menu,
then **Internet Options,** then the **Advanced** tab. Remove the tick next to
**Use AutoComplete** (in the **Browsing** section). If you're using the Mac
version of IE, select the **Edit** menu, then **Preferences,** then click on
**Browser Display** in the **Web Browser** section. Remove the cross in the
box next to **Use URL AutoComplete.**

## Tips – Internet Shortcuts

If you've downloaded two browsers so that you can cut between
the two, Internet Shortcuts will only work with the one nominated
as your default browser. Unless you tell it not to, the browser that
isn't the default will ask you whether you want to make it the
default every time you load it. So it's pretty easy to change things
around if you need to. ▲

< 136 >

## Troubleshooting

Sometimes you won't be able to get to a particular site. Your browser will usually tell you what the problem is and flash up some sort of error message. Here are a few problems you may encounter.

**Your browser says it is unable to locate the server or that the server doesn't have a DNS entry** – Check that you entered the URL correctly. Check for spelling and remember that URLs are case sensitive. If that's all fine, try again. If you still can't get through and get the same error message, it may be that the server at the site is down or that the site has closed down and vanished from the web (not unknown).

### Read about it online – Spelling Mistakes

We're always hearing that the net is home to innovative minds looking for new and clever ways to make money. So perhaps it shouldn't be surprising that companies have figured out a way to profit from your spelling mistakes. They have registered common errors and typos close to some of the biggest sites online, and put pages up at these destinations which feature advertising and re-direct you to the page you wanted. Go to **http://www.typo.net** to see what such companies think they are up to (they're free online spell checkers, apparently). ▲

< 137 >

### Read about it online – Real Names

If you have trouble writing out URLs without making mistakes, there are several companies that feel your pain (and hope to make money out of it). Real Names have created a piece of nifty technology that is supposed to let you just type a brand name into a browser and go directly to the site in question – for more information and a test run, go to **http://www.realnames.com/**. ▲

**A message comes up saying that the "Connection was refused by Host"** – Don't take it personally. The problem here is that the site you're trying to access is probably very busy. Try again and if you get the same message, leave it until the site is likely to be less busy.

**You seem to get through to the site but a page comes up saying File Not Found** – It may be that the site has been reorganised and that the page you're looking for has been moved. You can usually find your way to the document by working back through the site URL. For example, if you can't get anywhere with the URL – **http://www.hipsite.com/index/television/ simpsons.html**, it may be that the document simpsons.html is now in a different directory. Click in the location bar, delete **/index/television/ simpsons.html**, leave **http://www.hipsite.com** intact and hit the **Enter/ Return** key. This will take you to the front page of **hipsite.com.** From there, look around for links that might take you to the page you're looking for.

< 138 >

**You get an error message saying that the Document contains no data** – Most URLs end with a web document – in the example above, the document is **simpsons.html**. Usually with URLs that don't end with an **.html** or **.htm** document, the browser will hunt around for a default document – something like **index.html** – which it can display. If there isn't one, it can get confused and show the above error message. The best bet is to go to the front page of the site (by taking the directory path out of the URL, as in the previous example) and hunt around for a link to the page you want.

**You get into the site you want but things move very slowly and the page seems to seize up** – Again, a problem caused by excess traffic on a site. Sometimes all you can do is wait – and keep track of progress by checking the **Status** bar in the bottom left of the browser, which will tell you roughly how much of the page has loaded. Sometimes you can get somewhere by hitting the **Stop** button, then the **Reload** button (in Navigator)

---

### Tips – Hit the Stop Button

Some sites move very slowly and, as suggested above, the best thing to do is to click the **Stop** button, then **Reload/Refresh** and have another go. One thing to look out for – sometimes, the thing holding you up can be a big graphic file. If you hit the **Stop** button, the text on a page will load anyway – and that might be the thing you're interested in. ▲

< 139 >

or the **Refresh** button (in Internet Explorer). Your browser will try to get the page again and this time you might be able to get through.

**You're on a page, you click a link and nothing happens or the wrong page comes up** – This is probably down to dodgy programming on the site. Broken links are less common nowadays, but they're still around. The average website usually offers several different routes to its various sections. So look around for an alternative link to the page you want.

## Customising your Browser

When you get your browser, it will be set to do certain things by default – for example, load your ISP's site as the homepage. You can personalise your browser and speed up your web surfing by making a few changes. The first thing you might want to alter is your browser's homepage. Clearly, many ISPs and online services hope that you won't do this. Their business models are built on you always starting your surfing at their site (where you'll be exposed to the advertising they've sold). I haven't experienced this personally, but friends have told me that some ISPs go so far as disabling your ability to change the homepage on your browser to something you want. If an ISP tries to pull that on you, it's a good reason to try someone else.

▶ In Internet Explorer, select the **Tools** menu, then **Internet Options**. In the **General** dialog box, in the **Home page** section, enter the URL you want in the **Address** box. The **Use Blank** button means your browser will show a blank page as its home page, which will make it load quicker.

< 140 >

### Tips – Bookmarks

In Navigator, you can also use your bookmarks as a homepage. They're stored in a page called **bookmark.htm**. So in the **Navigator** dialog box, click the **Browse** button to look for this file – it should be in the **Default** folder within the **Program** folder in **Communicator**, then click **Open**. ▲

▶ In Navigator, select the **Edit** menu, then **Preferences**. In the **Navigator** dialog box, you can choose a blank page or, in the **Home page** section, enter your chosen URL in the **Location** box.

▶ In the Mac version of Internet Explorer, select the **Edit** menu, then **Preferences**. Then in the **Web Browser** section, look for **Home/Search**. You can choose not to have a homepage by click the **Use None** button.

Another simple way to speed up your surfing is to tell your browser not to bother with the visual or multimedia elements of a web page.

▶ In Internet Explorer, select the **Tools** menu, then **Internet Options**, then **Advanced**. In the **Multimedia** section, remove the ticks in the boxes next to **Show picture**, **Play animations**, **Play videos** and **Play sounds**.

▶ In Navigator, select the **Edit** menu, then **Preferences**, then **Advanced**, then remove the tick next to **Automatically load images**.

▶ In the Mac version of Internet Explorer, select the **Edit** menu, then

< 141 >

**Preferences**. Then look for the **Web Content** page in the **Web Browser** section.

When pages come up, you'll see a small icon where the image should be and possibly a caption describing the image. If you want to see a particular image, click on it and it will load. Alternatively, in Navigator, select the **View** menu, then **Show Images** and all the pictures on a particular page will load.

You can also mess around with the general look and feel of your browser. Both Navigator and Internet Explorer let you change colours and fonts.

▶ In Internet Explorer, select the **Tools** menu, then **Internet Options**, then click the **Colours** and **Fonts** buttons at the bottom of the **General** dialog box.

▶ In Navigator, select the **Edit** menu, then **Preferences**, then either **Fonts** or **Colours**.

▶ In the Mac version of Internet Explorer, select the **Edit** Menu then **Preferences**, then click on **Browser Display** or **Language/Fonts**.

You can also remove some of the toolbars so that you can see more of the web page you're accessing. To try out the various toolbar options, in Internet Explorer and Navigator, select the **View** menu. Try out various permutations here to see what you're comfortable with (i.e. which of the scores of buttons and menus you actually need when you're wandering round the web). You can also drag and drop the toolbars around if you

< 142 >

feel you need to change the way they are stacked up. Navigator can even be set to show text-only toolbar buttons – select the **Edit** menu, then **Preferences**, then **Appearance**, then under **Show toolbar as**, tick **Text only**. Actually, there's nothing to stop you removing all the toolbars.

▶ In Internet Explorer, select the **View** Menu, then **Full Screen**. You'll still see a small toolbar of buttons. You can remove these by right-clicking on the toolbar and selecting **Auto-hide** from the mouse menu. The toolbar will disappear, but it will come back if you move the cursor to the top of the screen. To return to the standard set of toolbars, click on the **Maximise** icon in the top right hand corner of the screen.

▶ In Navigator, just click on the little raised tags at the left end of each toolbar. Then click them again to make them reappear.

▶ In Internet Explorer for the Mac, there's no **Full Screen** option via the **View** menu, though you can use it to remove all the toolbars for a less cluttered view.

If you do hide all the toolbars, you can use keyboard commands to navigate. People who are comfortable with the keyboard often find this quicker and easier than using the mouse. Here's a quick list of useful keyboard commands (or shortcuts):

< 143 >

## INTERNET EXPLORER

| | |
|---|---|
| **Alt + Left Arrow** or **Backspace** | Move back one page |
| **Alt + Right Arrow** | Move forward one page |
| **Ctrl + Tab** | Move forward within frames |
| **Shift + Ctrl + Tab** | Move back within frames |
| **Alt + A + A** | Add the current page to your favourites list |
| **Esc** | Stop loading a page |
| **Ctrl + O** | Open a new location or file |
| **Ctrl + N** | Open a new browser window |
| **Ctrl + R** | Refresh the current page |
| **Ctrl + S** | Save the current page |
| **Ctrl + P** | Print the current page |
| **Ctrl + F** | Find something on the current page |
| **Ctrl + I** | Open your Favourites list |
| **Ctrl + E** | Open the Search Assistant |
| **Ctrl + H** | Open History |

## NETSCAPE NAVIGATOR

| | |
|---|---|
| **Alt + Left Arrow** | Move back one page |
| **Alt + Right Arrow** | Move forward one page |
| **Ctrl + A** | Highlights the text on a page |
| **Ctrl + C** | Copies highlighted text to the clipboard |
| **Ctrl + I** | Pulls up the Page Information |
| **Ctrl + O** | Open a new location or file |

< 144 >

| | |
|---|---|
| **Esc** | Stop loading a page |
| **Ctrl + N** | Open a new browser window |
| **Ctrl + R** | Reload the current page |
| **Ctrl + S** | Save the current page |
| **Ctrl + P** | Print the current page |
| **Ctrl + F** | Find something on the current page |
| **Ctrl + B** | Open your Bookmarks file |
| **Ctrl + H** | Open History |

There are more keyboard shortcuts you could use. Check in your browser's help file for details.

### The Cache and Saving Documents and Images from the Web

Every page you access on the web is saved by your browser in a temporary file known as a cache. (In its bid to seem different even when it's the same, Internet Explorer calls the cache its 'Temporary Internet Files'.) The idea is to speed up your browsing and do a little towards saving the net's limited resources. So whenever you direct your browser to a site, it will first check in its cache to see if it already has the relevant page. The most obvious way this is used is when you click the **Back** or **Forward** button. Rather than go to the trouble of heading off to get the page all over again, your browser gets it from the cache. You can improve your browsing speed by changing some of the cache settings.

▶ In Internet Explorer, select the **Tools** menu, then **Internet Options**, then the **General** tab. In the **Temporary Internet Files** section, click

< 145 >

the **Settings** button. You can then specify how much disk space you want the cache to use via a small slider control. The bigger you make the cache, the more pages it can store to call on during revisits. On the other hand, you don't want to overload your hard disk, so don't go mad. In the **Check for newer versions of stored pages** section, make sure that **Every time you start Internet Explorer** is selected. This means that your browser will check the page if you haven't yet visited it in the current session on the web, but if you have, it will get the stored version from the cache.

▶ In Navigator, select the **Edit** menu, then **Preferences**, then **Cache** (it's in the **Advanced** section) to call up the relevant dialog box. With Navigator you have to type in the amount of space for both the **Memory Cache** and **Disk Cache**. This is obviously a little trickier, since you need to know how much space you have to play around with. It's probably not a good idea to go for less than the default. With the line **Document in cache is compared to document on the network**, make sure that **Once per session** is ticked.

▶ In the Mac version of Internet Explorer, select the **Edit** menu, then **Preferences**. Then click on **Advanced** in the **Web Browser** section.

Once you've specified the size of the cache, your browser will fill it up, then as you add new pages it will dump the old files. However, this process can slow down your browsing. You may see everything slow down onscreen and hear your computer rattling away as it sorts out the browser cache and gets rid of old files. To avoid this and to free up disk space –

< 146 >

▶ In Internet Explorer, click the **Empty Folder** button in the **Temporary Internet Files** section.

▶ In Navigator, click both the **Clear Memory Cache** and **Clear Disk Cache** buttons in the **Cache** dialog box.

▶ In the Mac version of Internet Explorer, in the **Advanced** section, click the **Empty Now** button.

Since it automatically saves copies of pages you visit, the cache is a potentially useful resource. Rather than going to the trouble of saving individual pages, you could go and check them out in the cache. That's the theory, anyway. Both browsers (in their Windows version, at least) make it easy to get to the files in the cache.

▶ In Internet Explorer, select the **Tools** menu, then **Internet Options**, then **General**, then click the **Settings** button, then the **View Files** button.

▶ In Navigator, select the **File** menu, then **Open Page**, then click the **Choose File** button to look for the **Cache** (it's in the **Users** sub-directory of the **Netscape** folder).

Once you get there, you'll see that it's rather difficult finding the page you want because of the computer-ese of Netscape's file-labelling system. Internet Explorer handles this a little better – it shows the name of the file and the URL it came from. But it's still not a patch on the **History** file, which is the thing to use if you want to check back on pages you've previously visited. Of course, then you have to remember when you visited them. So if you find a page you know you'll want to refer back

< 147 >

to, it might be easier to go ahead and save it anyway. That way, you will know what it's called and where it is. To save a web page:

▶ In Internet Explorer, select the **File** menu then **Save As**. Then pick a name and a location on your disk for the saved file. You can choose to save the page as a complete web page (or 'web archive'). If you choose the former, when you open it again (with an application that can handle HTML, like your browser), it will retain the basic formatting it had on the web. If you choose text, all you get is the text and some basic formatting.

▶ In Navigator, select the **File** menu then **Save As**. You can then choose to save the page as either HTML or text. If you want to save a page complete with the images, you need to select the **File** menu, then **Edit**. Then select the **File** menu, then **Save As**.

If you're saving a page with frames, make sure you click in the frame you're interested in before you start the saving process. You can save a link without actually going to it. Right-click on the link, then choose the **Save Target As** (in Internet Explorer) or **Save Link As** (in Navigator) from the mouse menu. Your browser will get the page at the end of the link and you can then choose the format, name and location as above. You can also save just the images from web pages by right-clicking on the image, then choosing **Save Image As** (in Navigator) or **Save Picture As** (in Internet Explorer) from the mouse menu. Some web pages feature sound and video files and you can save these. However, since you'll often need special plug-in programs to play these, it's best to use those to save these

< 148 >

sorts of multimedia files. There's more on this on page 313. Rather than save web pages that seem particularly useful, you can always print them out for future reference. Make sure you have plenty of paper. Web pages seem a lot shorter on screen than they are in real life.

▶ In Internet Explorer, select the **File** menu, then **Print**. On the **Print** dialog box, in the **Print range** section, make sure **All** is ticked. If you want to see whether the page is going to look something like it does on screen or if you want to pick out certain pages to print, select the **File** menu, then **Print Preview**. Then select the **File** menu then **Print**, then specify the pages you want. If you want to print an individual frame, right-click in the frame, then select **Print** from the mouse menu.

▶ In Navigator, the easiest thing to do is use the **Print** button on the toolbar. If you only want to print a few pages from a big web document, select the **File** menu then **Print Preview**. You can then find out the page numbers you want. Then select the **File** menu, then **Print**, then specify the pages you want.

Finally, if you get particularly obsessed with speeding up your browsing, it might be worth investigating Web proxy servers. These are local servers that keep copies of the most popular sites. You can set your browser to get those copies rather than going out on to the net proper. Some ISPs have their own web proxies, so ask about it. To set your browser up to use a proxy -

▶ In Internet Explorer, select the **Tools** menu, then **Internet Options**, then **Connection**, then click the box next to **Access the Internet using**

< 149 >

a proxy server, then enter the details your ISP will give you in the relevant text boxes.

▶ In Navigator, select the Edit menu, then Preferences, then Advanced, then Proxies. Mark the box next to Manual proxy configuration then click the View button, then enter the details of the proxy – your ISP should supply these.

▶ In the Mac version of Internet Explorer, select the Edit Menu, then Preferences. In the Network section, look for Proxies. Put a tick next to Enabled then enter the address your ISP has given you.

## A few last browsing tips

Browsers offer lots of different ways to do the same thing. As you spend more time online, you'll probably find yourself choosing one particular way over another. You'll also pick up shortcuts and habits to make things go quicker and more smoothly. Here's one thing that I find particularly useful. Remember that your browser is a multi-tasking device. Don't sit there waiting for another page to load. Open another window (or two or three) while you're waiting and chase down something else. Once you've tracked down the pages you want, log off and read them offline.

Here's an interesting tip I found in *.net* magazine. Sometimes, you come to a page where the designer has gone a bit over the top with his backgrounds, the result being that it's impossible to actually read the page. Navigator allows you to do something about this. Select the Edit menu, then Preferences. Select Appearance from the category box on the left. Then use the Fonts and Colours sections to make sure you see black

< 150 >

text in the font you like on a white background. The in **Fonts**, put a tick in the box next to **Use my default fonts, overriding document specified fonts** and in **Colours**, put a tick in the box by **Always use my colours, overriding document**.

In fact, you can do all sorts of things with your browser. There isn't space to cover the whole lot here. The specialist internet magazines, .net and Internet are always good for picking up browser tips and tricks. Incidentally, .net does a great page about Internet Explorer 5 **http://www.ie5.co.uk**. It's worth a look if you want to find out more about IE5's hidden depths. If you want some more Navigator information, try Netscape's own page **http://home.netscape.com/browsers/using/** or the Unofficial Netscape FAQ **http://www.ufaq.org**.

### Next Step?

By now, you should be comfortable with your browser and the web. The next step is to learn how to find your way to new sites. For that, go to the next section on search engines. It may have occurred to you that, with things like the cache and the **History** file, your browser is saving a lot of information about you which could tell someone else what you've been up to online. For more on this and on browsing and privacy in general, go to page 379.

< 151 >

## Searching The Web

Neo-Luddite critics often moan that the net is just a vast, disorganised mess, that even when there is useful information online it's impossible to get to it. If all the search engines and online directories disappeared overnight, they might have a point. As it is, as usual, they're getting rather melodramatic. The truth is that modern net search tools now make it easy to find information. Like a lot of things online, they could be a lot better. But if you take the time to learn how to use them, they work well enough. In fact, you really can't get by without them.

That's why companies in the net/web search industry are among the most successful of net businesses. The market leaders (Yahoo and, to a lesser extent, Excite) have experienced phenomenal growth over the last few years and are among the best-known online brands. The big search sites are among the busiest on the web. Some even turn a profit (a relative novelty in the net business). That's why venture capitalists still queue up to throw money at start-up companies with new ideas for searching and ordering the web. And there are plenty of new ideas out there, mainly because online searching still needs to improve a lot.

Internet search tools were around before the web caught on. The first really popular net search engine, Archie, appeared in 1990. Archie helped people locate files online. They had to know the exact file name first, but using Archie they could quickly locate an FTP site where it was stored and then go there and download it. Once the web emerged, web search engines soon followed – even in the web's infancy (in 1993), it became clear that logging its various sites was going to be beyond mere human capabilities.

< 152 >

**Tips – Gopher**

If you feel like trying out another archaic online search tool, you could mess around with Gopher. This was/is a sort of web-like (but very un-visual) way of finding text files. Basically you click links to track down the file you want. Before the web turned up, it was going to be the next big thing. Now gopherspace is the equivalent of an online ghost town. However, it is still used by academics and it can still be useful. You can try it out via your browser. For a chance to surf 'gopherspace', try **http://giaspn01.vsnl.net.in/links/ind.html**. ▲

The first web search engine was something called the World Wide Web Wanderer. Strictly speaking, it didn't start out as a search engine – it was designed to keep track of the web's growth. However, it did work in roughly the same way as the big modern search engines. It consisted of a 'bot' – an autonomous, automated software program, which went out on to the net and performed a particular task (in this case counting web servers) then reported back with its findings. After a while, the Wanderer was tweaked so it collected URLs too. These were then added to a database, called the Wandex.

The Wanderer showed how web search engines might work. The first to make a big impact was called the WebCrawler. It was developed by students and staff at the University of Washington Computer Science department and was released in April 1994. The WebCrawler is still

< 153 >

around today (though it's not one of the better engines). It made such a big impact because it was the first search engine that could do a full text search on the web. Within a year, various competitors appeared – Lycos, Infoseek, OpenText, all touting roughly similar technologies and the search business was born.

## Search Sites on the Web

In theory, there are two distinct types of search site – search engines and directories. Both let you search through vast databases of links to different web sites. They differ in the search methods they offer and how they assemble their databases of links. As mentioned before, search engines rely on autonomous software programs (aka bots, spiders or crawlers) which roam the web (and other places on the net) collecting details about different pages – the URL, the title, the keywords chosen by the creator of the page as a summary of its content, known as meta tags,

### Tips - Specialist Search Engines

There are now all sorts of specialist search sites that target online resources devoted to a particular theme. Exes **http://www.exes.com/** is a travel search engine. Leisure Hunt **http://www.leisurehunt.com** lets you search for hotels worldwide, then book a room. For more links to specific search engines, try CNet's Search.com **http://search.cnet.com/**. ▲

< 154 >

and usually these days, the whole text of a page. A database is created from the bot's findings. Users can then search this database and turn up links to different sites, grouped in order of relevance.

Directories offer collections of links, arranged into different categories and themes. The directories employ people to do their searches and assemble their lists of sites. But some also use bots. They also accept submissions sent in by the webmasters responsible for particular sites. You can use a search engine to search a directory's links. But you can also drill down through different directories looking for the sites you want. Directories may deliver less information than search engines, which can turn up thousands of sites that are apparently relevant to your enquiry. They generally make up for this in the quality of the information they deliver – i.e. the search results usually have something to do with the original enquiry, not always the case with search engines. Aside from general directories, there are lots of specialist sites that index links in a particular field.

In fact, the distinction between search engines and directories is so blurred nowadays as to be pretty useless. You should perhaps just refer to them all as search sites. There are still a few 'pure' search engines out there, but most also come with a directory of some sort as well. These days, the big search sites feature all sorts of other services from free email to chat rooms. The people behind companies like Yahoo don't even like to use the word 'search' any more; they refer to themselves as a 'media company'. Indeed, the leading search sites are amongst the biggest of the portals, those all-purpose destination sites that aim to be the homepage of choice for mouse-clicking masses. The best known are:

< 155 >

| | |
|---|---|
| AltaVista | **http://www.altavista.com** |
| Hotbot | **http://www.hotbot.com/** |
| Infoseek | **http://infoseek.go.com** |
| Excite | **http://www.excite.com** |
| Lycos | **http://www.lycos.com** |
| WebCrawler | **http://www.webcrawler.com** |
| Yahoo | **http://www.yahoo.com** |

By the way, Yahoo, Excite, Lycos, and Infoseek all have UK-based sites up and running too. Just substitute **.co.uk** for **.com** in the URL. (Rather unluckily for Hot Bot, the **http://www.hotbot.co.uk** address has been taken by a novelty hot water bottle company).

Over the last year, these sites have been joined by various new contenders, many of whom seem to be putting less stress on being portals or 'media' companies in the making. Instead, they're trying to make an impact by delivering better searching (not a bad idea, when you think about it). Google **http://www.google.com** has probably made the biggest splash. It claims to be able to deliver more relevant results than the other search engines. As you'll discover shortly, the main problem with most search sites is that you get too many 'results' that have nothing to do with your original query.

In part this is down to the fact that search engine technology is still rather crude. But it's also caused by something rather more basic – human duplicity. Unscrupulous web designers set out to deliberately mislead search engines and get their sites higher up the lists of results by

< 156 >

misusing the meta tags on a web page. Meta tags describe the content of a page and are used as a reference point by search engines. In a practice known as spamdexing, some web designers deliberately assign inaccurate meta tags to their pages, hoping to draw some more traffic. For example, one site used its meta tags to suggest it was useful for parents worried about child care. In fact, it was a site that sold kids' clothes and was trying to divert more people its way.

In part, Google is a reaction to all this. Basically, it ranks its search results according to how many other sites link to each entry. It also takes into account the ranking of those sites doing the linking. The idea is that if a lot of highly ranked sites link to a particular site in a particular field, it's more likely to be relevant in some way to the original query. If this sounds over-complicated, why not give Google a try. At the moment, it's still testing and is one of the simplest search engines around.

It will be interesting to see how it develops. In the mean time, other new sites that have made an impact this year include Northern Light **http://www.northernlight.com**, now rated as one of best search sites, and Look Smart **http://www.looksmart.com**, which offers an interesting service along with the usual searching. With Look Smart Live, you email the site with your search query and one of its editors will send something relevant back within twenty four hours. Another new contender FAST Search **http://www.alltheweb.com** was launched recently with the promise that it would index the whole web, unlike the others which still only cover a fragment of what's up there.

GoTo **http://www.goto.com** has also had an impact. Here, companies

< 157 >

**Read about it online - Paid searches**

Salon's technology editor Scott Rosenberg wrote a typically sharp column about the minor fuss around Alta Vista's paid results proposal and the general failure of most search sites to really deliver. Read it at **http://www.salon.com/tech/col/rose/1999/04/22/altavista**. ▲

can pay to be ranked higher in the search results (and users can find out how much the company in question handed over). At least GoTo are up front about this. Many well-known search engines commonly sell 'keywords' to advertisers. So if you search for a particular topic, an ad relevant to that topic will appear on the results page. Earlier this year, Alta Vista tried the idea of letting businesses pay to be listed higher in the results. Their plan was to indicate when a result had been paid for. Some critics pointed out that this was far from a bad thing, that it might actually serve up something useful for search site users bogged down in pages of useless or misleading results. Nevertheless, Alta Vista has now backed away from the idea, saying that it wasn't that effective.

## Using a Search Engine

Superficially, search engines look pretty easy to use. Just enter your subject in the text box, click the button and in a matter of moments you'll be on the way to a set of sites that are exactly what you're looking for. That's the theory. The reality is a results screen which tells you that

< 158 >

the search engine has found several hundred thousand pages which contain the terms you entered. And if you start clicking the links to some of these pages, you will discover pretty quickly that many have little or no connection to the subject you're interested in.

This doesn't seem to trouble journalists who, in the past, have shown remarkable stupidity when using search engines, quoting huge search engine results (6 million pages found!) as proof that the micro-trend they're discussing is socially significant. For example, if you go to Alta Vista and do a search for 'fans of Jeffrey Archer's novels', you get back a results page which says that the search engine has found 1,730,430 pages that match your query. Seeing this in the past, many hacks would then have rushed off to write the deadline-busting piece about the massive Lord Archer craze on the net. These days, thank-fully, most (but not all) know a little more about the way search engines work.

There may be a few sad souls out there who have put up a Lord Archer page (He's put up one of his own). But there aren't that many. If you don't use the search engine properly, it will do a general search on all the words in your query. It will turn up pages that feature them all, pages that feature some and pages that feature only one. As you can imagine, that's a lot of pages. So if you want to get useful results, first learn to use a search engine properly. Whichever one you pick, read the help file first so you know how to refine your search – in other words, how to make your search terms more specific so that the engine in ques-tion at least has a fighting chance of turning up something appropriate.

< 159 >

Let's stick with AltaVista. When you go to the main page, you're offered the chance to do a standard search. Alternatively, you can choose to do an **Advanced Text Search** (more about that shortly). With the former, the first thing you can do is to specify where you want to search (the web or Usenet) and in what language, by using the drop-down menus above the main text box. The main thing to remember is that if you're searching for a particular phrase or group of words, put quotations marks around the phrase in question – as in "the novels of Jeffrey Archer". You could just start by searching for that phrase. Alta Vista now also lets you try a natural language query. "Where can I find a website about Jeffrey Archer?" for example. By the way, this doesn't turn anything up on Alta Vista. If you know an exact phrase or proper name you want to find, stick that in quotation marks and search for that, as in "Jeffrey Archer". Try this and the first site listed on the results page is The Greater London Forum, Archer's site for discussing London issues (and promoting his mayoral campaign).

## Read about it online – Ask Jeeves

For another search site that lets you ask natural language questions, try Ask Jeeves **http:// www.askjeeves.com/**. Here you ask things like 'Where can I get a cheap computer?' and Jeeves will do his best to find a site that supplies an answer. It's amusing though not always that useful. Think of it as a search toy. ▲

< 160 >

Of course, you aren't always searching for a proper name (and when you do, you often turn up pages put up by American academics and computer programmers who happen to be called Chris Evans and Martin Amis). Most of the time you're after something less specific. When you enter search terms, using several can help you focus your search – for example, **cats pets homes** might yield more relevant results than just **cats** on its own. You can make your search more specific by using various characters. A + sign before a word means that that word must be included in the search. A – sign means that a word must not be included. So **+cats +breeders** should turn up sites devoted to breeding cats; **+cats -musicals** should make sure you turn up sites devoted to pets and avoid accidental exposure to Andrew Lloyd Webber. You can use capitals (AltaVista does searches for words as they appear and does recognises cases), though if you want your search to be wider, use the lower case throughout. You can use the * sign as a 'wildcard'. Tack the asterisk on to the end of a word and AltaVista will search for other similarly spelled words that contain up to five additional letters. So **breed\*** will look for breed, breeders and breeding. Some search terms don't need to be refined that much to yield good results. Entering proper names will usually turn up the person you're after.

Aside from refining your search terms, you can also constrain your searches to specific areas. For example, to restrict your search to the titles of documents, put title: before the words you're searching for. For example, **title: 'World Wide Waste of Time'** will search for a web page called **World Wide Waste of Time**. Use **anchor:** to restrict your search

< 161 >

## Tips - Be a Web Voyeur

If you're having trouble with your search, why not amuse yourself for a while with the WebCrawler search ticker **http://webcrawler.com/SearchTicker.html**. It lets you sneak a peek at other people's searches by flashing up keywords currently being searched for in their databases. ▲

to the words found in links. To search for a web address, use **url:** followed by the word you want to find in the web address. To restrict your search to a country, use **domain:** then the domain name for the country in question – for example, **domain:uk**. Use **image:** then the name of the image to search for images. You'll find more about this in AltaVista's help file.

When you've sorted out your search terms, click the **Search** button. After a while, AltaVista will take you to a results screen which will probably tell you that it has found tens of thousands of pages that fit your search. It ranks the pages found in terms of relevance and shows you links to the top ten (along with a short description of what's on the page). Relevance is determined in a fairly straightforward way. If all the search terms appear on a page, it comes higher than if only one or two appear. If a unique term (e.g. a proper name) appears on a page, then it will move up the rankings. Usually, you can find what you're after in the first twenty or thirty links turned up by AltaVista.

< 162 >

**Tips - Direct Hit**

Another interesting search tool you should look at is Direct Hit's Popularity Engine. You can find this at **http://www.directhit.com**, though the technology is used by some of the big search engines. This aims to 'show you highly relevant results based on the search topics that other people have researched.' In other words, the results take into account which sites other people who did a similar search actually chose to look at. If one site was looked at by more people, it will be ranked higher. ▲

AltaVista's **Simple Search** will often be enough. If you're very keen, you can try an **Advanced Text Search**. For this, you need to construct your search terms using something called Boolean logic. It sounds slightly forbidding but what it basically means is that you don't use + or – to refine search terms but words – AND, OR, NOT and NEAR – which are known as Boolean operators. These work in roughly the same way as + or -. Using AND (you can write it in lower case if you want) means that the engine will search for all the words in a search. OR means it will search for either. NOT is used to exclude certain terms but it can't be used on its own. So you have to write **cats AND NOT musicals**. NEAR can be used to search for words or phrases that occur within ten words of each other in a document. AltaVista suggests that this is useful when you're doing a search on names (for example, **John NEAR Kennedy**), which

< 163 >

might occur in a document in various forms. Advanced searches let you look for documents modified within a specific time frame – just enter the required dates in the appropriate boxes. They also let you specify your own ranking words, which will determine the order in which your results are listed. To use the example AltaVista gives, with a search on **COBOL AND programming**, you can use **advanced** or **experienced** as ranking terms so that those pages will come first in the results page.

The other search engines work in roughly the same way, though each has it own quirks, so read those help pages. If you want to keep track of which is currently deemed to be the best, try Search Engine Watch **http://www.searchenginewatch.com/**. Hosted by MecklerMedia, this has a search-engine status report that regularly ranks the big names, lots of general search tips and a good explanation of how search engines work.

Navigator and Internet Explorer both have **Search** toolbar buttons which provide quick links to search sites.

▶ In Internet Explorer, click the **Search** button and a browser bar with a search box inside it will open. Use the box and your search results will appear in the browser bar. Click on the links shown and the site comes up in the main window (while the search results remain in the browser bar). If you want to see the search engines you're using (and remove one or two you don't like), click the **Customise** button. You'll notice that the search engines listed are mostly UK-based and there aren't that many. If you want to access a better list, here's another useful tip from .net magazine. Select the **Tools** menu, then **Internet Options**, then the **General** tab then the **Languages** button. Then add

< 164 >

'**English** – **United States** (**en-us**)' and move it to the top of the list, then click **OK**. Then when you use the **Search** button, you'll access a much larger group of US search engines.

▶ In Navigator click the **Search** button and you go to the Netcenter search page where you'll find links to all the big sites.

Both browsers will also let you do a quick search via the location bar.

▶ In Internet Explorer, enter the terms you want to search then hit **Return**. Internet Explorer will use its AutoSearch function and list the results in a browser bar on the left. It may also load a page in the main window, if you searched for a particular word and that word is also a **.com** address. For example, enter the word 'soccer' and hit **Return**. AutoSearch will find various football-related sites and list them in the browser bar. But it will also load **http://www.soccer.com**.

▶ In Navigator, enter the terms you want then hit **Return**. You will then go to a search results page at Netcenter.

Mac Users – aside from the **Search** buttons, if you have a newer Mac, you can also use its built-in search tool Sherlock.

▶ In Internet Explorer, you can start it up via the button with the magnifying glass on it to the right of the **Go** button

Both browsers now have a nifty little **What's Related** function. This uses technology from a program called Alexa to call up lists of sites that previous users thought were similar to the site you're accessing now. It can point you in interesting directions, though it often delivers nothing at all.

< 165 >

▶ In Internet Explorer, select the **Tools** menu, then **Show Related Links**.
▶ In Navigator, click the **What's Related** button on the right of the location bar.
▶ In the Mac version of Internet Explorer, you can access **What's Related** via the 'magnifying glass' button to the right of the **Go** button.

In a similar vein, site that feature collaborative filters can sometimes point you towards interesting pages. Collaborative filters work by pooling recommendations from individual users then cross-referencing them. If you like records A, B and C and another person likes records B, C and D, there's a chance that you may like record D and that the other person might go for record A. Most of the collaborative filters you find online these days are attached to retail sites. One exception is Movie Critic **http://www.moviecritic.com**. Once you sign up, you have to rate various films and then you'll start to get suggestions of other films you might like. Alternatively, you could try Jester, a collaborative joke filter

### Read about it online – Search UK

If you feel like trying a few home-grown engines, you could always give Search UK a whirl **http://www.searchuk.com/**. Alternatively, try UK Max **http://www.ukmax.com**, which will let you search for UK sites or go more global. ▲

< 166 >

**http://shadow.ieor.berkeley.edu/humor/**. Log on here and you have to rate 15 sample jokes, then Jester will start recommending new gags to you. For some thoughts on whether this might tell us something about the nature of jokes, try The Humor Quotient, a feature at the webzine Feed **http://www.feedmag.com/essay/es231_master.html**.

The NEC Research Institute at Princeton now publishes a regular survey of search engines. The search sites didn't come out of it too well this year, with even the best search engine – Northern Light – apparently only covering around 16% of the web. You can read the report at **http://www.metrics.com/**. People have argued about the report and its conclusions. But it's hard to disagree with one of its recommendations – that if you really want to make sure you search more of the web, you should use one of the MetaSearch sites, which allow you to combine the results from several of the major engines. Of course, merely covering

---

**Tips - Trading Names**

You don't always have to turn to a search engine. In some cases, a little thought will get you to the site you're after. If you're searching for a business site, their trading name will probably be the domain name. So if you're looking for the site for Dave's Hot Pies, try something like **http://www.daves-hot-pies.co.uk**. If you don't get any joy, try substituting the **.com** top-level domain. This often gets you to the site you're after pretty quickly. ▲

< 167 >

more sites doesn't necessarily guarantee end results will automatically be better, but it's certainly worth trying a sites like MetaCrawler **http://www.metacrawler.com/**, Dogpile **http://www.dogpile.com**, and Savvy Search **http://www.savvysearch.com**. If nothing else, it means you only have to learn one set of search guidelines.

## Using an Online Directory

Those who shrivel at the thought of something called a 'Boolean search' will probably get on a lot better with online directories. Yes, they do tend to have their own site search engine, and yes, there are a few guidelines to follow if you want to get the best out of them. But you don't have to sit there messing around with + and – signs. You can just click through various directories and sub-directories in search of the subject you want (and the links to the sites that cover it).

Take the opening page of Yahoo **http://www.yahoo.co.uk**. Here you'll see fourteen or so general headings – Arts and Humanities, Business and Economy, Education, News and Media, Reference, Society and Culture and many others. Under each general heading is a selection of sub-headings. So under Society and Culture, you see People, Environment, Royalty and Religion. Each of these headings and sub-headings is a clickable link. Click one and you move to that area of the directory, where you'll be presented with more links.

As an example, let's look for Yahoo's list of web search tools. Look for the **Computers and Internet** heading. Underneath you'll see several sub-headings – **Internet**, **WWW**, **Software**, **Multimedia**. Click on **WWW**.

< 168 >

That will take you to the general **World Wide Web** section. At the top you'll see links which take you to UK or Ireland-only sites in the general category. Below is another set of general categories to do with the web, from **ActiveX** and **Announcement Services** to **Web-based Entertainment** and **XML**. By some of these categories, you may notice the **@** sign. This indicates that this section cross-references with another general category. So if you click **ActiveX@**, it will take you to the **Computers and Internet: Software** section.

Actually, if you want to be specific, the exact location of this section is shown at the top in a list of all the directories it is nested within, as in **Home > Computers_and_Internet > Software > Operating_Systems > Windows > Windows_95 > Information_and_Documentation > ActiveX**. This kind of directory chain appears at the top of every page in Yahoo. If you follow a wrong turn, you can just click the previous term in the chain to go back or click **Home** to go the Yahoo homepage. Alternatively, click the **Back** button. Do that here and go back to the **WWW** section and click **Searching the Web**.

This takes you to a page that features more categories – from **All-in-One Search Pages** to **Web Directories** and **Weblogs**. Beside each heading is a number which tells you how many links are in that section. Click **Indices to Web Documents** and you'll be taken to a page which features more categories (**Best of the Web** to **What's New**) along with a huge general list of links to different types of web index sites. At the top of each page, incidentally, there's a search engine that lets you search the whole web, UK sites or just sites in the particular category you're investigating.

< 169 >

Good online directories are like well-designed libraries. In real-world
libraries, you often arrive at a shelf stacked with scores of titles relating
to a field you're researching. Unless you know beforehand what title
you're looking for, the only way to find out if a book is suitable is to take
it down and browse. Similarly, when you're faced with a list of 30 or so
links to sites offering to tell you 'What's New on the Web', a list which
only gives you the title, you don't have much choice but to click the links
and have a look. And that can be a bit hit and miss. Yahoo is great at
cataloguing sites, but it isn't in the business of quality control.

Some directories attempt to offer a bit more information. A slightly
different, more personal approach is offered by About.com **http://
www.about.com** (it used to be The Mining Company). Here guides put
together lists of sites in a particular area and write regular features on the
subject. It's worth a look, as are several British directories, which claim

< 170 >

to do a better job of classifying home-grown content than the UK version of Yahoo. Try UKPlus **http://www.ukplus.co.uk** or Yell **http://www.yell. co.uk**, the website for the Yellow Pages, which has a directory covering thousands of UK sites, the Electronic Yellow Pages (a searchable directory of UK businesses) and various other search services.

If Yahoo seems too big and baggy, you could try one of the specialist directories. Many of these are laid out in the same way as Yahoo but confine themselves to specific subjects and hence usually have the space and time to deliver a bit more information about the sites they list. As you might expect, Yahoo is good place to go to find specialist directories (there's a section in the Searching the Web category we were looking at earlier). You'll find that there are online directories covering pretty much everything you can think of. Here's a few to be going on with:

**The Media UK Internet Directory – http://www.mediauk.com/directory/** A useful collection of links to British TV and radio stations, magazines and newspapers and much else besides.

**Seniors Search – http://www.seniorssearch.com/** The Internet directory for the over-fifties, laid out like Yahoo but with categories like 'Just for Grandparents' and 'Seniors Personal Homepages'. There's a UK area too.

**WWWomen – http://www.wwwomen.com/** Bills itself as the 'premier search directory for women online'. Again, set out like Yahoo but with categories like 'Women in Business' and 'Personal Time for Women'.

< 171 >

FIND – **http://www.find.co.uk** The Financial Information Net Directory, this has links to all sorts of UK-based financial services resources online.

Shopguide – **http://www.shopguide.co.uk**

Entertainment City – **http://www.entertainment.city** These two shopping directories offer links to and reviews of online retail outlets in the UK that offer secure shopping.

## Listings, Web Logs, Awards and Web Rings

One of the first things people used to do when they got on the web in the early days was make a list of the sites they found, then group them under a heading – cool sites, new sites, underground links or some such. Presumably it was a way of helping them get to grips with the growth of the web. Maybe there wasn't much else to do on the web back then. More to the point, perhaps they weren't quite sure what to put on a web page. So they just created helpful lists of links, which soon became lists of links to lists of links, and so on.

The first What's New page came out of the National Centre for Supercomputing Applications – the place where Mosaic, the first big web browser, was developed. It was maintained by Marc Andreessen (one of the Mosaic team) and was essentially his bookmark file. It started up in the summer of 1993. By December, Andreessen was complaining that maintaining the list was a full-time job and left shortly afterwards to start Netscape. I guess he had bigger fish to fry, but lots of other people saw that they might be able to get ahead online by compiling lists which told people

< 172 >

which sites were cool, new or even useless. There's lots of these listings sites around now. They're not exactly a serious search tool, but they can be fun and they can point you towards sites you might otherwise never find.

As ever, Yahoo provides an exhaustive set of links to listings sites – look in the Searching the Web directory as before. What's New and What's Cool sites are the most common sorts of online listings. But they can be about anything. If the people who put together the big directory sites are like online librarians, then the linkmeisters behind listings are more like editors. The best ones take a particular angle and show you something about the web you hadn't seen before. Take Steve Baldwin's excellent Ghost Sites of the Web **http://www.disobey.com/ghostsites/**, a site of links to other sites that are still online but no longer breathing; in other words, they haven't been updated in ages, but live on, a relic of earlier web times. Listings are also a great source of what you might call the online trash aesthetic. For every linkmeister dutifully logging his cool sites of the day, there's another one totting up the web's worst pages (and adding sniggering captions to the links). Try the Useless Pages **http://www.go2net.com/internet/useless/**, which specialise in highlighting all the supremely pointless sites on the web.

Listings sites with pretensions tend to move into the online awards business. As you move around the web, you see sites sporting lots of little logos that proclaim that they are in someone's top 5 per cent of sites or that they are Dave's Animated Site of the Week. The first awards site to become really popular was the Cool Site of the Day, which turned its creator, Glenn Davis, into something of a net celebrity. (He now runs a

< 173 >

site called Project Cool **http://www.projectcool.com/**). Dreaming of micro-fame (or of the ad dollars a site with his traffic could garner), amateur web users and gamey corporations followed Davis's example and set up various awards sites.

Like all awards scams, they generally share the same secret purpose. It's often not so much about recognising excellence; it's about showing that you, the judicious authority handing out the gongs, know what you're talking about (and might be available for online consultancy, if the price is right). A lot of web awards sites are harmless fun. Many are pointless and have come in for some serious ridicule. But a few carry some authority and are genuinely useful. If you're interested in web design, it's worth looking at High Five **http://www.highfive.com/**, which hands out awards for the best designed web pages. For a general list of awards sites, try Yahoo (there's a Best of the Web category in the WWW section. Alternatively, go to **http://www.thecorporation.com/**, one of the many awards parodies, where you can download various joke award icons (e.g. 'Sell Out Site of the Month') to put on your homepage.

For an interesting extension of the basic listing idea, try a weblog. These are pages of links, usually updated on a daily basis, to stories and articles on the web. Where old listings pages used to link to sites, cool or otherwise, weblogs instead link to good pieces of writing. In contrast to the old listings, they tend to represent the dynamic nature of the web. According to Jorn Barger, whose Robot Wisdom is one of the most popular web logs **http://www.robotwisdom.com**, the name refers to the fact that these sites simply log someone's surfing. Certainly, a weblog is often

< 174 >

a very personal edit of the web, featuring comments on and critiques of the material linked to. But that isn't always the case. One of the best weblogs, Memepool **http://www.memepool.com** is a collective effort.

Taking things even further, Slashdot **http://www.slashdot.org** links out to stories about Linux and other 'news for nerds' and on its own pages features discussions about those stories, the result being threads that often dwarf the essay or news story originally linked to. Often weblogs focus on one subject or industry. For example Dave Winer's Scripting News **http://www.scripting.com**, often celebrated as one of the first weblogs, high-lights stories about programming. Jim Romanesko's Obscure Store **http://www.obscurestore.com** links to offbeat stories located in the middle pages of America's myriad local papers. At its most minimal, a weblog can be just a list of headlines/links, in which case the site is sometimes referred to as a newslog. Leaving aside the terminology, weblogs can be a great way of finding interesting material online. For a useful list of links to some of the best examples of the genre, try CamWorld **http://www. camworld.com**, which is itself one of the better weblogs

For more fuzzy but occasionally useful searching, you could try web rings. These are loose collectives of sites (often personal homepages put up by fans) all devoted to the same basic subject. Once they might have been deemed to be in direct competition with each other. But someone somewhere rather cleverly figured out that, as the web got bigger and more corporate, small pages might make more impact and draw more traffic by sticking together. In a web ring, sites are connected so that you can move from one to the other by clicking the **Next Site** link at the

< 175 >

bottom of a page. Alternatively, the starting-point of the ring usually offers a link to a master list of all the sites involved.

There are web rings devoted to all sorts of subjects – from Afro-American issues **http://www.halcon.com/halcon/1ring.html** to the 'Rugrats' TV show **http://www.geocities.com/Hollywood/Set/9404/webring.html**. These rings can get very big (there are almost 800 sites in the Afro-American web ring) and you might find yourself browsing more than searching. And they're a bit hit and miss. Some amateur/fan sites seem deranged, but others are brilliant mini-archives of useful material. So web rings are definitely worth investigating. For general links, once again, look in Yahoo. Alternatively try WebRing **http://www.webring.org/**, a web ring directory which lets you search web rings or find the one you want, Yahoo-style, by going through various subdirectories.

## Research Online

Most search sites are good for moving you on to other locations. But what about research sites proper, sites that are destinations in their own right and offer searchable databases of information? There are plenty of these online – look under the **Reference** category on Yahoo. As you might expect, you can research all sorts of things online, from films at the Internet Movie Database **http://uk.imdb.com**, to technical terminology at the PC Webopaedia **http://www.pcwebopedia.com/**. However, it's no surprise that one of the areas in which the net is strongest is searchable archives devoted to itself. Try the Usenet newsgroup archives at Deja.com **http://www.deja.com**. Alternatively, take a look at the excellent

< 176 >

## Read about it online – Search Tips

One of the best sites I've found for advice about searching is About.com's Web Search page **http://websearch.about.com/**. This has news and reviews, plus links to all sorts of useful resources. Look for the **Web Search Articles by Topic** link for an archive of past reviews. In the archive, look for the **Beginning to Advanced Tutorials** link. Click that and you'll find all sorts of useful stuff, everything from tips from professional researchers to a fascinating article on 'The Invisible Web', the web that the search engines never reach. Highly recommended. ▲

Research-It **http://www.itools.com/research-it/research-it.html** – a self-styled 'one-stop reference desk' which lets you search dictionaries, a thesaurus, collections of quotations, maps and much else, all from the same page. Finally, an awards-laden British business search site you shouldn't miss is Scoot **http://www.scoot.co.uk/**.

## Next Step?

Now you're on top of search sites, you could take a break from the web for a while and learn about online communication in the next section on email. If you want to learn more about the web, go to page 252 and the chapter on Downloading.

< 177 >

## Email and Mailing Lists

When I got online, the first thing I did was send some email to a friend who'd been connected for a while. It wasn't much of a message – the epistolary equivalent of those telephone calls you used to get from people where the first thing they said was, 'Hey, I'm calling on my mobile'. But he wrote back. And when his reply appeared, I'll admit that I was blown away. Back then, the web was only just getting started and email was one of the more immediate things you could do when you got online. That's my excuse, anyway. Today the web has become the thing most people go for when they first get online. But lots of people still think email is the net's killer app (as techno-pundits put it). Even those who make a profession out of net-bashing usually make an exception for email, which they 'really couldn't live without'.

Email has been around almost as long as the net. When ARPANET (a trial network that was essentially the beginning of the net) was set up in 1969, it was supposed to enable the sharing of scarce computing

### Jargon File – Killer App

As in 'killer application' – the piece of software that works well enough to convince people they need to spend lots of money on the hardware needed to run it. So, according to some accounts, the spreadsheet was the killer app which sold the business world on computers. ▲

< 178 >

---

**Jargon File - ARPANET**

ARPA stands for Advanced Research Projects Agency, essentially the Pentagon's R&D department during the cold war So, as you might expect, the ARPANET was the network it set up to test out new computer communications technology. ▲

---

resources. But the researchers who used it soon began to send messages across the trial network, first about official business, then about office gossip, then about the science-fiction novels they were reading.

Today, every major business and institution has an email contact address. TV and radio programmes, newspapers and magazines can't do without them. Email regularly features in Hollywood films, though for obvious reasons it always looks a lot flashier and more exciting than the thing you get on your desktop. This year, it was even the central device in 'You've Got Mail', the latest blockbuster romance featuring the Hollywood everycouple Tom Hanks and Meg Ryan. Email is now a part of best selling novels and the daily papers. Take the Monica Lewinsky affair. Part of Kenneth Starr's investigation into her affair with old Slick Willy involved recovering deleted email from a computer hard drive. Over here, the email leak that backfires has become a regular news story, with both a Tory party employee and a member of staff on the C4 show 'The Big Breakfast' getting caught out by the fact that email at work is never as private as it may seem. Melissa, a particularly nasty computer virus

< 179 >

that spread via files attached to email even made the front pages this year.

Email is a part of our lives now. And it's not hard to see why email has caught on. For the cost of a local telephone call, you can send messages to someone on the other side of the world in a matter of minutes. It's easy to save email and keep track of your correspondence. It's cheaper than faxing someone and you don't have to worry about paper and ink. You can also send more than plain text – attaching image and sound files to mail is simple. For no extra cost you can send mail to lots of people at the same time, building up informal mailing lists where you can thrash out political problems or discuss last night's TV. You can also subscribe to more formal mailing lists devoted to particular subjects and receive regular updates and news. The arrival of HTML mail means that web pages can be delivered directly to you. You can also sends your friends mail that resembles web pages, with flashy graphics, images and hyperlinks.

Email's attraction isn't just to do with speed and ease of use. Perhaps because it sits somewhere between speech and writing, because it's like a

### Read about it online – Email fiction

To sample an experiment in using email for fictional purposes, go to the site run by net celeb Carl Steadman and try Two Solitudes. Subscribe and over the next few days you'll be sent a series of emails in which two people play out an email romance – look for the link on **http://www.freedonia.com/**. ▲

< 180 >

---

**Jargon File – HTML Mail**

Email that doesn't come in the form of plain text but is formatted using Hyper Text Markup Language, the computer code used to create web pages. ▲

---

letter with the immediacy of a telephone call, it seems to encourage directness and intimacy. People get to the point quicker in email and sometimes seem more open and accessible. Email can also be less potentially painful or embarrassing than face-to-face contact, which might be one reason why it's apparently finding favour as a way to ask people out on a first date. Incidentally, email is also being used by some to dump boy or girlfriends. When it is, this hugely intimate form of communication can seem paradoxically impersonal; the absence of face-to-face accountability makes it all the harder to bear for the person on the receiving end.

Perhaps because it's less of an intrusion than a telephone call (generally, you can't just phone up your boss to tell him what you think), email seems to break down barriers and cut across hierarchies, especially in offices and the business world in general, where it has helped some to communicate more effectively. Telephoning someone on the other side of the world always involved negotiating time zones and inflated call charges. Email means you don't have to lose sleep (especially over your bank balance) to stay in touch with friends and business colleagues abroad.

< 181 >

## What software do you need?

All you need really is your web browser. The latest versions of Netscape's Navigator (4.6) and Microsoft's Internet Explorer (5.0) both come with mail packages (called Messenger and Outlook Express, respectively). In the past, these were a bit weak. But now they're pretty good – as good as most of the standalone specialist mail programs. So save yourself some time and use your browser.

▶ To start Outlook Express, just click/double-click on its icon on your computer desktop.

▶ To start up Messenger, start up Communicator first by clicking/ double-clicking on the icon on your desktop, then select the **Communicator** menu, then **Messenger**.

I'll come clean and say that, though I've been a Netscape user in the past, at the moment I think Outlook Express is slightly better than Messenger. It lets you do a bit more with your messages and mail accounts and it's got a lot easier to use. That said, Messenger is still only on version 4.6. Version 5.0 may catch up. You could install both and switch between them to see which you prefer. If you have lots of disk space, there's nothing to stop you running both browsers and another mail program as well, but you will have to nominate one as your default, so that when you click an email link on a web page (for example, to send mail to the person responsible for the page), the computer knows which program to start up. All very simple, or it ought to be. However, rather irritatingly, Netscape have made it very difficult for you to use their Navigator browser and have Microsoft's

< 182 >

**Tips - Try Eudora**

If you want a specialist mail program, go for Eudora, which is available for both PC and Mac. There are two versions – Light, which is free and fine for most people's purposes and Pro, which has lots of snazzy extra features which you may or may not use and is free for the first thirty days. You can download Eudora from the web at **http://www.eudora.com/**. ▲

Outlook Express as your default mailer. It requires some technical fiddling. For similar reasons, Microsoft don't go out of their way to make it easy for you to use the Explorer browser with Netscape's Messenger mail software.

Finally, just to complicate things, the version of Outlook Express available to Mac users is currently 4.5 (5.0 is apparently on the way). As ever, the Mac version is slightly different to the Windows version in all sorts of little ways. It's still easy enough to figure out, but where there might be potential for confusion I've tried to include specific instructions for Mac users of Outlook Express. As usual, there isn't that much of problem with differences between the Mac and Windows versions of Netscape's Messenger, so covering those in detail doesn't seem necessary.

## Configuring Your Mail Software

If you're going to use the mail program that came with the browser/internet suite supplied by your ISP, you may find that it was

< 183 >

configured during the general installation process. Similarly, if you're using an online service, everything will be sorted out during the main installation. However, if you're installing something from scratch, you will need to enter a few personal details before you can send any mail.

You may have to enter any and all of the following:

**Your name**: As in Jim McClellan

**Your email address**: Your ISP will have given you this when you signed on – something like **yourname@yourserviceprovider.net**

**Your return email address**: Usually the same as above, though you can enter something different if you're going to be picking up replies at another location (e.g. work)

**Your user name (also known as the account name)**: This is the first part of your email address – i.e. **jim.mcclellan**

**Outgoing Mail Server (SMTP)**: The computer at your ISP that handles the mail you send to other people. This will usually be something like **mail.yourserviceprovider.net**

**Incoming Mail Server (POP3)**: The computer on which the mail sent resides. Again, this will be something like **mail.yourservice provider.net**

**Password**: The password your ISP gave you when you signed up.

▶ With Outlook Express, the first time you use it, the **Internet Connection Wizard** should take you through configuration. If it doesn't you can start it up yourself, by selecting the **Tools** menu, then

< 184 >

---

**Tips – Outlook Express 5**

If you do try Outlook Express 5, you'll see that the opening screen is rather cluttered. There's lots quick links, a contacts lists and a regular 'tip of the day'. If this kind of thing bothers you, scroll to the bottom of the page and put a tick in the box next to 'When Outlook Express starts, go directly to my Inbox'. ▲

---

**Accounts**. Click the **Add** button, then **Mail**. If you need to change any account information (you might change ISPs and email address), select the **Tools** menu, then **Accounts**. Pick your account, then click on **Properties**.

▶ In Messenger, select **Edit**, then **Preferences**. Then click on **Identity** and **Mail Server** in turn to enter the relevant information.

▶ In the Mac version of Outlook Express, click the **Preferences** button, then select **E-Mail** from the **Accounts** section. If you're using a new Mac/iMac, you can also do all this via the **Apple** menu. Select **Control Panels**, then **Internet** and you'll call up a dialog box where you can enter details about your email account, amongst other things.

### Your first message

If you've got friends who are already online, now's the time to bug them with those 'Hey, I just got on the net' messages. (If you really want to wind them up, you should call them up repeatedly to see

< 185 >

whether they actually got your mail.) If you don't have any friends who are online (or want to avoid irritating those that are), you could always send a message to yourself. Alternatively, why not send a message to the Guardian.

We've set up a program which will automatically send out replies to all mail sent to the Guardian at the address given in this book. It may be a touch impersonal but at least you can check quickly and easily whether your first mail reached its destination. Open your mail program and click the **New Message/Compose Message** button. A window will open which is split into two parts. The bottom part is where you write your message. The top part is where you enter details about the address to which you're sending your mail. Click in the **To:** field to move the cursor there, then enter the address – **guidetest@guardian.co.uk** – making sure that you don't capitalise anything (net addresses are case sensitive). Don't add an extra period at the end – however they may appear in books or the papers, email addresses do not end in full stops. If all this looks rather confusing, go back to page 25 for more information.

Your own address may already be in the **From:** field. In the **Subject:** field, enter a brief description of what your message is about – My First Message or some such. When you come to file mail sent to you, you'll realise how useful the **Subject:** field is and you'll curse people who don't bother entering anything there. Ignore the other fields in this window for the moment. Once you've filled out the address information and the subject line, click in the bottom part and write your mail. What you put here is up to you – you might want to tell us whether you think this book

< 186 >

is any use. On second thoughts, perhaps you should just say what sort of day you're having.

### Email style

At school, you may have been given advice on how to lay out a letter. None of that really applies to email. When it comes to layout, you don't need to start by writing your address in the top right-hand corner. When people get your email, before they open it, their mailbox will show them who sent it and what it's about (if you enter something in the **Subject:** field). Some people don't bother opening their mail with a 'Dear Jim' and just get straight to the message.

Email purists also don't sign off with a 'Yours, Dave' or whatever, but instead include a personal 'signature file', aka 'sig file'. This usually contains your contact details – name, email address, perhaps snail mail address and telephone number(s) – all the stuff you might put at the top

---

**Jargon File – Snail Mail**

Snide net slang for old-fashioned mail that comes in envelopes, is delivered by the Post Office and takes a lot longer than email to arrive. Actually, in the past, some well-known UK ISPs have had problems with mail at particularly busy times of the year and some unlucky users found themselves waiting two weeks and longer for their email. ▲

---

< 187 >

right-hand corner of a piece of snail mail, plus a jokey/deep quotation that shows what an interesting/deep/sexy individual you are. A few years ago, 'So long and thanks for all the fish' from Douglas Adams' Hitchhiker's Guide to the Galaxy was a popular sig file choice, so popular that it has now been officially outlawed, along with all quotations from Monty Python, Blackadder and Shooting Stars. Some sad folk also include ASCII art – those 'clever' little pictures made up with keyboard characters.

Your mail package will let you compose a signature file and save it. When you write mail, you will automatically be able to paste it in at the end of the message.

▶ In Outlook Express, select the **Tools** menu, then **Options**, then the **Signatures** tab. You can then compose your signature and choose to add it to all messages.

▶ In Messenger, select **Edit** then **Preferences**, then **Identity** in the **Mail and Newsgroups** section.

▶ In the Mac version of Outlook Express, select the **Tools** menu then **Signatures**. When you compose a new message, there's a **Signature** toolbar you can use to add your sig file or not.

In terms of general style, brevity and directness are key. People are paying to download your mail, so the idea is not to add to their bills, in however minuscule a way. Perhaps because it hovers somewhere between speech and writing, email tends to be more informal and slangy than snail mail. In theory, you don't need to take quite as much care with your grammar

< 188 >

**Tips - Email conventions**

The thing to remember about email style conventions is that you don't have to follow them rigidly. Don't be intimidated by people who babble on about netiquette and insist that email should look a certain way and should end with a sig file. If you don't want to turn out something conversational, if you want your email to be like your snail mail, fine. The only principle you should stick to is to keep things brief wherever possible. ▲

and upper and lower cases. You don't need to go back over your messages and make sure everything is just so. Of course, sending illiterate pieces of doggerel isn't good email style either and won't make that good an impression. Both Messenger and Outlook Express have spell checker programs that will automatically go over messages before you send them.

## TLAs and Smileys

There are a few distinctive elements of email/online style you should know about – probably so that you can ignore them. You can compress messages even further by using TLAs, as in Three-Letter Acronyms. This includes things like WRT – with regards to; IMO – in my opinion; LOL; OTOH – on the other hand; RTFM – read the f- manual. (OK, so they don't always have three letters.) Most of these can be understood quickly, without resorting to some kind of TLA dictionary. That's the theory,

< 189 >

anyway. Interestingly enough, they've started to spread to print prose. The journalism written by the American novelist David Foster Wallace is packed with wrts.

The TLAs above are all capitalised, though people tend to write them in lower case. In fact, email, and online communication in general, often seems to be a lower-case medium. Capitals are reserved for emphasis. Writing something in capitals is the online equivalent of shouting. You'll notice that most junk mail features capitalised 'subject' headings – MAKE MONEY FAST!!! You should shy away from it, unless you really need to make a point. It can look rather rude and people do get the hump. It may sound daft if you've never been on the net, but a splurge of capitals in an online message does feel hectoring and confrontational.

When you're writing your email (or chatting or posting to a Usenet newsgroup), you can also use emoticons, aka smileys. These are little sideways-on faces constructed from keyboard characters, which are used to indicate emotion – :-) means happy; :-( indicates sadness, and ;-) is supposed to signal irony. The prevailing theory about this is that sometimes it can be hard to tell what a person mailing or chatting to you

**Read about it online – TLAs**

For a pretty comprehensive list of smileys and TLAs (and a useful glossary of general net jargon), try Netlingo at
**http://www.netlingo.com**. ▲

< 190 >

online means exactly, or it can be hard to grasp their tone, especially if they're trying to be funny or sarcastic, mainly because you're not face to face and hence can't pick up on the physical/facial cues they're giving. Hence smileys.

Of course, most people over the age of fourteen don't feel the need to pepper their ordinary paper letters with little faces to help the recipient understand when they're being ironic. And I can't remember the last time I got some mail with a smiley in it. So it may be that smileys are just a product of the novelty/strangeness of email. They can be useful, though there is sometimes something slightly bogus about them, especially the irony smiley that some people use as an all-purpose get-out clause. As the science-fiction writer Bruce Sterling once pointed out, writing 'you, sir, are a complete asshole', then following it up with ;-) to show that, hey, you didn't really mean it, is probably not going to go down that well with the recipient of your message.

## HTML or Plain Text Mail?

Email used to be plain ASCII text. But now we have HTML mail, which means letters with pictures, links and more. Most new mail programs – e.g. Messenger and Outlook Express – automatically use HTML mail for email unless you tell them otherwise. Some older mail programs may have difficulties with this. It's not that big a deal. If you send HTML mail to someone whose software can't handle it, it will appear in their inbox as text plus an attached HTML file. However, to save on aggro, you can

< 191 >

always check that the person you're mailing can receive HTML mail. If they can't, choose to send just plain text. (This is generally the best option when sending messages to mailing lists.)

▶ In Outlook Express, once you've opened a **New Message** window, select the **Format** menu then either **Plain Text or Rich Text (HTML)**.

▶ With Messenger, when you're writing your mail, click on the **Message Sending Options** button in the bottom-left corner of the **Address** window. Then look for the drop-down **Format** menu on the left that will let you pick text or HTML or both.

For the moment, you should concentrate on sending a simple message. However, thanks to HTML, you can produce very flashy email, complete with different fonts and colours, much like the kind of thing you can do with a modern word-processing program. Once you're used to email, try the options available via the **Format** menu. In Outlook Express, select the **Format** menu, then **Apply Stationery** and you'll be able to use various standard templates for your email – party invites with coloured balloons, snow scene Christmas cards and the like.

## Sending your first message

You're happy with your message. Click on your mailer's **Send** button. Your connection software should now kick into gear. You can now choose to go online and send the mail straight away. Alternatively, you can stay offline and choose to send your mail later. It will be transferred

< 192 >

to your **Outbox** or **Unsent Mail** folder, depending on which mail program you're using. You can then write more messages and stack them up in the **Outbox** to send all at once. Alternatively, you can wait and send them later. If you close your mail program without sending your mail, you may get a brief reminder asking whether you want to send it now. With unsent or queued mail, most mail software will send it automatically the next time you check your own mail. Alternatively, with Messenger, you can select the **File** menu, then **Send Unsent Mail**.

Let's say you choose to send your mail straight away. You may have to enter your password, then the mail software will send your mail and check to see if you have any messages as well. There might be something from your ISP welcoming you aboard.

Most mail software is set up by default to save a copy of mail you send, usually in the **Outbox** or in the **Sent Items** folder. Some older programs used to automatically send you a **Carbon Coby** (aka **cc**) of any messages you sent. Either way, it's a good method of keeping track of

---

**Tips - Cut and Paste**

You can always write your mail in your word-processing package, then cut and paste it to the **New Message** window. But all that clever formatting you spent hours on won't come out, especially if your mail software is set to send plain text. You could always attach particularly flashy documents. ▲

---

< 193 >

mail. However, if you don't want to save your mail:

▶ In Outlook Express, select the **Tools** menu, then **Options**, then click the **Send** tab, then remove the tick in the box next to **Save copy of sent messages in the Sent Items folder**.

▶ In Messenger select the **Edit** menu, then **Preferences**, then **select Copies and Folders** (it's under **Mail and Newsgroups**). Then remove the tick in the box next to **Place a copy in folder 'Sent' on 'Local Mail'**.

▶ In the Mac version of Outlook Express, click the **Preferences** button, then select **General** in the **Outlook Express** section then look for the relevant text box.

After you've sent your mail to **guidetest@guardian.co.uk**, go and make yourself a cup of tea. With luck, if everything's working, you should get

---

### Tips – Reading Mail Offline

Perhaps this sounds a bit obvious, but whenever possible work on your mail (i.e. read and write it) offline. Once you've downloaded mail sent to you, disconnect and then read it. Some programs log off automatically. But if you have one that doesn't, don't get your mail and start reading it, forget you're still connected and then write the reply online. It's easy to do and then you end up paying BT or whoever for all that time puzzling over the mot juste or the right smiley. ▲

---

< 194 >

a reply from us in the next couple of hours – perhaps quicker, though don't hold me to that.

## Troubleshooting

Email is one of the more glitch-free parts of the net. Occasionally, mail might be bounced back to you unsent. Usually, the problem is caused by errors in the address. Remember that email addresses are case sensitive. Also, don't add spaces or extra periods. If you've checked everything and it appears ok, it may be that the person you're sending it to has changed address. If that isn't the case, the problem may be at the ISP where your intended recipient has his or her mailbox – their computers may be down – in which case, try sending your message later.

## Getting your mail

Email sent to you sits in your mailbox on your ISP's mail server until you go and get it. If you want to see if you have any email:

▶ In Outlook Express, click **Send and Receive**.
▶ In Messenger, click the **Get Message** button

You'll connect to the net and your messages will be downloaded. Log off. A window should open showing the new mail in your **Inbox**. If not, click on your **Inbox** icon or button. For each piece of new mail, you'll see a line of information, telling you who sent it and when and what it's about. Double-click on that and the message will open in a new window.

Most people prefer to check their mail manually. However, you can

< 195 >

get your mailer to pick it up automatically at regular intervals – every hour or so, or whatever you decide. This is mainly of use if you (a) get an awful lot of mail and (b) are online all the time because it doesn't cost that much where you live or because someone else is paying your bills. If that sounds like you:

▶ In Outlook Express, select the **Tools** menu, then **Options**, then click the **General** tab. Make sure there is a tick in the box next to **Check for new messages every X minutes** and change the figure to suit your requirements.

▶ In Messenger, select the **Edit** menu, then **Preferences**, then **Mail Servers**, then click the **Edit** button, then tick/change the line **Check for mail every X minutes**.

▶ In the Mac version of Outlook Express, click the **Preferences** button, then select **General** in the **Outlook Express** section then look for the relevant text box.

When you're reading your mail, before you get to the message proper you may encounter a lot of technical-looking information known as the 'header'. This gives details of when the message was sent and by whom, the path it took on its way to you and other bits and pieces. You don't really need to see all of this and by default most mailers remove or trim down the headers. However, the header can sometimes be a useful starting-point, if you're on the receiving end of junk email or abusive messages and want to find out more about where they're coming from. To display the full header if you need to:

< 196 >

---

**Tips – Multiple Identities**

Outlook Express 5.0 makes it very easy to create a different
"identity" for each person who uses the program – something that's
useful for families all using the same PC and the same internet
account. It means each person can use the same program but
maintain separate messages, contacts, and personal settings. To
create a new identity, select the **File** menu, then **Identities**, then
**Add New Identity**. You can also choose to password this. To switch
to a particular identity, select the **File** menu, then **Switch Identity**.
You can also do this via the **Identities** quick link at the top right of
the main Outlook Express window. ▲

---

▶ In Outlook Express, open the mail you're interested in, select the **File**
menu, then **Properties**, then click the **Details** tab.

▶ In Messenger, click on the message, select the **View** menu, then
**Headers**, then **All**.

## Replying to your mail

A friend has emailed you and you want to reply. You don't need to open
a **New Message** window, then write his or her address in the relevant
section. You can just click on the **Reply To** button. This will open a **New
Message** window with your friend's address already filled in. In the
**Subject:** field, it will say 'Re: whatever your friend entered in the Subject

< 197 >

line in the mail they sent you'. When replying to mail, it can be helpful to quote from the previous message – especially if you're writing to someone who gets lots of mail and thus may lose track of their correspondence. If you use the **Reply To** button on some mailers, when the message window opens it will display the past message – indented with what are known as 'quote tags', as in:

>Jim
>blah blah blah
>Wally

You can then edit this, selecting the bits you want to keep, then adding your own contributions, as in:

On the 10th March, Wally wrote
>blah blah blah
See what you mean, Wally.
Jim

The end result simulates a kind of conversation and helps to keep track of ideas over several messages (as a result, it's indispensable when it comes to posting messages to Usenet newsgroups – more on this on page 222).

When replying to email, conventional wisdom says you should reply quickly, if only to confirm you received the message. I was once berated by a famous author I was interviewing by email when I took a few days to reply to one of his messages. 'Bad email etiquette, Jim' he wrote in a mildly tetchy mail asking why I hadn't replied yet. 'If you're going to take that

< 198 >

**Tips - Editing Replies**

Make sure that you edit down the previous message so that only the appropriate bits are included. Don't just automatically send people back a complete copy of their previous mail when replying.
Obviously it's not such a problem if the first mail was a few lines.
Several thousand words is something else entirely. ▲

long to reply we might as well use regular mail'. This was stretching it a bit, since he lives on the other side of the Atlantic. But I could see his point.

Sometimes, if a reply doesn't appear for a while, you start to wonder whether your mail actually reached its destination. Then again, just because email goes a lot faster, it doesn't automatically mean you have to. One of the few bad things about email is the way it often carries a kind of implicit pressure to be more productive, the way it can feel as if it is bullying you to get cracking, speed things up, write back NOW!

## Carbon Copies and Forwarding

One of the good things about email (though it is open to abuse, as you will unfortunately discover) is that it is very easy to send the same message to large groups of people. One way to do this quickly is to use carbon copy (CC) or blind carbon copy (BCC). If you use the Cc option, recipients will be able to see who else got your message. If you use Bcc, they won't know who else got a copy.

< 199 >

▶ In Outlook Express, you'll see a **Cc:** line underneath the **To:** line. Type in the addresses you want here. If you want to use the **Bcc** option and you can't see it, move your cursor over the **Cc:** – it will turn into a button. Click on it and you'll be able to access the **Bcc:** line.

▶ In Messenger, to add **Cc** and **Bcc** addresses, just click the **To:** button in the **Address** window.

It's also easy to forward mail. Once a message is open, just click the **Forward** button and a new message window will open with the old message in quote tags. You can then enter the address of the person you want to forward it to and add any comments. Some mail packages also let you redirect messages to someone else. Click the **Redirect** button and a window will open containing the message you want to send on, this time without the > tags.

## Address Books and Email Directories

If someone sends you mail, you can add their contact details to an address book for future reference – helpful if you find it difficult to remember email addresses or type them out without making mistakes.

▶ In Outlook Express, click the **Address book** button. (In the Mac version try the **Contacts** button). To add a new entry to the book, click the **New** button, then select **New Contact**. To send a message to someone, click on their name then click the **Action** button, then select **Mail**. To add more information to their entry, click on their name then the **Properties** button. Outlook Express also keeps an easy-

< 200 >

access **Contacts** list on the bottom left of the screen. To write to someone on this list, double click on their name.

▶ In Messenger, select the **Communicator** menu, then **Address Book**. To add someone to the book, select **Personal** from the browser bar on the left, click the **New Card** button then fill out the relevant details. To send a message, click on the person's name then click the **New Msg** button. To add more detail to their entry, click on the name then the **Properties** button.

Outlook Express and Messenger also give you the option of specifying whether the person in question can receive HTML mail, which is useful.

You can also search online directories for email addresses. Both Outlook Express and Messenger are set up to allow you to search various directories – Big Foot, Four11, WhoWhere, Switchboard, Infospace. These are a bit hit and miss. Some rely on submissions from users who want people to be able to find them. Others use software that trawls the net, in particular Usenet newsgroups, for addresses. They all have a definite American bias. Big Foot is probably the best for British users, though there's not much in it. All of them will turn up plenty of results – especially if you do a simple search on a name. Of course, you then have to figure out which, if any, might belong to the person you're trying to contact.

Once you're online:

▶ In Outlook Express, click the **Address Book** button, then click **Find People** toolbar button. A **Find People** dialog box will come up. Click

< 201 >

the **Look in** drop-down window to pick a directory to search, then enter the name of the person you're searching for and click the **Find Now** button. (This works slightly differently in the Mac version but it's easy enough to understand).

▶ In Messenger, get online, then select the **Communicator** menu, then **Address Book**. In the dialog box that comes up, you can click on a directory in the left frame, then write a name in the text box, then click the **Search For** button

## Email and Attachments

You can send more than just text using email. It's possible to attach all sorts of different files to your messages – everything from images and sounds to video and programs. However, there is a size limit for email messages of 64Kb – generally fine for most text messages, but not for images, programs and the like. In addition, most files you might want to send are binary (8 bit), whilst email is all 7 bit ASCII text. So before files can be sent, they have to be converted into ASCII. Then they'll be converted back to their proper form by the person who gets your mail. In theory.

Attaching files to email has been made easy by modern mail software. In Outlook Express or Messenger, just click the **Attach** button on the toolbar (the one with the paperclip on it), then find the file you want to send in your directory, then click on **Attach**. However, problems are caused by people not checking whether recipients of their mail have software that can cope with the type of attachments they're sending.

< 202 >

**Tips - Mailing URLs**

Messenger lets you attach a web page to mail you're sending to a friend. Get online, then write your mail. Click the **Attach** button, then select **Web Page**. Write the web page URL or address in the **Please Specify a location to attach** dialog box, then click **OK**, then send the mail. Messenger will then go and get the page and attach it to your mail. This can be a fun way to tell people about a good page you've found. But check they can receive HTML mail and think about the size of some of the pages before you send. It might be better just to send the URL. You can also do this via Internet Explorer. If you're browsing and find a page that might interest a friend, select the **File** menu, then **Send**, then choose whether to send the page or the link. Then Outlook Express (or whatever your default mailer is) will open and you can write your mail and send it. You can also do this via the **Mail** button on the toolbar. ▲

A few years ago, most PC mail programs converted attachments using something called UUencode. Newer mail programs use something called MIME which is becoming the standard. Mac mail programs also used something called Bin Hex. Modern mail programs can cope with all of these. However, many people don't religiously upgrade their software. Especially with something like email, they're happy chugging along with the mail program they've always used. Until they get a chunk of indecipherable gibberish in their mailbox.

< 203 >

So before you send an attachment to someone, find out what conversion method their mail program uses. If they use a newer mailer, there should be no problem. If they have an older program, you'll have to use UUencode. To use UUencode for attachments

▶ In Outlook Express, select the **Tools** menu, then **Options**, then the **Send** tab. The **Mail sending format** will be set to **HTML**. Click the box by **Plain text** to change it, then click **Settings**. You can then specify either MIME or UUencode.

▶ In Messenger, click the **Message Sending Options** button in the bottom-left corner of the **Address** section of the **Composition** window then click in the box next to **UUencode instead of MIME for attachments**.

▶ In the Mac version of Outlook Express, click the **Preferences** button, then select **Message Composition** in the **Outlook Express** Section. Then make the changes as required.

If you use an online service rather than an ISP, attaching files to messages to members of the same service is no problem. However, in the past, you did encounter trouble, especially when receiving attachments from friends elsewhere on the net. Most of the online services have sorted things out now and can handle MIME files but you could always double-check if you're sending to a friend on one of the online services. When it comes to receiving mail with attachments, both Outlook Express and Messenger will usually show picture attachments in the body of the message. If the attachment isn't an image, there should be a paperclip

< 204 >

**Tips - Viruses**

Always virus-check Microsoft Word documents that are sent to you as attachments. They can be host to various macro-viruses. These are more irritating than dangerous, but they're still a pain. Even if the document was sent by a friend, check it. Often people pass these on without knowing. ▲

icon at the top of the message when you open it. Click that. The file's name will appear. Click that and you'll be asked if you want to open it or save it.

You can attach large files to email but sometimes you have to break them up into parts. (What qualifies as large? Most people say 1MB per message, including attached files, though some say 2 to 4MB per message. In part it depends on your ISP and email system.) Your mail program may break up a large file and send the parts, but check in the **Help** file for details. For example, if you want to set Outlook Express to break up a large message, select the **Tools** menu, then click **Accounts.** Then click the **News** tab, the **Properties** button, then the **Advanced** tab. In the **Posting** section, you can tell Outlook Express to break up messages above a certain size. Then when you try to attach a large file, it will kick into gear.

When it comes to receiving attached multi-part files, check your mail software's **Help** files to see how it handles them. If you try to open one part of a multi-part attachment, some programs will automatically open the rest and put them together. With others, you have to mark the various

< 205 >

## Tips - Compressing Files

If you are going to send a large file via email, to speed things up, you might want to think about compressing it. The best way is with a program called WinZip (evaluation copies are available for download from **http://www.winzip.com/**). Check that the person you're mailing can deal with zipped files. For more on downloading files and using WinZip, go to page 263. Incidentally, if you are using an older mail program that has trouble with MIME, UUencode or BinHex and you have a PC, you can use WinZip to convert all these file types and more. ▲

parts before your software can deal with them. For example, in Outlook Express, click on all the parts (press the **Control** key, then click on each header), then select the **Message** menu, then select **Combine and Decode**.

## Managing your email

Obviously, it's up to you how hard you work at filing your mail. There are people who let months of mail pile up in their Inbox without doing anything about it. It's easily done. Email doesn't exactly clutter up your office the same way as the stuff that comes on paper. But it can get out of control. Anyway, it's very easy to organise and file email.

First, try to read messages as soon as you get them and reply quickly. Messages in your **Inbox** will most likely be sorted according to the date they were received. If it helps you get through them quicker, you can

< 206 >

order them in another way – by sender, subject, etc. In Messenger or Outlook Express, select the **View** menu, then **Sort** or **Sort By**. Be ruthless when it comes to deleting messages you don't need. It's easy to save your mail, but often you don't need to. If you do want to keep mail, file it when you've read it. You can set up specific folders for mail from different people, organisations, mailing lists or subjects, then transfer it easily as you read it. To create new folders, select the **File** menu, then **Folder** or **New Folder**. To file a piece of mail:

▶ In Outlook Express, select a message, then select the **Edit** menu then **Move to Folder**.

▶ In Messenger, click the **File** button on the toolbar.

You can create filters that automatically direct incoming mail into specific folders rather than the **Inbox**. Here you have to tell your mail software to look out for messages that carry certain keywords in the subject line or come from a particular person or place.

▶ In Outlook Express, select the **Tools** Menu, then **Message Rules**, then **Mail**.

▶ In Messenger, select the **Edit** menu, then **Message Filters**. Click on the **New** button to create a filter.

▶ In the Mac version of Outlook Express, select the **Tools** menu, then **Mail Rules**, then click on **New Rule**.

From here you have to specify what you want your software to look for and what it should do with a message that fits the parameters you set.

< 207 >

## Tips - Filters

Filtering messages directly to specific files may make you feel as if you've dealt with them, so you might not actually read them for a while. Cue a huge email backlog. For some people, it may be better to read stuff as it comes in, then file it manually. On the other hand, filters may do the job for you. ▲

Say you get a lot of mail from a particular business colleague. You can put his or her email address in the **Sender** category, then arrange to transfer it to a special mailbox/folder. Alternatively, if they never say anything interesting, you could get it diverted straight to the trash. Outlook Express can even be set up so it won't even bother to download certain messages from your ISP's mail server. Actually, there are now many filter programs specifically designed to block junk mail, which generally work better than the filters in your standard mail package. For more on this, go to page 413.

## Free Mail, Redirection and Other Mail Services

You already have an email address/account. But do you want another – for free? Of course you do. Start up your web browser and go to Mircrosoft's Hot Mail **http://www.hotmail.com**. In a matter of minutes you can set up an email account (with your own password). You can then use your web browser to read and send mail.

< 208 >

Web mail has now gone from being incredibly popular to being totally ubiquitous. Interestingly, many computer industry analysts failed to predict its success, though perhaps you can't blame them. After all, most people online already have an email address. In general, ISPs don't offer the option of not having an email address and paying a little less. So why bother with an extra one? Never underestimate the hypnotic power of that word 'free'. Nevertheless, a web-based email address offers a few tangible advantages. First, it makes it very easy to get your mail whilst travelling. All you need is a computer with a connection to the web. You don't need separate email software any more – you can use your web browser.

You can change your ISP without having to inform friends and colleagues of your new email address. You can create multiple email addresses on the same net connection – for example, for family members. You can 'maintain your independence' from work or college, according to one Free Mail site. Translation: if you have an official mailbox at work and if that's your only connection to the net, you can set up something for your personal mail on the web. It's also true that if you have an account at home that you share but you want to keep some mail private, a web mailbox is a good option. Then the mail you want to keep private won't be sitting around on your machine at home, waiting to be discovered.

Not all of these benefits stand up to scrutiny. Take the basic attraction – that Hot Mail and others offer a 'free' service. Clearly they don't charge up front. What they do is sell advertising space, so you have to look at ads while you get your mail. Sometimes your mail may also contain ads. Given the way web mail works, you'll inevitably end up

< 209 >

---

**Tips - Global Net Cafes**

Web mail is a great tool for staying in touch with friends and family
at home when you're off travelling the world. You just need an
account and to know where the cybercafes are in the city/country
you're headed to. It might be worth doing a bit of advance research
at the Internet Café Guide **http://www.netcafeguide.com/**. The site is
based around a book but also features a useful online list of
cybercafes around the world, along with a few mail services. ▲

---

composing some of your mail online – which obviously means a bigger
telephone bill. As you may already have discovered, the web can be
slow, which means getting your mail will be slow too, perhaps consid-
erably slower than downloading it from an ISP. And sometimes servers
can be down, which means you won't be able to get your mail at all.

Given that the big browsers come with mail software attached, the
advantages of being able to deal with everything via the browser are
minimal. Many ISPs now allow you to create multiple email aliases on
the one basic account, so that other family members can have their own
addresses. Some free web mail services give users the chance to send mail
anonymously and claim this as a benefit. There's more on why you might
want to do this and how on page 403. However, there has been some
abuse of web mail in this respect and some of the bigger players will not
now let people send messages anonymously.

< 210 >

If you use web mail for personal purposes at work, your mail will remain private, but if the boss is keeping tabs on your time online, he or she will know that you keep making repeat visits to the Hot Mail site and might wonder why. On the subject of privacy, you hand over a certain amount of personal information in return for your free mail account and you can't always be certain how that information will be used in the future, or if it will be adequately protected.

It's also become clear, following the high profile Hot Mail hack this summer that web mail is not as secure as it could be. Of course, many users already realised this and used it mainly for personal chat, figuring that there was safety in numbers (e.g. the millions who use the web mail services). However, it you are sending important business messages online, it might be best to avoid the standard web mail services and try something more secure, like Hushmail – see below for more detail.

---

### Read about it online – Self Destructing Web Mail

With some many free web mail services around, you have to offer something pretty special to make a splash these days, like 1on1mail, who began to offer secure, encrypted email that also self destructs after a while – so it won't be sitting around on a server somewhere waiting to be discovered. For more information, go to **http://www.1on1mail.com**. For something similar, but without the Mission Impossible trappings, try Hushail **http://www.hushmail.com**. ▲

< 211 >

So what you're left with is a separate address where you can receive mail you might not want to show up in your standard mailbox and the ability to change ISPs without hassle and to pick up mail while on the move. These are considerable benefits, so you should definitely have a free web mail account or two. Most of the big portal sites now offer them. Alternatively, try the following:

| | |
|---|---|
| Hot Mail | **http://www.hotmail.com** |
| iName | **http://www.iname.com** |
| Rocket Mail | **http://www.rocketmail.com** |
| MailCity | **http://www.mailcity.com** |
| Net@ddress | **http://www.netaddress.com** |

Some web-based mail services are designed not to replace your ISP mail account but to work in tandem with it. Take Big Foot (**http://www.bigfoot.co.uk**), who do one of the better email directories and will also let you create what it calls an email address for life –

### Read about it online - Fun Mail

Here's an amusing (sort of) free mail service you can try – register at the Fun Mail site **http://www.funmail.co.uk** and you can choose various email addresses that suit your mood (or say something about you), as in **sid@ilovestarwars.co.uk** or **jim@ihatestarwars.co.uk**. ▲

< 212 >

---

### Read about it online - Electronic Postcards

To amuse or irritate your friends, why not try the Activegrams web mail service and send them a deeply naff animated greetings card? Choose from a variety of cards to suit all occasions and locations at **http://www.activegrams.com/**. For a more useful email service you can access via the web, try Remind-U-Mail. Here you create a kind of personal calendar filled with important dates (e.g. your mum's birthday). Then you'll get an email reminder so that you don't forget it. It's free, so you have no excuse – **http://calendar.stwing.upenn.edu/**. ▲

---

**jim.mcclellan@bigfoot.com** or some such. This is what you give out to people. Mail arriving at this address is then redirected to your ISP mail account. Once again, this reduces hassle when it comes to changing ISPs. Other companies (e.g. iName) give you the opportunity to pick a name that sounds a bit better than the thing your ISP lumbered you with (in certain cases, charging you for it). Once again, this address is the one you give out and mail is redirected to your ISP mail account.

Bigfoot also offers a variety of other useful services. It's very good when it comes to blocking junk mail and spam. When you go on holiday, it will automatically send out messages to people who mail you, telling them you are away until a certain date. Many ISPs will do the same and if you think email is going to be particularly important to you, check to see what special services are on offer. For example, some ISPs will also redirect mail

< 213 >

to another address for you and send notification about new mail to your pager (which could be useful for business people on the move).

## Mailing lists

Mailing lists are one of my favourite things about the net. At their best, they can offer quick and painless access to high-quality information about a particular subject. When they're open to contributions from all subscribers, the discussions that are generated are more focused, productive and friendly than the free-flowing anonymous brawls you often find in Usenet newsgroups.

There are thousands of mailing lists online. Some are one-way only. You subscribe and everything from product information to news bulletins is sent to you on a regular basis. Many webzines run mailing lists which update you about content and even send web pages direct to your mailbox. Plenty of excellent electronic zines exist only as mailing lists.

With two-way lists, the content of the list is generated by the subscribers. You send a message about something on a particular topic or event. It goes to everyone on the list. Then someone might respond and over time – hours or days, depending on how active the list is – a discussion builds up. Some of these can be pretty serious affairs where people try to thrash out theories and ideas. Others are more relaxed and the ostensible subject of a list – a local pop group, gardening, whatever – often takes a back seat to general chatter.

Two-way lists can either be moderated or completely open. The former are controlled by a moderator who tries to keep discussions on track, and

< 214 >

weeds out posts that are off-topic or deliberately abusive. The latter are completely open. Everything anyone sends in to the list goes out to everyone else, which can lead to huge amounts of mail. Moderated lists seem preferable – so long as the moderator is accountable for the decisions he or she might make. Moderated lists appear to be much smoother. People fall out less. And though there's often less traffic, it seems to add up to more.

Subscribing to a list is easy. The general information about the list that you find at a site like Liszt.com will tell you what to do. You send mail – usually with something like 'subscribe' in the body of the message – to the computer where the list is based. You will then receive mail notifying you that you have been put on the list. Save this message. It will contain important details about how to post to the list and how to cancel your subscription. One thing to look out for: lists have two addresses – one to which you send messages intended for the list proper and one for administrative queries. Don't get the two mixed up. Otherwise you may end up sending mail about how your attempt to cancel your subscription was unsuccessful to everyone on the list. More than likely, they will not be too pleased.

## Read about it online – List Directories

The web is the best place to go for information about different lists, and there are thousands you could join. Try the excellent Liszt – **http://www.liszt.com/** or Publicly Accessible Mailing Lists at **http://www.neosoft.com/internet/paml/**. ▲

< 215 >

## Read about it online – Web-based mailing lists

Lots of sites on the web now offer free mailing list services. You can set up your own list or subscribe to the ones already established there. Try Topica **http://www.topica.com**, eGroups **http://www.egroups.com**, Cool List **http://www.coollist.com** or One List **http://www.onelist.com**. ▲

Online mailing lists are usually automated. The two most popular list software programs are Listserv and Majordomo. They basically do the same sort of things but respond to slightly different commands and requests. The main difference is that Listserv is a connected system, which means that if you don't know which computer houses a list you want to join, you can send your subscription request to any Listserv computer. (Of course, you still have to know the name of the list, in which case you're likely to know the proper address.) With Majordomo lists, you need to know where the computer hosting the list is.

## Tips – Access

Remember that most lists are public forums. They're easily accessible and easily searched. In other words, the things you write might be found by someone using the net to check you out. So you might want to watch what you say. ▲

< 216 >

## Read about it online – Email Genres

For an antidote to all those who go on about how productive email is, go to the webzine Suck and read Thinking Outside the Mailbox by Polly Esther, aka Heather Havrilevsky. A jokey run-down of email genres (the Long Lost Friend email, the Virtual Boss email, the Playing Hookey email), this contains the interesting theory that the After Work Plans email is a revolutionary act because it turns what used to be a two-minute conversation into an endless, time-wasting round of emails as you try to fix a time and a place **http://www.suck. com/daily/97/01/10**. ▲

It's pretty easy to join a list. Dealing with the number of messages it can generate might prove problematic, however. If you're going on holiday, sign off from high-volume lists before you go. Don't stay on the list and then use one of those services that automatically send people a little note saying you're on holiday: if you're on a high-volume list, in your absence you will end up sending your reply to every message – and you may make the list unworkable. If you find yourself on a high-volume list thats interesting but a bit overwhelming, check with the administrator to find out if there's a weekly digest of the list you can get instead. To avoid messages from a high-volume list clogging up your **Inbox**, set up a mail filter to divert it to its own box. Set the filter to look for the list address or the list name, which is usually in the **Subject** line of messages.

< 217 >

## How Not To Be A Slave To Your Email

Email is a wonderful thing but it will take over your life if you don't keep it under control. When you first get online, you may find yourself checking for new email every half an hour and feeling floored and friendless when you don't have any. Then suddenly there's too much of the stuff. You find yourself thinking back to the good old days when you got to work or came home in the evening, started up your computer and just got on with what you wanted to do. Now you start up your computer, get online and there are fifty emails fighting for your attention. Worse still, the important ones are often hidden under a mini-mountain of junk mail. There are things you can do to deal with spam but none of them are perfect. In the end, you have to learn to live with it.

Spam may turn out to be the least of your problems. As mentioned before, one of the potentially great things about email is the sense of intimacy it can generate. But this can cut both ways. In other words, it's remarkably easy to annoy people with email without really meaning to. Some people argue that this may be something to do with the fact that it's often hard to catch the exact tone of certain messages. You may think you're being cleverly ironic, but the plain text in the mailbox of your soon-to-be-former friend might end up looking pretty insulting. So what you need is a little smiley to let someone know exactly what you did or didn't mean.

There's another school of thought that says that all the smileys in the world won't help. These people believe that, by filtering out the distractions and diversions of the real world, people get to the point in email, say what they really mean and that's why there are so many bust-ups.

< 218 >

---

**Read about it online - Bryan Winter**

Recently a man called Bryan Winter apparently sent an arrogant brush-off email to a woman he had met at a club. So what, you may say. Well, that email has since been circulated widely online and taken as proof of the general awfulness of modern males. Meanwhile real people called Bryan Winter have started to get hassled. And a few cool heads have pointed out that the original Bryan Winter email could have been fake. But people still pass the mail around. For an interesting analysis of a modern email myth in the making, head to Salon and read 'The Humiliation of Bryan Winter' at **http://www.salon.com/health/sex/urge/1999/05/11/ bryan_winter/index.html**. ▲

---

People don't agree on things. In the real world, they cover things up and try to get along. But in email, they can't cover things up. The truth is that though email is great for creating and maintaining friendships and romantic relationships, it can also be pretty good at wrecking them.

Aside from arguments over semantics, there's the potential for accidents email opens up. Netiquette says you have to deal with those fifty messages in your **Inbox** quickly or people might get the hump. So you do, but in a rush you send mail to the wrong people. On one mailing list I subscribe to, a message appeared from one list member that was clearly intended for a friend. It was a previous post from one of the more

< 219 >

deranged members of the list, plus a few comments on what a wacko this bloke was. Common knowledge on the list, but something that was left unsaid. Consequently, the poor guy who made the mistake had to issue a public apology.

Things get worse in the office. Never, ever assume that email in a business environment is either private or your property. Your boss probably thinks that he owns all electronic communications made on his computers and that he has a perfect right to read them. At the moment, the law backs him up. So if you have to send a friend memos about what a fool he is or about a juicy job offer from a competitor, do it on paper. At least you can eat that if the going gets rough. Email will sit on the system in all sorts of places. It's really difficult to delete it completely. And you may end up thinking the boss is the least of your troubles if your steamy emails to the marketing manager in the cubicle down the corridor are discovered and sent to all and sundry by your office colleagues.

Actually email can even get the bosses into trouble. During the Microsoft anti-trust trial, both sides have made great use of thousands of private email messages from the big computer companies involved, email messages in which CEOs drop their PR-friendly banality and say how they want to crush the competition. It seems that Bill Gates and his competitors really do say what they think in email. Or rather did say. With that particular court case and its demonstration of the way email can bounce back at you, the golden age of business idealism about email has probably officially come to an end.

< 220 >

There has been lots of talk about how email flattened office hierarchies and liberated ordinary office drones. It can do just that. But now companies are wary of what their employees are doing online. They send round memos telling people to button their lips when they're sending email, just in case. Actually a rather more basic sign that all the hype about email revolutionising workplace efficiency was rather overstated is provided by the messages that turn up in your office mailbox everyday. For every useful communication, you'll find ten lame email jokes that are currently doing the rounds and, if you're really unlucky, several files of stupid animated cartoons.

So, great as it is, email can cause a few problems. Here are a few survival tips that might help. Be sensible about the mailing lists you subscribe to. Don't take on more than you can handle. If you're up till two in the morning trying to stay on top of your lists, you're on too many. Remember that email in the office environment is not private and could be saved and used against you. And although you're supposed to answer email quickly, think before you press **Send**.

### Next Step

Now you've mastered email, Usenet newsgroups will be a doddle. So you could go straight to the next section. Alternatively, if you're worried about email and privacy, or dealing with spam, go to page 413. ▲

< 221 >

## Usenet Newsgroups

When people try to explain Usenet newsgroups to first-timers, they usually reach for some sort of helpfully recognisable real-world image. They talk about Usenet as the world's biggest conversation, one that ranges across national boundaries and takes in everything from who killed JFK to how to cook a curry. Others talk it up as a kind of transnational think tank, a global groupmind, a place where experts collaborate on solving problems, where you can find the answer to just about any question you might want to ask. Others less enamoured of the whole thing call it the world's biggest slanging match or dismiss it as a multinational rumour mill, where the daftest kind of disinformation can gain currency.

Let me add my own real-world analogy to all this. Another way to get your head round Usenet might be to think of it as a virtual equivalent of Speaker's Corner in London. It's similarly rowdy and anarchic. Log on and you'll find people standing on their digital soapboxes, holding forth. There are plenty of hecklers who take over the soapbox to have their say. There are also loads of people who don't say anything but are just there to take in the show.

However, in the virtual Speaker's Corner that is Usenet there's space for 30,000 different soapboxes, all devoted to different topics and themes. And if you get on the wrong soapbox, people get cross. Every now and then someone gets up on a soapbox and says 'Testing, testing, testing'. Then all the other speakers get really mad and yell at him or her for so long that they lose track of what they were talking about. If that didn't

< 222 >

make things chaotic enough, every few minutes all the speakers are simultaneously pushed off their soapboxes by people holding up big advertisements for get-rich-quick schemes or porn shops. Then a bunch of people show up to chuck blankets over the get-rich-quick/porn people and push them off the soapbox, so that the original speakers can start up again.

Actually, all this goes to show is how limited real-world metaphors are when it comes to explaining what happens on the net. Let's try something more basic. Usenet is a kind of text-based global bulletin board. It consists of around 30,000 different newsgroups. The name itself is misleading. Groups can cover pretty much everything – not just the latest stories placed in the papers by political spin doctors.

With most groups, people log on to read and respond to previous messages, known as posts or articles. Some groups are one-way affairs, for announcements only. Others are primarily for exchanging files (which could be anything from images to software). People often talk about the anarchic nature of Usenet and it's true that most groups are pretty free and easy. But a few are strictly moderated. Usually this is not primarily from a desire to censor discussions but to make sure that, for example, a group devoted to cooking doesn't keep circulating recipes that have appeared before. There are also fairly rigid conventions governing everything from how to post messages to how to create new groups, so rigid in the latter case that some Usenet users created a much more open set of newsgroups in protest (known as the alt groups).

Usenet isn't the same thing as the internet. It's better to think of it as one of the many kinds of communications traffic carried by the net. Your

< 223 >

ISP keeps a database of newsgroup postings on its news server, a computer running the Usenet news transfer protocol. Your ISP's news server is connected to others and a steady flow of postings to the newsgroups is passed between them. You connect to the news server to access the various groups and read the latest postings.

When you send a post to a particular group, it goes to your ISP's news server and is then passed on to others. As a result it can sometimes take a while before everyone on Usenet gets to see your wittily phrased deconstruction of Jerry Springer's haircut. If they don't access Usenet on a regular basis, they may miss it altogether. There's so much traffic (i.e. so many messages) generated on Usenet that ISPs clear out their databases fairly frequently.

Usenet was created in 1979 by some American computer science graduates. Their idea was that, via a computer network, the geeks of America (and the world) could bring their collective brainpower to bear on the multiple bugs and quirks of the Unix operating system and gradually make it better. This original, idealistic vision survives in many newsgroups, where people do attempt to collaborate and help each other out.

### Jargon File – Unix

The computer operating system of choice for hackers and geeks, who spend hours tinkering with its various versions. ▲

< 224 >

But as Usenet has spread to the mainstream, it's become clear that plenty of people don't want to be 'constructive', or use technology in such a benign way. Either that, or they have their own, rather odd idea of what being constructive means (for example, putting together lengthy theories to show how the spread of cashpoint machines is hastening the advent of a United Nations take-over of America). Plenty of people get completely caught up in the newsgroups but the bulk of users (90 per cent according to some estimates) are lurkers. Drifting round Usenet can be one of the more diverting modern spectator sports. If nothing else, it alerts you to the incredible variety of things people can find to argue about.

Usenet is one of the more controversial areas of the net, mainly because a large chunk of it is driven by uncensored human desire. Yes, there are groups where pornography is exchanged. Unlike web sites, where people are trying to make money, the stuff in Usenet is often given away for free and is easy to download if you're using the latest software. There are also newsgroups devoted to child pornography and paedophilia. It's more than likely that your ISP won't carry these. A few years ago, British ISPs came under police pressure not to carry news-

---

**Jargon File - Lurkers**

Net slang for those who hang around in newsgroups (and chat rooms), read what other people have to say but don't actually post anything themselves. ▲

< 225 >

**Read about it online – Wendy Grossman**

She wrote an award-winning account of the online scrap over Scientology which formed the start of an excellent book called net.wars – an account of the various battles being fought on the borders between cyberspace and the real world. The whole book is available online and it's a great source of information on the history and culture of Usenet and the net in general – **http://www.nyupress. nyu.edu/netwars.html**. ▲

groups that contain illegal material and most have complied. As for newsgroup porn, be aware that it is there (especially if you have children who use your net connection), but don't get it out of proportion. For more on dealing with it, go to page 403. Incidentally, Usenet controversies don't begin and end with porn. The newsgroups have been the scene of some ferocious online spats, like the battle between the Church of Scientology and its critics in **alt.religion.scientology**.

People are always saying Usenet isn't as good as it used to be. They were saying it when I first got online at the start of 1994, mainly because the newsgroups were being visited by more people like me (i.e. non-techie types) and that inevitably caused a few growing pains. People are saying it even more now, not without reason this time. Newsgroups have been hit by a plague of bulk junk messages (aka spam) touting get-rich-quick schemes and pornographic web sites amongst other things. As a result,

< 226 >

some groups have become unworkable. Some gloomier net users have concluded from this that Usenet is doomed.

Obviously spam has caused serious problems, but people are also going elsewhere for the kind of conversation and community they once got from the newsgroups. There are now all sorts of web sites where you can go for newsgroup-style discussions – try Talkway **http://www.talkway.com** or RemarQ **http://www.remarq.com**. Many big web sites have their own discussion boards where users can post their thoughts. There are even special browser add-on programs that let people add newsgroup style discussions to the web sites they visit, for example Third Voice **http://www.thirdvoice.com**.

Despite all this, people shouldn't be too quick to write off the newsgroups. Usenet users have developed some ways of dealing with spam – a few volunteers spend hours of their own time sending out 'cancel messages' that remove unwanted spam. In the spring of 1998, these spam

---

**Read about it online – Usenet II**

According to its creators, Usenet II was set up 'to create a structure where the traditional Usenet model of co-operation and trust can be made to work in the internet of the 21st Century'. This means lots of moderators and rules (no crossposting articles to more than three newsgroups, no binaries – e.g. pictures – text postings only) and much else. Read about it on their website – **http://www.usenet2.org/**. ▲

< 227 >

cancellers went on strike to force ISPs to take more action to tackle spam. Despite predictions of infocalypse, Usenet didn't collapse. What the cancel strike did reveal is that most spam goes to newsgroups devoted to sexual subjects. However, some people still think spam has made Usenet unworkable and in response have set up something called Usenet II.

People often talk about the net in general as a new interactive public realm where free expression rules and everyone can have their say. This is often wishful thinking. Many don't have the time to learn how to put up a web page. However, pretty much everyone who gets online can figure out how to send a message to a newsgroup. As a result, Usenet is one of the things that lives up to the rhetoric . . . sort of. It also shows you the consequences of that rhetoric. If you want to see what a people-driven info-anarchy actually looks like, check out Usenet. It can be both heart-warming and kind of scary. It isn't always pretty, but it is interesting.

## Choosing a newsreader

To access the newsgroups, read what people are saying and stick your own oar in, you need a newsreader. As with email software, it's probably easiest to use the newsreader that came with your browser/internet suite. Microsoft's email package Outlook Express is also a newsreader and is pretty good. Netscape Communicator's mail software Messenger is also a newsreader and also works just fine. To access your browser's newsreader:

▶ Start Outlook Express then look for the **Read News** link on the introductory screen once you've launched the main program. Alternatively, click on your news server's name in the **Folders** window on the left

< 228 >

▶ Start Navigator, then select the **Communicator** menu, then **Messenger**.

To make things go smoothly, your newsreader should be able to search the list of newsgroups, read offline and filter messages i.e. block messages from particularly irritating people. It's also helpful if it can handle postings in HTML, messages that resemble web pages and feature graphics and links. On this basis, there isn't much to choose between the current versions of Outlook Express and Messenger. If you do install both, you will need to nominate one as your default newsreader. This will be the one that starts up if you click a link on a web page to a particular newsgroup. As with email software, there can be problems if you want to browse with Navigator and use Outlook Express for the newsgroups, or vice versa. If you're using Outlook Express, there can sometimes be problems if you don't also make it your default email program. Once again, if you use Outlook Express for the Mac to read the newsgroups, you'll find that it doesn't have all the features you find in the Windows version

---

### Tips - Standalone Newsreaders

For an alternative to the big two, PC owners should try the excellent Agent. There's a free version, called, not surprisingly, Free Agent **http://www.forteinc.com/getfa/getfa.htm**. Mac users could try Newswatcher **http://www.best.com/~smfr/mtnw/**. ▲

---

< 229 >

and that it is organised slightly differently. Where there are differences that might cause confusion, I've tried to indicate as much.

## Configuring Your Newsreader

This is very similar to configuring your email software. You need to enter details about yourself and the address of your ISP's news server – the computer that maintains a database of newsgroups. Your news server address is usually something like **news.yourisp.net**.

▶ In Internet Explorer, select the **Tools** menu, then **Internet Accounts**. Then click the **News** tab. To add a new news account, use the **Add** button, then **News** then the **Internet Connection Wizard** will start up and walk you through it. To change an old one, click the **Properties** button and follow the directions.

▶ In Messenger, select the **Edit** menu, then **Preferences**. Then go for the **Mail and Newsgroups** section and add in details of your news server address. Use the **Newsgroup Servers** category to add in new servers or edit details on existing entries.

▶ In the Mac version of Outlook Express, click on the **Preferences** button on the toolbar then click on **News** in the **Accounts** section. Click on **New Server** to add in a new server.

The first time you start up Messenger or Outlook Express as a newsreader, they should both automatically download a complete list of newsgroups available from your ISP's news server (something that may take a few minutes). Once you've got a list of groups, log off. It's easy to forget you're connected and start searching for groups you want.

< 230 >

## Getting started

You've downloaded the complete list of newsgroups and are ready to get involved in that big global conversation. First, you need to find the groups that match your interests – not an easy task given that there are tens of thousands. Though it may not look like it at first, there is an order to the newsgroup list – an address system of sorts, though it refers to subject matter, not actual locations.

Groups are ordered into a number of hierarchies – fairly wide-ranging thematic categories – followed by more specific detail about what the group discusses. For example, **uk.politics.censorship** would, as you might expect, be devoted to discussing the politics of censorship in the UK only. There are plenty of hierarchies – some easy to decipher, others rather mystifying. Many refer to discussions specific to a partic-ular country, some to a specific university or company. Here are a few of the more popular ones.

| | |
|---|---|
| **alt** | As in alternative – the place for discussions with a non-conformist/ anarchic/funky flavour |
| **biz** | You can send your commercial messages here |
| **comp** | Discussions about everything to do with computers |
| **microsoft** | Get your product support advice here |
| **misc** | Catch-all category for stuff that doesn't seem to fit in elsewhere |
| **news** | Home to announcements about Usenet, debates on what's wrong with it, how to fix it, make it better in the future, etc. |
| **rec** | Recreation, as in sports, hobbies and the like |

< 231 >

| | |
|---|---|
| **sci** | Science |
| **soc** | For socio-cultural discussion (and a bit of religion as well) |
| **talk** | The place to argue out more controversial issues – gun control, for example, though that particular debate seems to occur pretty much everywhere on Usenet |
| **uk** | Devoted to UK-specific discussions |

Of these hierarchies, the **alt** groups are far and away the most popular and also the most controversial, mainly because they're not subjected to quite the same controls as the other groups. The **alt** hierarchy was essentially started as a protest. Frustrated by the rigid nature of the system by which new groups were created and approved, angered by the fact that a proposed **rec.drugs** group was blocked by the Usenet powers-that-be, even though it had passed the vote of users that all new groups have to undergo, a few net users created the alt hierarchy on their own computers in 1987.

**alt.drugs** came into being and a year later, when the proposed **soc.sex** was also blocked despite succeeding in the general vote, **alt.sex** got started. In contrast to the formal procedures for creating new news-groups, **alt** groups can be created by anyone whenever they want. What this means is that many groups are actually gags and wind-ups, there for the sake of the name and not thriving communities, though many jour-nalists don't realise this and take some of those groups listing bizarre sexual practices rather more seriously than they should.

When it comes to finding a newsgroup, you could flick through the general list, which if nothing else will give you a good idea of the

< 232 >

variety of discussions going on. However, most newsreaders let you search the list.

▶ In Outlook Express, select the **Tools** menu, then **Newsgroups**. Alternatively, just click on the **Newsgroups** button above the main window. A **Newsgroups Subscriptions** dialog box will come up. There's a search box at the top. You search via simple key words – comics, 'The Simpsons', shopping. Once you find a group you like, you need to subscribe to be able to read it. Click on your chosen group then click on the **Subscribe** button.

▶ In Messenger, select the **File** menu, then **Subscribe**. A **Subscribe to Newsgroups** dialog box will come up. Then click the **Search** tab. You can then search on simple key words you're interested in. Once you find a group you like, you need to subscribe to get the messages. Click on your chosen group then click on the **Subscribe** button.

▶ In the Mac version of Outlook Express, just click on the name of your news server in the left-hand window. The newsgroup list will come up in the main window with a search box above it. Then highlight a group and click the **Subscribe** toolbar button.

You may find the same subject coming up in different hierarchies. One **sci** group might discuss the science of genetics, for example, whilst in a talk forum people might be thrashing out the political implications of gene trademarking and the like. Sometimes the same subject gets chewed over in groups which don't look that different – you might find an **alt** group and a **soc** group devoted to drugs, for example. Check out each group to

< 233 >

see which one suits you best. Finding the right newsgroup is a hit-and-miss affair. This isn't the fault of the labelling system, which is admirably specific. It's more that each group has a flavour of its own, its own history and culture, which determines how it treats a particular subject.

Your ISP might not provide access to all the available newsgroups. In part, this may be due to space. There are so many newsgroups, you can't blame ISPs for attempting to ease the strain on their bandwidth. So it may be that some specialist or foreign-language groups aren't available. If you want access to those groups, ask your ISP. They will usually oblige. If they don't, consider changing to another ISP.

Of course, another reason why groups may not be available is that your ISP has taken the decision to censor its newsfeed. It may not carry

---

### Tips - Finding Newsgroups

You run a search on the newsgroup list and there doesn't seem to be a group devoted to Namibian woodworking technique. That doesn't mean there isn't one in existence, just that your ISP doesn't carry it. Get on the web, go to **http://www.jammed.com/~newzbot/** and you can search for such a group. It could be that someone before you has recognised the need for a Namibian woodwork group and is trying to start one. To find out if that's the case, look in **news.announce.newgroups** to see which new groups are being proposed and to vote on whether they should be accepted. ▲

---

< 234 >

some groups because they contain illegal material (i.e. child porn or pirated software) and/or because they don't fit with its image/marketing strategy. Some ISPs and online services specifically target the family market and as a result don't allow access to whole chunks of Usenet that they think may carry porn and the like. Hence, they block all the **alt.sex** groups or whole chunks of **alt.binaries** (one of the places people exchange images).

There are problems with this kind of blanket censorship. For example, some of the **alt.sex** groups are devoted to worthy nattering about sexuality and aren't particularly salacious or pornographic. However, your ISP gets to decide which newsgroups it carries. If it's an issue, try to look for an ISP that doesn't censor the groups so rigorously. Of course, with the internet, there's always a way round censorship. You can always try a publicly accessible news server. Again, try **http://www. jammed.com/ newzbot/** for information.

## Reading newsgroups

Once you've subscribed to a few groups, you need to get online to download the most recent messages. Once you're connected:

▶ In Outlook Express, in the window on the left of the screen, you should see a list of the news groups you have subscribed to. Connect to your ISP then click on one of these groups. Outlook Express will now download the headers from the newest messages. Click on the header of an individual message and the whole thing will be downloaded. Outlook Express should be set to download 300 headers by default, usually enough to get a feel for most groups. You can change

< 235 >

it to a higher or lower figure. Select the **Tools** menu, then **Options**, then click the **Read** tab and change the line **Download 300 headers at a time**. In the Mac version, to find a similar section, click the **Preferences** button, then click **General** in the **Outlook Express** section.

▶ In Messenger, to the left of the window, under your news server's name you'll see a list of the news groups you've subscribed to. Double-click the one you want to read. A dialog box may come up asking you how many headers you want to download. Usually Messenger is usually set by default to ask you before it downloads more than 500 messages or message headers. To change this, select the **Edit** menu, then **Preferences**. In **Newsgroup Servers** change the figure in the line **Ask me before downloading more than 500 messages**. Once you've decided how many headers you want, a window will open, showing a list of the messages in that particular group in the top part of the window. Click on a message on the list and its contents will appear in the bottom part of the window.

The most sensible way to consume Usenet is offline. Once you've subscribed to a few groups, you should go online, get the latest messages from those groups, log off and then read them.

▶ In Outlook Express, download the headers from your newsgroup, as detailed above then log off, if you're really keen to save every last penny. Set Outlook Express to work offline, via the **File** menu. In the main window, you should see a list of headers. Some will have a + sign next to them. Click on this and you'll see the rest of the thread

< 236 >

### Jargon File – Headers

In this context, headers are the basic details about the message: what it's about, who sent it and when. They are not the message itself. You'll need to go back online to get that. ▲

(i.e. the various replies) that this particular message has generated. Scroll through them and you'll be able to see what's being discussed and by whom. Next you need to mark the postings you're interested in. To the left of the headers, click in the column underneath the arrow pointing downward. A little blue arrow will appear to the left of the header. Once you've marked the messages, then select the **Tools** menu, then **Mark for Offline**, then **Download Message Later**. If you want to get messages from more than one group, open another group and mark the posts there. Then once you're done, go online, select the **Tools** menu then **Synchronize Newsgroup**. Outlook Express will then go online and get the stuff you want. Once your messages have been downloaded, you can log off and enjoy the witty badinage and thoughtful discussion that is Usenet's stock-in-trade. Actually, if you want to simply this a little, just mark the messages for download, then select the **Tools** menu then **Synchronize Newsgroup**. A dialog box will come up asking if you want to download all the marked messages. Click **Yes**. Outlook Express will go online and get what you want.

< 237 >

▶ In Messenger, select the **File** menu, then **Go Offline**. Then select the newsgroup you're interested in, so that the headers are displayed in the main window. Then mark the messages you want. There are several ways you can do this. The easiest is probably to hold down the **Control** key, then click on each of the messages you want. Once that's done select the **File** menu, then **Offline**, then **Get Selected Messages**. Your newsreader will download the messages. Then you can log off and start reading.

Both newsreaders offer several ways of reading newsgroup messages offline. It might be worth trying each out to see which you like best. For more information, look in the help files. After a while, you may find that you really enjoy one particular newsgroup and consequently want to download all the messages posted to it on a regular basis to read offline.

▶ In Outlook Express, the quickest way to do this is to use the **Synchronize Account** and **Settings** buttons at the top of the main window. First, highlight the newsgroup you're interested in. Then click the **Settings** button. You'll be given a choice of downloading the headers, all the messages or just the new messages. Choose **New Messages**. You'll see it marked in the **Synchronize Settings** column. Now just click the **Synchronize Account** button. Outlook Express will go online for you and get what you want. Incidentally, now you've chosen a particular synchronize setting, you don't need to do it again. Each day, just press **Synchronize Account** to get the latest from your group.

< 238 >

▶ In Messenger, highlight the newsgroup you're interested in, then select the **File** menu, then **Offline** then **Synchronize**. A dialog box will come up asking you to specify a category for synchronization. Choose **Newsgroup messages**. Then click the **Select Items** button. You can then specify the group you want to keep tabs on. Tick the box next to **Work offline after synchronization**. Then click the **Synchronize** button. Incidentally, you can also specify exactly what get's downloaded via **Preferences**. Select the **Edit** menu then **Preferences**, then select **Download** from the **Offline** category. There you can choose to get messages according to date.

▶ In Outlook Express for the Mac, though you don't have that many options when it comes to specifying that certain messages be downloaded for offline reading, you can quickly get the new messages from a newsgroup you're following. Highlight the group you're interested in, then select the **View** menu, then click **Refresh Message List**.

## Reading the newsgroups

With most newsgroups, it can take a while to get into some of the discussions. When they respond to a previous message, as with email, people quote relevant sections of that message using the quote tags (>). Again, the theory is that it makes it easier to keep track of the discussion. Stick with a group over a few days and it should start to make sense.

After a while you may realise that some people in the group are complete timewasters. To preserve your sanity and good temper, you can create a bozo filter/kill file – i.e. you can set your newsreader up to filter

< 239 >

their messages so that they are deleted before you see them. It has to be said that, in general, this is one area in which standalone newsreaders have the edge. Outlook Express isn't bad, though.

▶ In Outlook Express the simplest thing to do is to block messages from individuals. Highlight a message by the offending individual, then select the **Message** menu, then **Block Sender**. Alternatively, to create more versatile filters, select the **Tools** menu, then **Message Rules**, then **News**. Then you just need to tick off the various categories. You can choose to delete messages from certain people or messages that have certain words in the title.

▶ In the Mac version of Outlook Express, you can block certain messages by selecting the **Tools** menu, then **Newsgroup Rules**. Then click **New Rule**, then specify the criteria for blocking messages.

## Tips - Newsgroups

When you're just starting out, try the **news.announce.newusers** and **news.announce.important** groups. The former is a good place for general introductory information about Usenet. The latter is the place to go for important news and developments – all newsgroup users should make a point of checking in here. It's also worthwhile keeping abreast of what's happening in the UK hierarchy, so make a point of checking out the **uk.net.news.announce** group.▲

< 240 >

### Tips - ROT13

Every now and then you may encounter a newsgroup posting which looks even more like gibberish than usual. It's more than likely been 'rotated' – encrypted using ROT13, which replaces each letter with the one thirteen steps ahead of it in the alphabet. People use ROT13 if they're sending a posting that some people might think is offensive. To decode ROT13 postings, in Outlook Express, select the **Message** menu, then **Unscramble**. You used to be able to do this in Messenger by selecting the **View** menu, then **Unscramble**, though that doesn't appear to be on offer in the newer versions. It's true that you don't see ROT 13 that much these days – at least not in the newsgroups I occasionally look at. ▲

To keep track of discussions, you need to check your groups on a reasonably regular basis, depending on how active they are. To save on bandwidth, messages tend to be removed after a few days, though the headers remain. Indeed, the first time you download some groups, you may find you have downloaded a pile of headers but can't actually get the messages they refer to.

You can sort the messages in a group according to date or sender. Don't bother with that unless you're trying to keep track of a particular person. The best way to view newsgroups is by thread – most newsreaders have that as the default option. If you want to change it:

▶ In Outlook Express, select the **View** menu, then **Sort By**.

< 241 >

▶ In Messenger, select the **View** menu, then **Sort**.

To find a particular message:
▶ In Outlook Express, select the **Edit** menu, then **Find Message**.
▶ In Messenger, select the **Edit** menu, **then Search Messages**.

## Newsgroup Style and Netiquette

Once you've perused the newsgroups for a while, you may be ready to have your say. But before you do, you need learn a bit about newsgroup style and netiquette.

When it comes to general style, the advice given for writing email applies to newsgroup postings. If you didn't read that section, go back to page 187. Newsgroup netiquette is similar but more complicated than its email counterpart. They might look like chaotic free-for-alls, but newsgroups are very big on manners and conventions. And if you do something wrong or ask a silly question you will inevitably be flamed by someone.

---

### Read about it online - Netiquette Guide

Boning up on newsgroup netiquette is a full-time job. There certainly isn't the space to go into it all here. But you can find a lengthy guide to Usenet netiquette, as well as some amusing parodies and lots of other useful information on the UK Usenet homepages at
**http://www.usenet.org.uk**. ▲

---

< 242 >

Actually, if you're starting out on Usenet, it's more than likely that whatever you do someone will find a reason to flame you. One of the drearier things about Usenet is that it is packed with the sort of sad fools you could call 'netlier than thou'. They want to prove themselves part of the online old school. The best way to do this is to beat up (virtually speaking) the new kid on the block – aka the 'newbie'. In the end, you just have to put up with this. However, you can make sure you don't present too obvious a target.

First, read the newsgroup for a while before you send a message. Find out what gets discussed and how. You will then have a good chance of posting something people will find relevant. Each group will have an FAQ – a file of Frequently Asked Questions, which details what the group discusses and how. The latest versions are usually posted to the group in question on a regular basis. Read the FAQ for any group you're interested in. That way, you will have a chance of avoiding sending in messages or questions which people will dismiss as obvious or already dealt with. The web is a good place to get FAQs. Try **http://www.lib.ox.ac.uk/internet/news/**.

Don't post a message to an ongoing thread about something completely different. If what you've got to say goes off at a tangent, start a new thread. Most importantly, don't spam. In other words, don't send advertising, commercial messages or junk mail to a newsgroup or a group of newsgroups, even if it seems relevant. It is ok to do some discreet personal advertising – i.e. include references to a personal homepage in your sig file, which, by the by, should be kept small. Don't post private email to a newsgroup without getting permission. Generally you're ok re-

< 243 >

**Tips – Flames**

If you do feel like arguing, trading insults and generally winding people up – if that's why you were interested in Usenet in the first place – try the **alt.flame** groups. There are plenty devoted to trading abuse on all sorts of topics. ▲

posting material that has appeared in a newsgroup already: it's deemed to be in the public domain. But before you do, check its copyright status anyway. It's beginning to be accepted that posting a message to a newsgroup is equivalent to publishing it, which means you shouldn't post illegal or libellous material. On a more down-to-earth level, if you're discussing films or books, specifically how they end, indicate this in the subject line of your posting (i.e. put the word 'Spoiler' in there somewhere). And don't criticise spelling or grammar. There is nothing that upsets people more and it generally leads to inane, tit-for-tat arguments. There's enough of those on Usenet already. You don't need to start any more.

Knowing all this is obviously useful. But the most important thing is just to think a bit before you post. Remember that there are people on the other side of the screen. Online communication is a paradoxical thing. It can seem both impersonal, as if it doesn't quite matter, and peculiarly intimate at the same time. As a result, it can become rather hurtful. So – and I'm sorry to sound like some sort of cheery teacher – try to be constructive. Some people in Usenet do spout the most incredible rubbish. But it is possible to point this out to them without adding a

< 244 >

series of ever more baroque insults. Before you get involved in a flame war, think about the rest of the group. Sometimes it's amusing to watch two people slugging it out. But mostly it's a bore.

## Posting messages

So you now know enough not to upset those sensitive souls in your newsgroup of choice. You've read a message you want to reply to. It's pretty simple, virtually the same as replying to someone who's sent you email.

▶ In Outlook Express, click the either the **Reply to Group** button (this will send your thoughts to the group) or the **Reply to Sender** button (this will send your message to the author of the post you're responding to – it's considered good netiquette to do this). You can do both by at the same time by selecting the **Message** menu then **Reply to All**. (In the

---

**Tips - Cancelling Messages**

You got steamed up and sent a message you now regret. You can do something to retrieve the situation by sending out a cancel message. This will remove the posting (although it takes time and if someone downloads the message before your cancel message reaches the group, there's nothing you can do). In Outlook Express, highlight the message you posted, then select the **Message** menu, then **Cancel Message** (At the moment, the Mac Outlook Express doesn't offer this function). In Messenger, select the offending message, then select the **Edit** menu, then **Cancel Message**. ▲

---

< 245 >

Mac version, select the **Message** menu then **Reply to Newsgroup and Mail**). Whatever you choose, a new window opens, with the address filled out and the previous message quoted. Trim that down and add your response. Then click the **Send** button on the toolbar.

▶ In Messenger, click either the **Reply to Group** button (which send the message just to the newsgroup) or the **Reply to All** button (this simultaneously sends messages to the newsgroup and the original author of the post you're responding to. A new window will open, with the address filled out and the previous message quoted. Trim it down and add your response. Then click the **Send** button on the toolbar.

Messages to newsgroups are often crossposted, which means that they're sent to a variety of groups that share some interest in a general subject. When you reply to a crossposting, your message will be sent to all the groups the previous message was crossposted to. You'll see them entered in the address field.

To post an original message:

▶ In Outlook Express, in the window on the left side of the screen, where the list of your subscriptions is, click on the group you want to post to. Then click the **New Post** button on the toolbar. Remember to write something suitably pithy in the **Subject** line, write your thoughts in the text box at the bottom then click the **Send** button.

▶ In Messenger, select the group you want to post to from the list on the left side of the browser window and then click the **New Message** button. Again, remember to write something in the **Subject** line and click **Send** when you're done.

< 246 >

When you send an original message you may be tempted to crosspost it to several groups. Think before you do this. Don't crosspost to groups you don't know. If you're not sure it fits in with the discussions there, don't bother. It's a very good way to annoy people. Remember, they have your email address and they will let you know how they feel. If all this sounds a bit daunting, you might want to try a test post first. Some ISPs have their own test newsgroups where beginners can find their feet. There's also an **alt.test** group you can try. But whatever you do, don't send a test post to a regular newsgroup, another sure-fire way to upset people.

## Getting answers from newsgroups

Newsgroups are, so people tell you, packed with experts ready and waiting to give up their time to help you. All you have to do is ask. On one level, this is true. But there is a correct way of asking. It's good form, if you have a question, to specify in your original postings that people should answer with private email and that you will post a summary of responses. That way, the newsgroup doesn't become clogged with people sending the same answer. When it comes to posting a summary, trim down the answers you received and avoid repetition.

Incidentally, students shouldn't assume that all those experts in the newsgroups are just dying to help out with their dissertations. In other words, don't send a questionnaire on a particular subject to a series of groups. This annoys newsgroup users (understandably) and you probably won't get any useful replies. An alternative might be to hang out in relevant newsgroups, locate the more active/knowledgeable members

< 247 >

and send them private email asking if they have time to answer a few questions. Then send your questionnaire.

If you're looking for answers, your best bet may be to tap the archived collective wisdom of Usenet via Deja.com **http://www.deja.com**. Here you can search several years of postings to Usenet. It's more than likely that someone in a newsgroup somewhere has kicked around the query that's troubling you, so give it a shot. You can also access the newsgroups via Deja.com. However, the web can be slow – slower than downloading messages from your ISP's server. Other companies are attempting to do something similar, offering snazzy web interfaces to Usenet which let users collaborate to filter out spam and idiots – try Talkway **http://www.talkway.com**, Realize **http://www. realize.com** or Supernews **http;//www.supernews.com**.

## Attachments and HTML

Newsgroup postings can come with attached binary files, just like email, and there are plenty of newsgroups whose purpose is exchanging files, not ideas. These files could be anything from images and sound samples to shareware games and programs. But mostly they're images, often pornographic. Groups devoted to exchanging pornography (e.g. many of the **alt.binaries** groups) do account for a sizeable amount of newsgroup traffic. You should be aware of this, especially if your kids are using Usenet. But don't assume that's all there is to newsgroups that swap files.

In the past, dealing with files attached to Usenet postings could be tricky, but the latest newsreaders make the whole thing easy. They work

< 248 >

in exactly the same way as email attachments. If you skipped the email section, go back to page 187 for general advice. UUencode has been the standard way to convert attachments on Usenet for a while. However, MIME is becoming more popular. Outlook Express and Messenger can handle both, but if you're using an older newsreader you may experience some problems. A group FAQ might have advice on how to convert attachments posted to the group. Alternatively, you could hang out in the group for a while and see what everyone else does. Outlook Express is set by default to encode newsgroup attachments with UUencode. Messenger uses MIME as the default for attachments. There's advice on how to change them if you need to in the email section on page 202.

In the dim and distant past of the net (three or four years ago), Usenet newsgroups mainly involved text postings and UUencoded attachments. Now the new generation of newsreaders let you send postings that are formatted in HTML and hence look a bit like web pages (they have links, flashy graphics and embedded images). Both Outlook Express and Messenger can handle HTML. When you're composing a reply or a new message to a newsgroup, you can format it in HTML. However, before

## Tips - Viruses

People sometimes worry unnecessarily about viruses and the net. However, you should worry about software or games that you download from a newsgroup. Always run a virus check on it. ▲

< 249 >

you send off your dazzlingly colourful posting to your newsgroup, think about whether it's appropriate. Many groups prefer plain text. Again, see what seems to be acceptable in the group in question. For information on how to change the format of your newsgroup postings from HTML to text or vice versa, go to page 191 in the email section.

One thing to look out for is that if you decide to configure Messenger to send postings to newsgroups in plain text, it will mean that Messenger will send all your email in text as well. So if you want to send text to a newsgroup, it might be best to specify it on a message-by-message basis. In the **Composition** window, click the **Message Sending Format** button in the bottom left of the **Address** window and then look for the **Format** drop-down menu in the bottom right. You don't need to worry about this with Outlook Express. You can choose to send text to newsgroups and use HTML for your mail. To check on this, select the **Tools** menu, then **Options**, then **Send**.

## Coping with newsgroups

The net makes a lot of things in life easier. However, newsgroups are one of the few things online that still require some effort and commitment if you're going to get anything out of them. You do have to spend some time with them. You have to get to know your newsgroup colleagues. In certain groups, you have to wade through megabytes of spam. But if you do take the time, it can be very rewarding, on an emotional and intellectual level. You may even get so caught up that you want to start your own newsgroup. For information on that, go to page 433.

< 250 >

If you want to get the most out of the newsgroups, there are a few things you should do. First, learn how to use your bozo filter and the **cancel message** function. Then find out as much as you can about Usenet culture. The UK Usenet homepage mentioned before is a good starting point. Make frequent use of the Deja.com archive. Aside from revealing the huge range of subjects covered by the newsgroups, Deja.com also makes you aware that postings to Usenet are public. Potentially, millions of people can read what you say there. Your postings will be archived and at some time in the future may be searched by other people with an interest in you.

So the basic message is, once again, to think before you post. This doesn't just mean taking time out before flaming. It means thinking about who might end up reading what you write. You could just write what you want but cover up your identity – by removing your return email details from any messages you send to newsgroups and not giving your real name. Many people now do this anyway, in an attempt to avoid spam. Those responsible for junk email build up their lists of victims via programs that suck up all email addresses posted on Usenet. So keeping your email address to yourself could help. But it also stops you from tapping into the full potential of the newsgroups.

## Next Step

If you're worried about privacy and the newsgroups, go to page 403. Alternatively, now you've got the hang of Usenet, you're probably ready for the real-time rough and tumble of online chat, so go to page 278. ▲

< 251 >

## Downloading Files from the Net

Browsing the web is all very well. But what about making your time online more practical and useful? Not a problem. Go to the right places on the web and you can come back with something a little bit more tangible than a long history file and a pile of pages stored somewhere in your cache. You can download software programs, sound files, video clips and animations, even text versions of classic novels. And you can do it in the much the same way that you browse the web. Just click on the appropriate link and after a while you'll have something potentially useful/entertaining sitting on your hard drive.

If you do that, you'll have actually been using something called FTP. FTP is one of those bits of net jargon that the acronymically challenged love to hate. The letters stand for File Transfer Protocol, something which enables you to shift files around a network – either upload them to another computer or download them on to your hard drive. A few years ago, you had to use a specialist FTP program and go to an FTP site – a sort of online file library – to download something from the net. But these days, though you can still do all that, you don't really need to bother. Pretty much everything you need is on the web. You can get it with your browser. And much of it can be downloaded for free. So let's get moving.

## How free is free software

You may have heard someone describe the internet as a gift economy. It's a nice idea, though it does seem to mean rather different things to

< 252 >

different people. For some, it seems to mean that you can download lots of stuff from the net without having to pay for it. On one level, that's true. There is plenty of 'free' stuff online: Shakespeare plays, amateur artwork, customised levels from computer games like Doom and all sorts of software – screensavers, personal organisers and pretty much everything you need for the net. And, if you agree to discount telephone charges, it is all free.

However, more often than not, items on the net loudly trumpeted as 'free' come with some kind of cost. Frustrated artists give away their art online in the hope that someone somewhere will pay them a bit of attention. As it turns out, multinational corporations aren't all that different. The first version of Microsoft's Internet Explorer web browser was given away for free because it was the only way Bill Gates and co. could hope to get people to use their software and so start to catch up with Netscape, who by that time had begun to charge for their then-dominant web browser Navigator.

The first incarnation of IE may have been free but you definitely paid some kind of price when you actually used it (in terms of stress, irritation and general frustration). Internet Explorer has got an awful lot better and is still free, but now its hidden cost (as more people understandably give it a go) is an online world in which Microsoft is the dominant force and alternative ideas are squeezed out. However, Gates and his crew are only doing what everyone else does. Giving away product has become a standard business strategy in the computer software industry. The idea is that you give away stuff now in the hope of getting something back later.

< 253 >

At first it was software developers who gave away versions of their products online to build market share. Their plan was that punters would get attached to their product and ultimately pay for upgrades or add-ons. Now everyone connected to the net seems to be working the same strategy. The UK's free ISPs give away the kind of service that subscription-based ISPs had been charging for. The aim is to 'acquire' as many users/customers as possible (and thus go on to start making some money via advertising and online shopping commissions). In the States, net service companies have started to give away computers to build their market share. Of course, to get your free PC, you generally have to sign up with a particular subscription-based ISP for a lengthy period of time. Usually, you also have to agree to look at certain ads and hand over personal data about what you do on the net.

It's a good illustration of the way that most 'free stuff' has some kind of price. As a result, some idealistic programmers suggest that we shouldn't really think about money when we hear the word 'free'. According to Richard Stallman, the founder of the Free Software Foundation, free software is really 'a matter of freedom not price – the freedom to modify the software, redistribute the software and release improved versions of the software'. The idea here is that free software is open, that its source code – the stuff that makes it run – is freely available and can be modified.

That's a big attraction for other programmers. If they find a problem with a free program, they can then mess around with the code, come up with a solution and pass their new, improved version on to other users.

< 254 >

As a result, say enthusiasts, where it has a chance to flourish, this kind of free software ends up being better and more reliable than commercial alternatives. After all, there's an army of programmers around the world beavering away on its problems and sharing their conclusions via the net.

Idealistic programmers like this (hackers in the old sense of the word) have a more high-minded interpretation of the internet gift economy. Their idea is that you give away your time and the fruits of your intellectual labour. But you don't lose out, because you benefit from the efforts of numerous other idealists who also do their bit. In the end, nobody gets 'paid' for their contribution but everybody gets by.

Obviously, this is a world away from the modus operandi of a company like Microsoft. It keeps a close guard on the source code of something like Windows 95/98 because it sees it as the rock on which its empire is founded. If you have a problem, you're supposed to call the Microsoft support line. Then they'll sort it out for you, perhaps issue a patch and ultimately charge you all over again for a new version of the

---

### Read about it online – Free Software Foundation

You can read an interestingly hardcore definition of what counts as free software (and what doesn't) at the Free Software Foundation's website at **http://www.fsf.org/**. A good place to start is the essay on 'words to avoid', and 'Categories of Free Software' in the Philosophy section **http://www.fsf.org/philosophy/philosophy.html**. ▲

< 255 >

### Jargon File - Hackers

In the press this has come to mean computer criminal, something which hugely upsets old-school hackers. Originally, hacker meant someone who loved programming and messing around with computers, someone able to make the old machines do all sorts of thing that weren't in the manual. People who identify with this like to dismiss younger hackers who get into headline-grabbing mischief as 'crackers'.▲

program in which all the old bugs have been fixed (and a whole set of new ones have been introduced).

It's easy to be snide. And the idealistic vision of the internet gift economy does sound great. But the truth is that ordinary punters generally prefer the commercial way of doing things. They don't have the ability or the desire to go fooling around with source code. As a result, free software is more of a techie pursuit and currently has more of an impact on the back end programs that keep the net running – for example, one of the more popular programs for running web servers is a piece of free software called Apache.

### Jargon File - Patch

A small chunk of code designed to fix a bug in a larger program.▲

< 256 >

That said, the Free Software movement, or rather the Open Source movement, as many now prefer to call it (the word 'free' comes with too much baggage) may soon start to have a more tangible effect on the way ordinary users access the web. Looking for a way to stay ahead of Microsoft, influenced by ideas generated by the movement, Netscape decided to make the source code of its Navigator browser available for free in the spring of 1998. Programmers can now produce their own versions of the browser. If what the free-software champions say is true, this might lead to a more interesting, useful and trim browser in the future. You can find out how the attempt to create a new Open Source version of Navigator is going at **http://www.mozilla.org**.

However, the idealism surrounding Netscape's embrace of Open Source was dissipated somewhat when AOL bought the company. That hasn't affected the Open Source movement in general, which seems to becoming more and more influential on the net. In some ways, as the online world is increasingly dominated by business concerns, Open Source has become the repository of all the vaguely nebulous idealism about individual empowerment, collective effort and the like that used to cluster around the net in general. It's been described as the net's first political movement.

Most of the attention now focuses on Linux, the free operating system developed in part by Linus Torvalds. This isn't really for beginners – you still need to use text commands to use it properly. But it is beginning to become more and more popular, mainly because it is fast, robust and just not as buggy as its commercially produced competitors. Microsoft is clearly

< 257 >

**Read about it online – Eric Raymond**

The people at Netscape were particularly influenced by 'The Cathedral and the Bazaar', an essay arguing the case for free/open software by Eric Raymond. You can check it out at his homepage **http://www.tuxedo.org/~esr/writings/cathedral-bazaar/**, which contains lots of other interesting essays and ideas. For more on this, look at the Open Source page **http://www.opensource.org**. For more on Linux, the free/open operating system that has Microsoft worried, try **http://www.linux.org** or **http://www.uk.linux.org**. You can read about the Apache Project, its aims and history (and download the programs) at **http://www.apache.org**. ▲

concerned about Open Source, something that was demonstrated in October 1998, when an internal company memo about the movement was leaked to Eric Raymond, one of OS's prime movers. According to this document, which became known as the Halloween memo, Microsoft was impressed with the performance of Open Source software and worried about its possible impact on its own products, impressed and worried enough to be thinking about ways to undermine the movement.

You can read the Halloween memo at The Open Source page **http://www.opensource.org/halloween/**. However a better introduction to the whole subject might be the archives of related articles maintained the big webzines – Salon has lots of OS articles at **http://www.salon.**

< 258 >

**com/tech/special/opensource/**. Wired keeps a similar archive of articles on Linux at **http://www.wired.com/news/news/linux/**. Another good place to look is the special Open Source edition of Feed, which you'll find at **http://www. feedmag.com/oss/ossintro.html**. Wired and Salon are good places to go to keep track of what's currently going on with Open Source. It's worth keeping tabs on it. Though the movement has its feuds and internecine battles (that isn't surprising, given the way it unites hard core libertarian capitalists and old style lefties interested in the 'public good'), it remains the standard bearer for those who hope that the net will offer some sort of escape from a world dominated by buggy software and big corporations.

To bring all this down to a more basic level, when you download something that calls itself 'free software' it's as well to be aware of what

---

**Read about it online – Neal Stephenson**

The SF author Neal Stephenson recently published 'In the Beginning was the Command Line', a fascinating and funny essay about his experiences using different computer operating systems (Windows, the Mac OS and Linux). Though it's good on the specifics of each system, it broadens out into a general critique of our reliance on computer interfaces, which Stephenson sees as infantilising. It's very long, but worth it. You can find it at **http://www.cryptonomicon.com/ beginning.html**. ▲

---

< 259 >

## Read about it online - Freeware

This doesn't have to be computer software. The SF author and critic Bruce Sterling made his book about hackers, The Hacker Crackdown, freely available online. Sterling called it 'literary freeware'. He argued that since no one would actually take the time to download the whole book and risk eyestrain by reading it all from the screen, his giveaway worked as a kind of ad for the print version. Certainly, it's meant that the book is everywhere online. For a web version, go to **http://www.mit.edu/hacker/hacker.html**. ▲

it is you're actually getting. Here are three basic types of free software you're most likely to find yourself downloading.

## Freeware

You don't have to pay anything for this, though sometimes the creators ask for a kind of forfeit. For example, you might be asked to send them a post-card of where you live. There are fully-fledged freeware programs but often many commercial software companies also release free patches. The people at the Free Software Foundation don't like this word – they prefer 'free software' which means not software that comes at zero price but software that comes with certain freedoms – i.e. the ability to monkey around with the code.

< 260 >

## Shareware

One of the more misunderstood terms in computer culture. Shareware is actually a 'try before you buy' thing. The idea is that you can use an evaluation copy of a program for a given period. Once the trial period is over, if you want to keep using the software you have to register it and pay something. Some pieces of shareware are set to 'time out': you can't use them after a certain point. Others continue to work just fine but with a few features disabled, so you could keep using them. The makers can't force you to pay up if you continue to use their program. Rather, they rely on you being honest. So, if you like a program, you really should pay your shareware fees. Plus, shareware is a clever way of keeping software prices down. It bypasses the regular commercial channels and all their built-in overheads. And it only works if everyone plays the game.

### Tips – Shakespeare

You don't want software, you want culture? Why not get some e-Shakespeare from the SUN site at Imperial College **http://sunsite.doc.ic.ac.uk/media/literary/authors/shakespeare**. Click on the comedies directory and you'll be able to download the complete text of the play that most sums up how you feel about the net – 'A Comedy Of Errors' perhaps, or 'Much Ado About Nothing' or 'As You Like It' or maybe even 'All's Well That Ends Well'.▲

< 261 >

**Tips – FTP Programs**

If you find that FTP is the thing for you, you may eventually want to get a proper FTP client. They're sometimes a bit quicker and have some nifty features. For PC owners, there's CuteFTP **http://www. cuteftp.com**, FTP Explorer **http://www.ftpx.com** or WS_FTP **http://www. ipswitch.com**. The most popular Mac FTP client is Fetch **http://www. dartmouth.edu/pages/softdev/fetch.html**. ▲

## Beta Versions

These are test versions of software currently in development and due for eventual commercial release. Betas let you see what's coming, but you also have to put up with occasional bugs and crashes. Some betas time out after a given period. Companies don't charge for them, but neither do they offer technical support. Some run competitions in which you can pick up rewards for identifying bugs. Though they can be buggy, often betas run just fine and it can be tempting to stick with them rather than fork out for the official version. When Netscape tried charging for Navigator a couple of years ago, a lot of net users got by without paying by using Navigator betas.

< 262 >

## Getting Started

When it comes to downloading files from the net, your web browser will do the job more than adequately, especially if you have Internet Explorer 5.x or Netscape Communicator 4.6. If you're going to use your browser, you can get moving straight away. You don't need to get any new software or spend time configuring it. But before you do, it's worth spending some time sorting out your computer so you know where to put all those files. If they're not there already, create directories or folders on your hard drive called **Download** and **Program Files**. When you download a file, stick it in the **Download** directory or folder.

## Downloading files from the Web

We'll start with this because the web is where you're likely to do most of your downloading. Start your browser and go to the WinZip website **http://www.winzip.com**. If you missed out the section on the web and came straight here, go back to page 101 for details on entering web addresses. To save space and speed up download times, files online are often 'compressed' into a smaller form – known as archives. Before you can use them, you need to decompress them. WinZip is the leading compression/decompression program for the PC. You can't really get by without it and you can download an evaluation copy from the website. Mac users could go to the Aladdin Systems website **http://www.aladdinsys.com** where they can get versions of Stuffit/Stuffit Expander, programs which will decompress/compress Macintosh files.

< 263 >

---

### Tips - Games Domain

While you're at the Games Domain site, it's worth looking at the
FAQ and 'Walkthrus' sections. These contain text files that tell you
how to get to the end of pretty much every game going. So if
you're stuck down a blind alley with Lara Croft or if you want to be
able to beat your kids just once, check it out. ▲

---

Once the page comes up, click on the **Download Evaluation Version**
link. The **Download** page contains links to details of new WinZip
features, FAQs and installation instructions. Check these out if you like,
then look for the link to the appropriate program for your machine
(Windows 95/98/NT or Windows 3.1). Click on that and the download
process will start. A dialog box will come up asking whether you want
to open the file or save it. Pick the latter. You'll then be asked to specify
where you want to save the file. Pick the **Download** directory you
created, then click **Save**. The program will begin downloading. Once it's
done, yet another dialog box will appear telling you so. Click **OK**.
Incidentally, if you find yourself stuck in the middle of a slow download,
you don't have to wait around doing nothing. You can open a new
browser window and get on the web, or start to download something
else. In both browsers, select the **File** menu, then **New**.

< 264 >

## Downloading files from an FTP site

Accessing FTP sites with a browser is similar to accessing web pages. You key in an address, click a button and go. FTP addresses are roughly similar to website addresses. (If you skipped the section on the web, go to page 101.) The differences are that they don't begin with **www** but with **ftp**. When you enter them you start with **ftp://** rather than **http://** (although with some browsers you don't have to bother with that). If they are for a specific file they can be rather long, since they specify all the directories and subdirectories it is stored in. One example might be **ftp://ftp.gamesdomain.co.uk/pub/patches/**. Tap that into your browser and it will take you to the FTP site run by Games Domain, specifically to a directory of patches, little add-on programs which will tweak well known computer games to make them run faster or look more gory.

FTP sites are a little more complicated to deal with than web sites. Some sites are private and to access them you have to enter your username and password. Sites that are open to the public are accessed via what's known as anonymous FTP. You still have to enter some details but you don't have to give your real name. When asked for your username, enter **anonymous**, and for your password, enter your email address. You can enter a fake address and still get in, but it's not good form. If you're using a browser, it will take care of anonymous FTP automatically.

FTP sites give you a glimpse of what the web was like before the arrival of all those animated corporate logos and flashy graphics we know and love: grey backgrounds, spidery text and long, vaguely impenetrable lists of links to files. It's enough to make an old geek get a little watery-

< 265 >

eyed. That said, the new version of Internet Explorer seems to make them all look like directories and folders on your own computer. When you first arrive at an FTP site, you should see something called the **Root Directory** – basically a welcome message, general information about the site and a list of the main directories. Some anonymous sites allow you access to everything. Others restrict some of their contents. The files that are open to all-comers are usually in a directory called **pub.**

Click on a directory name and you'll see the contents of the directory – perhaps a series of sub-directories, which you click to open until you track down the file you want. Beside a particular file you may see details of when it was uploaded on to the site and how big it is. If you follow a set of links and can't find what you want, retrace your steps with the **Back** button. Alternatively, look for a link that says **Up to a higher level direc-**

## Tips – Mr Cool

If you become keen on acquiring software via the net but become frustrated by the occasional lengthy downloads, it might be worth getting your files via email or even via Net Services' Mr Cool program. Basically, if you start a download and realise it's going to take a long time, you cancel it and kick it over to Mr Cool, which sends a request for the program to a server which emails the program to you. It works for web pages too, apparently **http://www.cix.co.uk/~net-services/mrcool**. ▲

< 266 >

tory, which is usually at the top of the page. On some sites you may see the following links – "." and "..". Click on the former and you will go back to the root directory. Click the latter and you'll go up a directory level. If this sounds complicated, rest assured it becomes easy after a while, rather like moving around in the files and directories on your own hard drive.

When you first access an FTP site, look around for a text file called **Index** or **ReadMe**. This will tell you how the site is structured and where everything is. Sometimes you might have the exact address for a file, in which case you can go to it directly. Often though, it's a better bet to rummage around a site and see what's there. When you find a file you want to download, click on it and the download process will start. Direct the file to your **Download** directory as before.

## Troubleshooting

**You can't actually get into the FTP site of your choice** – First, if you entered the exact location of the file, check that you got it right. If you did, it may just be that the site is busy. Like good web sites, the best FTP sites can get incredibly crowded at peak times. If the site is busy, a dialog box may appear telling you as much.

**The file you want isn't where it's supposed to be** – If you entered the exact address, it may be that the site has been reorganised and the file has been moved. Look for the index file and check there.

< 267 >

**You're halfway through a lengthy download and you lose your connection**
– This used to happen an awful lot and it was hugely irritating. It still
happens, but needn't be such a problem. Most specialist FTP programs have
a **Resume Download** feature. If you lose your connection and you've only
downloaded part of the file, reconnect and double-click on the file again. A
dialog box will come up and ask if you want to **Resume, Overwrite,
Rename** or **Cancel**. Click the first and the program will pick up where it left
off. Check the **Status** bar of your program when you first log in to a site to
see whether it will let you resume aborted downloads. Some sites still don't.

The latest versions of Navigator and Internet Explorer should let you
resume downloads. If you get cut off, just try to start the whole process
again and both browsers should pick up where they left off. Actually,
you're best bet here is probably to get a plug-in program called Get
Right. This boosts your browser's in-built FTP capabilities, adding lots
of useful features – you can resume downloads or automate them. Get
Right is available from **http://www.getright.com**. Unfortunately, at the
time of writing there isn't a Mac version, though it is on the way, apparently. Of course, if you start getting plugs ins (and there's more about all
this on page 315), you could argue that you should go the whole hog and
get a proper FTP program. Certainly, if you become more serious about
the net, if you want to create your own web page, you'll probably need
a decent FTP program. It will make uploading your homepage files to
your ISP's server a bit easier all round.

That said, if you're using Navigator, you can use its FTP program.
Open the directory on your computer that contains the file you want to

< 268 >

upload. Get online, use Navigator to connect the FTP site, then open the directory where you plan to upload your file. Drag and drop the file from your directory into the Navigator window. Incidentally, when you're uploading something – say your personal web pages – to an online space maintained by your ISP, that space will be private: you will need a password and user name to gain access. Your ISP will supply you with details.

## Working with downloaded files

So your **Download** directory is now bulging with all sorts of different files. Most likely, you've got a selection of **.exe, .zip** and **.txt** files. The latter present no problem, obviously. Click on them and an application on your computer should open them for you. Files with the **.exe** extension are also easy to handle. **.exe** indicates a self-extracting archive. Click/double-click on one of these and it should unpack itself automatically. **Setup** will kick in and on the way you'll be asked where you want to install the program. Pick your **Program Files** directory. Before you do this, run a virus check. Always virus check all **.exe** files you get from the net before you install them.

So far, so easy. **.zip** archives are a little more complicated. These are collections of files that have been compressed, using WinZip or something similar. You need to 'unzip' these archives before you can work with them. This is easy – especially since you have the latest version of WinZip. That's an **.exe** file, so it should be easy enough to install. The latest versions allow you to pick two different interfaces – Wizard or Classic. Wizard makes unzipping files incredibly easy and it's good for

< 269 >

beginners. Once you get used to it (and want to compress your own files), try the Classic interface.

Once WinZip is installed, just click/double-click on a file to unzip it. WinZip will start up. Then, if you're using the Wizard interface, just follow the directions and WinZip will decompress the archive and put its contents into a directory/folder called **Unzipped**. You can put it in a different folder if you wish. If you want to look at any text files in the zipped archive, click the **View Zip Documentation** button. Then click the **Next** button. WinZip is set by default to display the file icons after unzipping. So they will appear in a window and you can then click/double-click the **.exe** file (after virus checking it) to start installation. If you choose the Classic interface, you can do all this via the toolbar buttons. Just click the **Open** button and look for the archive you want to unzip.

Once your files are installed, you could clear out the **Unzipped** directory if that wasn't done automatically during installation. You could also delete the original archive from your **Download** directory. Alternatively, if you want to keep copies of files from the net (just in case something goes wrong and you need to re-install), why not create a directory called

**Jargon File – Extension**

As in File Extension. A group of letters that come after the file name and identify what type of file it is. ▲

< 270 >

**Tips - Virus Check**

Your computer should come with a pre-installed virus checker.
However, if it doesn't, you can download something from the net.
One of the most popular virus checkers online is the McAfee
VirusScan Security Suite. You can get an evaluation copy at
**http://www.nai.com**. ▲

Archive and put them there. You can use WinZip to compress files
(perhaps before attaching them to email, or just to save space). Use the
Classic interface and click the New button. A New Archive dialog box
will appear. Write the name of your zip file in the File name text box,
then click OK. The Add dialog box will appear. Use the drop down menu
at the top to find the files you want to put in your archive. Hold down
the Control key and click on each one you want to include. Then click
the Add button.

## File Types

You're most likely to come across **.exe** and **.zip** online, if only because PC
users are in a majority on the net. Macintosh self-extracting archives
come with a **.sea** extension. Archives compressed on the Mac using
Stuffit come with the extension **.sit** – you'll see a fair amount of them.
However, there are loads of other file types available online, either at web
sites or FTP sites. Here's a few you may encounter, with details of the
programs you need to view/open them.

< 271 >

**.arc** An older type of PC compressed archive. Stuffit Expander can handle this

**.arj** Another older PC compressed archive. Stuffit Expander also works here

**.au, .aif** Macintosh sound files. Double-click on these once downloaded and the Windows Media Player should play them

**.avi** Video for Windows file. Again, the Windows Media Player will play these once downloaded

**.bin** MacBinary files. Macintoshes can cope with these automatically

**.bmp** Bitmap files. Windows has something (e.g. Paintbrush) which will display these

**.cpt** Mac Compact Pro archive. Stuffit Expander can decompress this

**.doc** A Word file. WordPad on Windows 95/98 will cope with this

**.exe** A PC executable file, to give it its official name. This will self-execute or extract itself when you double-click on it

**.gif** As in Graphic Interchange Format, an image file found on web pages. Your browser displays this automatically

**.gz, .gzip** A Unix compressed archive. Stuffit Expander and WinZip will deal with these

**.hqx** A Mac BinHex file. Stuffit Expander will convert it

**.htm, .html** As in Hypertext Markup Language. Your browser takes care of it

**.jpg, jpeg** Another type of compressed graphic found on web pages. Browsers display these automatically

**.lha, .lzh** Yet another type of compressed archive. You can add an external program to Winzip so it can cope with these. For more infor-

< 272 >

mation, go to **http://www.winzip.com/xextern.htm** on the WinZip site

**.mid, .rmi** As in MIDI sound files. You need a external player/plug-in to handle these – for example, something like Crescendo

**.mov, .qt** QuickTime movie files. You can get a QuickTime player/plug-in to play these

**.mpg, .mpeg** Compressed video files. You can get a separate player/plug-in for these though these days your PC or Mac will come with something that can play these

**.mp2, .mp3** An MPEG sound file. You can get an external player for these (e.g. WinAmp). Windows Media player will handle these too

**.pdf** As in Portable Document Format. You need Adobe's Acrobat viewer to open this

**.pict** Macintosh graphics file. Macs handle these automatically

**.ra, ram** Real Audio sound files. You'll need the RealPlayer plug-in for these

**.sea** Macintosh self-extracting archive. Just click

**.sit** Macintosh compressed archive. Use Stuffit Expander

---

### Tips – Compression

You occasionally come across files with double-barrelled extensions – e.g. **.tar.gz**. This indicates that two levels of compression or encoding have been used. A good program like Stuffit Expander should automatically cope with both levels. ▲

< 273 >

**.tar** Another compressed archive you occasionally come across. WinZip will open it

**.txt, .text** ASCII text files

**.uue, .uu** UUencoded files. Winzip and Stuffit Expander can convert these

**.wav** Another type of Windows sound file. The Media Player will handle this

**.z** Another Unix compressed archive. Stuffit Expander will open it

**.zip** PC compressed archive. Winzip or Stuffit Expander will unzip this

Once you've got WinZip and Stuffit Expander, you can cope with a fair few of these. Browsers can also handle many of them. However, for some multi-media files you'll have seen that you need to augment your browser with various plug-ins or helper applications. There's more on this on page 313.

### Finding files on the net

Searching for files, especially from FTP sites, can be a bit hit and miss. It's fine if you know the exact name of the file you want. Then you can use an old piece of net software known as Archie to locate an FTP site that contains your file. There's a useful program which combines Archie with an FTP program (i.e. it finds the file, then downloads it) called fpArchie, available from fpWare's homepage at **http://www.fpware.demon.nl**. However, it's probably easier and quicker to use the FTP Search site at **http:// ftpsearch.lycos.com**. You could also try the big search sites. If you're looking for software, you'll probably find what you need at the 'software warehouse' web sites. Here are a few to be going on with. If you don't

< 274 >

**Tips – Doh!**

You don't have to restrict yourself to downloading useful bits of software. Want to make your computer say 'Doh!' when you start it up? Go to Tim's Simpsons' Page at **http://www.timtoews.com. index2.html** and download sound files from the TV show. After something so manifestly pointless, make yourself feel better by visiting the Project Gutenberg site and downloading the electronic edition of a piece of classic lit **http://promo.net/pg/**. ▲

want to use your browser to do everything and want to see what other programs you could use for mail, news, FTP and chat, these are great places to look.

**Download.com** – **http://www.download.com** Huge site maintained by C|Net. With a **Quick Search** and links to the top ten, newest and recommended downloads. While you're on the site, look out for a chart of the top fifty/hundred downloads. It can be interesting to see what everyone else is helping themselves to. Usually it's software. More recently, it's been bits of video from South Park and those Dancing Baby animations.

**Shareware.com** – **http://www.shareware.com** Another huge C|Net site with lots of stuff for PCs and Macs. Again, easy to navigate and search.

**Stroud's** – **http://cws.internet.com** The full name is Stroud's Consummate

< 275 >

Winsock Applications, which is a bit of a mouthful and not strictly accurate any more but we'll let it pass because Stroud's is a terrific site. Links to lots of useful internet apps plus reviews and information.

Tucows – **http://www.tucows.com** Another huge repository of net software for PCs and Macs and others. This link takes you to a general page. From here, click the links to find a UK mirror.

WinFiles.com – **http://www.winfiles.com** This was Windows95.com. (Either Bill's lawyers have been in touch or they just decided to broaden their remit to cover other Microsoft flavours.) Another very useful site.

When you go to a download site, you'll often be offered the choice of picking an alternative mirror site – i.e. a copy of the site maintained at another computer, perhaps on a different continent. The idea is that you can go somewhere less busy and save on download time. However, think before you pick a site. Don't immediately pick the nearest UK site. For

---

### Tips – Download Times

A friend who downloads a lot of stuff has this method for cutting download times. First find the file you want. If it's on an American site and you're looking at a serious download time, take a note of the file name and then go to the FTP Search site at **http://ftpsearch. lycos.com**. You can then use it to search for a nearer site that contains the file you want and then download from there instead. ▲

< 276 >

example, trying to download some software from the Demon Internet site in the early evening would be asking for trouble. Instead, try to find a site in a part of the world that's asleep, and hence unlikely to be online. Alternatively, pick a site in a country that's unlikely to have a huge net population. US sites can be fine if you're downloading in the morning, UK time, when most Americans should be asleep.

## Next Step

Now you've got the hang of downloading files, you're in the perfect position to start beefing up your web browser with all sorts of multimedia plug-ins. For more on that, go to page 313. ▲

< 277 >

## Online Chat

It may sound hard to believe now, but when the net was first hyped by the mainstream media it was considered exciting enough to be the centre-piece of nightclub events. People actually bought tickets for 'cyber nights' or 'interactive raves'. When things were just beginning to warm up at these events, everything would be brought to a halt and people would be directed to some bloke sat in front of a computer, who was 'accessing the future now'. (If you were really unlucky, this would be followed by a cyber fashion show.)

In a bid to make this rather dull spectacle more interesting, the bloke by the PC usually demonstrated online chat. The thinking must have been that at least chat was 'live', a (disjointed, disembodied, usually slightly daft) conversation, involving people from all around the world but scrolling out in 'real-time' text on your computer screen.

### Read about it online - Chat

Some academics have taken a particular interest in chat. MIT professor Sherry Turkle had some interesting chapters on chat and chat worlds in her last book, Life on the Screen. You can find out more at her home page at http://web.mit.edu/sturkle/www/. There are some good links to interviews with Turkle and some of her essays at **http://www.uiowa.edu/~commstud/resources/digitalmedia/ digitalpeople.html.** ▲

< 278 >

Unfortunately chat and chat rooms are also pretty unpredictable. The glowing reports about the net that first appeared in the press suggested that it was packed with articulate and witty people. But somehow, when you needed them, these people were always elsewhere.

At one net club night I attended, we all sat around and watched as the hapless demonstrator looked for a coherent conversation or someone willing to talk. He eventually started nattering with Jed from somewhere in Texas. He typed in his textual questions, which appeared on large screen projected above the desk. 'How's it going, Jed?' After a while the textual response blipped across the screen. 'Great. Hey this is really cool :-).' Cue a long pause as Jed thought of what to say next. 'So, what's the weather like over there?'

Not surprisingly, this kind of thing did lead to a sense of anti-climax and perhaps helped spark the backlash that British journalists were dying to unleash. Events like this were sniggeringly dismissed as symptomatic of the net as a whole, which was written off as a nineties version of Citizens' Band radio. What the sarcastic press pack didn't realise (and perhaps you can't blame them) is that the net is not a spectator sport. Online chat is particularly dull to watch. But if you do it yourself, even if you're exchanging banalities, it can be surprisingly exciting seeing words appear on your computer screen that come from someone else on the other side of the world (well, it is at first).

Many net users agree that online chat is a bit too close to 'breaker, breaker, ten four good buddy' nonsense for comfort. Occasionally, chat achieves a brief respectability – usually when there's a war on and people

< 279 >

are using chat rooms to get news out from the frontline. But in general, lots of net users think it's a bit of waste of (cyber)space. Perhaps there is a slight class dimension to all this. A sizeable part of the online population comprises of middle-class people whose business is information. For them, the net is an invaluable resource and they use it mainly for research (with perhaps a little online shopping/gaming/surfing for pleasure on the side). But what about people who aren't involved in 'knowledge work', people who get online in the evening for looking for entertainment and diversion?

Unless they're particularly obsessed, they aren't going to want to spend their time locating all the Quentin Tarantino interviews from the last three years. What ordinary people usually want to do when they get online is communicate with other people – in other words, chat. A while back a British TV programme about the net introduced a group of Welsh housewives with no previous computer experience to the online world. They remained pretty unimpressed by much of what they saw but immediately warmed to online chat.

Online services like AOL recognised the 'will to chat' of ordinary people, and built their businesses up by catering to it. Their chat rooms were (and are) a hugely popular part of their general operation. Indeed, in the early days of the net, it became clear that chat was one of the few online things people were prepared to pay for. That sparked a mini boom a few years ago, with companies looking for ways to make more money from chat. However, since then it's become clear that chat isn't quite the route to easy money many had hoped.

< 280 >

It worked for the online services because they used to charge by the minute for the time people were connected, but most web chat sites rely on advertising and it's becoming clear that when people chat, they stay in one place. They don't move around and hence don't see that many advertising banners. Consequently (and not without reason), many advertisers feel they're not getting value for money. Some also worry that chat rooms can be rather wild and might not create the right associations for their particular brand. As a result, even those companies who made a big success of taking chat to the web now see it as something of a dirty word.

However, a year or so ago, chat was anything but a four-letter word for British politicians who queued up to show how modern they were by 'interacting' directly with the people in a chat room. Usually they got someone else to type for them and the questions were vetted beforehand. Indeed, it's possible that the politicians weren't there at all but had sent

**Read about it online – Online Sex Chat**

For some interesting thoughts on online sex chat, try the excerpt from Lisa Palac's The Edge of the Bed published by the webzine Salon – **http://www.salonmagazine.com/21st/books/1998/04/ cov_27books.html**. Palac used to edit a magazine called Future Sex and is a little more open than most about the ups and downs of sex chat. ▲

< 281 >

their spin doctors instead. (The perfect way to stay on-message?) Indeed, when it comes to interacting directly with the voters, chat rooms are probably slightly below radio phone-ins.

Despite the politicians' love affair with chat, it remains one of the wilder things you can get involved with online. For beginners, simply following and then joining in a conversation can be tricky. Everyone seems to be talking at once, often in weird variants of something that once resembled English. In a chat room where everyone is telling jokey riddles, because of delays caused by the connection, the opening questions can come at once, followed by a jumbled set of punchlines – which is funny, though not in the way intended. Like everything else online, chat is constantly being upgraded. You can now chat in rooms that are presented onscreen as 2D or 3D environments. You can even send sounds to certain chat rooms (and as you might expect, a lot of fart noises travel down the wires).

Despite this kind of thing, chat rooms have been described like supermarkets and galleries, as 'the singles bars of the nineties'. It's true that a fair amount of chat online is about sex. In fact, to a lot of people it is a form of sex in itself. People meet online then head off to private rooms to type dirty to each other.

Some people get rather hot under the collar about one-handed typing, writing it off as perverse, empty, unreal and psychologically damaging. Other see no problem with consenting adults exchanging sexual/textual fantasies, so long as they keep a sense of proportion about it (though on one level, a sense of proportion is something clearly lacking in people

< 282 >

describing themselves as 'Busty Babe' and 'Big Boy'). Men hassling women with indecent propositions is another thing entirely.

However, in contrast to the real world, when you're on the net you can set your software to remove all traces of a person who's hassling you. Men who hit on women should be aware that you can never be sure who you're chatting with online. Those who make a big deal of presenting themselves as women are often men goofing around. If nothing else, this can help them to realise the amount of hassle women have to put up with in online chat rooms. For that reason, many women keep their gender secret.

Sexual deception is one thing. In some online chat rooms, you might even find yourself in conversation with something that isn't human – in other words, a chatbot, a program designed to greet new arrivals or even hold a sort of conversation. A small percentage of chat rooms are also home to hackers who indulge in silly but usually harmless mischief. For some people, chat can become incredibly compelling and end up taking over their lives. Even ordinary users who keep their chatting under control can find themselves facing sizeable telephone bills at the end of the quarter.

For that reason, parents should check on their children's use of chat rooms. Chat can be as compelling for teens as the telephone. And yes, there is some evidence that paedophiles frequent chat spaces trying to engage children in conversation. So children's chat use should be supervised in some way. Parents should not let their kids chat without giving them some general rules and tips about what to look out for or avoid. After you've read this section, go to page 389 for specific advice on this.

< 283 >

As ever with the net, don't get too hung up over the potential problems. For most people, online chat is an entertaining way to pass the time, make friends and build a sense of community. Take all those stories about online relationships that turned into real-world marriages. They usually started in chat rooms.

In the last year, chat has experienced something of a resurgence, thanks to Instant Message programs like ICQ and AIM. Simplifying things somewhat, they are essentially net pagers. Leave them on while you browse and they will tell you when your friends come online so you can page them to see if they want a chat. Though they started as geek toys, they're now hugely popular with all sorts, including business people who are beginning to see them as useful professional tools. AOL dominates Instant Messaging (it owns the two biggest programs AIM and ICQ), which is perhaps fitting, given its chat heritage. But this summer Microsoft decided to get into the game and released its own Instant Message program. The two big companies then spent a few months facing off over whether their competing programs should be compatible. It's the perfect emblem of how important chat still is online, how compelling (and useful) people still find it.

## Places to chat online and the software you need: Online Services

Beginners (with a bit of money to spend) might find the chat rooms at online services like AOL the easiest places to start. You get all the software you need when you sign up. They are easy to use. There are thou-

< 284 >

sands of different rooms, each devoted to different subjects. Chat in the online services is generally a pretty organised thing, with regular events in which users can get advice from experts and put questions to celebrities and, yes, politicians. Chat here is also subject to some control. If you're bothered by someone you can report it to a moderator who will take appropriate action. Parents who want to make sure their kids aren't exposed to dirty typing can take measures to block access to certain chat rooms. Of course, what some see as the advantages of the online services – that chat is easy to access and is controlled – may be a problem for others. Also, you pay extra for the online services' chat rooms, which may become annoying once you realise how easy it is to cope with the cheaper chat spaces on the net.

### Internet Relay Chat, aka IRC

IRC was given to the world by the Finnish programmer, Jarkko Oikarinen, in 1988. It was pretty popular with net users right from the start, though it started to get more attention from the mainstream world during the Gulf War when it was used to send out live (uncensored) reports about the conflict. To chat using IRC, you have to connect to a chat server. Groups of chat servers around the world are hooked up into networks, known as nets. Much like an online service, a particular net will host a bewildering amount of chat spaces (known as channels), each in theory devoted to a particular subject. Though they're nowhere near as organised as the online services, IRC nets do host celebrity chats, special events and even games. In general, IRC is very free and easy –

< 285 >

**Read about it online - IRC**

For an interview with Jarkko Oikarinen in which he talks about the
ideas behind IRC and how he thinks it will develop in the future, go
to **http://www.mirc.co.uk/help/jarkko2.txt**. ▲

which may attract some and worry others. Certainly, compared to the
online services, IRC is more confusing. However, it also offers a less
American experience.

To use IRC you need the right software. PC owners should go for
mIRC, available from **http://www.mirc.co.uk**; Mac users should try
IRCLE, available from **http://www.ircle.com/**. If you downloaded the full
version of Internet Explorer 5.x you should have Microsoft Chat, which
you can use to access the IRC network, but I wouldn't advise it. If you
skipped the section on downloading, go back to page 252.

## Web chat

Many web sites now feature chat rooms. You'll usually find a few chat
spaces on the big portals. The basic format is the same as IRC and the
online services – a selection of spaces devoted to different topics. Again,
they sometimes host special events; there will usually be details of these
on the website in question. The main attraction of web chat is that it's
happening on the web, so you can use your browser without resorting to
separate software. To access many web chat rooms, all you need at first

< 286 >

### Jargon File – Java, Javascript, Applet

Java is a programming language which, among other things, can be used to create interactive multimedia effects on the web. Javascript is a similar sort of language. An applet is a small program written in Java which can be placed on a web page. ▲

is an up-to-date browser – i.e. one that can run Java or Javascript. When you enter the chat room, a Java applet is loaded by your browser which enables you to participate in real-time chat. That said, many chat rooms will now also run in HTML too.

## Chat Style and netiquette

Chat style is very similar to email style. If anything, the TLAs and smileys people use in their mail are more useful in real-time chat. Once you get used to them, the former can speed up your typing; it still won't be anything like normal spoken conversation, but it helps. The latter can help resolve any potential misunderstandings caused by bad typing or delays on the line. (If all this sounds like gibberish, you probably skipped the chapter on email. Go back to page 178 for some general style tips.)

As for chat netiquette (or chatiquette), again it is really an extension of email and newsgroup netiquette. So typing using capitals is the equivalent of shouting and should be avoided. Similarly, you should

< 287 >

always think a bit before you type. Don't immediately kick off a flame war in response to something that seems like an obvious insult. It may not be intended that way and even if it is, sometimes it's best to ignore it anyway.

As with newsgroups, the best policy when you join a group is to lurk for a while, not say anything and find out what the group is talking about and what kind of language is acceptable. Each chat room or channel has its own codes of conduct, so in some bad language may be fine. One difference between chat rooms and newsgroups is that in the former everyone knows you are lurking; your arrival in a chat room/channel is always announced to all the other users. So if someone does say hello, it's bad form not to respond. In fact, it's generally considered rude to ignore people (unless you're being hassled).

The basic idea with chat is to keep the conversation going smoothly and to remember that it is a conversation. Don't change the subject of an ongoing chat or start talking about something unconnected with the

---

### Read about it online – Chat Netiquette

For an exhaustive (and somewhat specialist) guide to chat/IRC netiquette, which advises you to 'Consider the lag factor', avoid 'attention-seeking gimmicks' and much else, go to **http://mirc. stealth.net/mircrulz/**. For more general tips on netiquette, try **http://www.albion.com/netiquette/index.html**. ▲

< 288 >

room's designated subject. Attention-seeking pranks that break up the collective flow are frowned upon. It's bad form to 'flood' a chat room or channel – i.e. dump a huge amount of text (or even your latest piece of ASCII art) into a conversation. If you have a lot to get off your chest, it's better to break it down into shorter chunks. Keeping things short is always the best policy with chat.

With each kind of online chat there are specific things you can do to protect yourself (and your computer) from potential hassle. Here are a few all-purpose tips that hold for all chat spaces. Never, ever give out personal information in a chat room or channel – i.e. your real name, address, credit card number or details of your net account and password. The person asking for such information may flash what seem like authoritative credentials, but don't believe them. (This scam has been particularly common in the American chat rooms on AOL). Most chat programs let you create a personal profile. Think about the details you include if you choose to put one together. Putting details of what you do or your hobbies is fine. Don't put your address and telephone number or any other important personal details.

Think about the nicknames you pick for yourself. If you call yourself something like 'Hot Hunk', you are asking for a certain kind of attention (and signalling that you are a sad fool in the process). Women should go for chat room nicknames or screen names that don't indicate their gender. Otherwise, they will be hassled by the troglodytes who populate some chat rooms. Finally, don't always believe everything you read in a chat room. People are often not really what they say they are.

< 289 >

## Read about it online - Web Chat Listings

A good place to find out about chat (and various other live events) on the web is Yack **http://www.yack.com/**, a kind of chat listings site. Alternatively, try Talk City **http://www.talkcity.com/**, a kind of chat community site which features all sorts of themed chat rooms (accessible via a directory) and various celebrity chats and advice forums. ▲

## Which Chat Service?

Obviously, this is up to you, but I'd advise starting out with web chat. It's free and you don't need extra software. You can do it via your browser. It's true that web chat rooms aren't as controlled as the chat spaces in online services as AOL. But they're not quite as forbidding as the IRC network. I've decided to focus on web chat first here, mainly because it's immediately accessible to everyone. It also works in roughly the same way as AOL chat. So if you learn to chat on the web, you'll be able to hack it in the AOL chat rooms.

## Chat on the web

For those who don't want the full-on chat experience of IRC but also don't want to sign up with an online service, the web offers a good halfway house. You don't need to get new software but you can do a little bit more than just type without having to learn lots of text

< 290 >

commands. Web chat has a little of the free-and-easy feel of IRC chat but it also has the structure, the big-name celebrity chats and special events you associate with the online services. Web chat rooms are generally hosted by well-known companies who have rules about appropriate conduct and mechanisms for reporting those who get out of line. If, after chatting on the web for a while, you decide that chat is your thing, you can always go on to sign up with AOL. That said, if you do get serious about chat (and you do want to talk to a wider range of people), it might be better to go for IRC. As I said, it's your choice.

Perhaps the only difficult thing is finding the right place to chat. There are chat spaces all over the web these days. Yahoo's chat rooms are as good a place as any to begin. (Others work in roughly the same way.) Go to the US Yahoo site **http://www.yahoo.com** and click the **Chat** link. You'll need to register first. Once you've done that, you'll go to the Chat front page. Here you'll see details of upcoming events, links to chat rooms covering different themes and much else. There's a link at the top that also

---

### Read about it online – Roving web chat

Several new browser add-on programs have recently appeared which let you chat with other users who happen to be looking at the same website as you. The best known is probably Gooey **http://www.gooey.com**. ▲

< 291 >

allows you to change the 'identity/profile' you created during registration. For example, you can set up a new nickname and chat under that. You can also put together a list of favourite rooms and put together a list of friends so that you can go to them quickly if they're on Yahoo and chatting. In addition, at the top of the page, there's a menu that lets you choose whether or not you chat via Java (which is the default) or HTML. Don't worry too much about this unless you're using an older browser.

Pick a room and click on to get moving. When the chat window proper loads (which may take a while), it will be packed with frames. To the right of the window, you'll see a list of people in the particular room you're in. To the left of this, taking up the bulk of the window, is the chat proper. Yahoo uses a colour-coding scheme to make chat easier to follow. People are shown in red type, what they say is in blue and the emotions they send are pink. You can however change the way all this appears, if you wish, via the buttons at the bottom of the main window. The Emotions button calls up a list of emotions you can send with your chat message. These are gestural messages, things like 'cackle', 'cringe', 'snicker' and 'snivel'.

Below the buttons, you'll find the text box. Type your contribution in here then press the **Send** button to get involved. To send a private message to someone, click the **PM** button below the Chatters list. Then fill out the pop-up box that appears. To 'send an emotion', select one from the scrolling menu then double-click on it. It will appear on the screen in pink next to your name. If you want to send an emotion to another user, click on the emotion from the list, highlight their name in

< 292 >

**Read about it online - Celeb Chatbots**

For some chatbot fun, try out the Robbie Williams website at **http://www.robbiewilliams.com**. In the chat rooms here, you can shoot the digital breeze with various Robbie fans. You might also find yourself talking to a Robbie chatbot, programmed to talk/type like him. ▲

the **Chatters** box, and then press **Emote User** at the bottom of the **Emotions** box. If you want to see if any of the people on your Friends list is online at Yahoo, click the **Friends** button below the main chat window.

Below the main chat frame, in the bottom left-hand corner, is a general navigation menu. The buttons are generally pretty easy to understand. Clicking on **Who's Chatting** calls up a vast list of everyone currently on Yahoo, along with the chat room they're chatting in and some information from their personal profiles. Click on **Create A Room** and a menu comes up which lets you choose a name for your chat room,

**Tips - Help Files**

This may sound obvious, but with web chat sites, always start by reading the help files/introductory guides. They're all slightly different and if you don't read the guides you won't know what you can do, or what other people might be able to do to you. ▲

< 293 >

specify whether it is public or private, describe it and pick a 'rating' which allows you to choose whether you want bad language in your room to be automatically filtered. If you create a public user room, it appears on the general rooms list. A private room won't. The only way people can enter it is if you tell them you're there via a private message. To invite somebody to the chat room you're in, just click on the **More** button under the **Chatters** List. Type in the name of the person you want to invite and click the **Invite** button. Alternatively, you can invite other chatters to your room through the **Who's Chatting** list. Locate a name in the list and click the **Invite** link.

In a way, the biggest problem with web chat is finding a place where coherent chat is going on. Many web chat rooms don't seem to draw crowds of regulars or build up a real sense of community. They often seem to be populated by people who are there on a whim. As a result they can be chaotic. Since they are so easy to access, you get a few people dropping in to shout rude words or otherwise wind people up. You can choose to ignore people who are a pain. Click on their name in the **Chatters** box, then press the **Ignore** button. If someone is hassling you with private messages, you can also click the **Preferences** button and uncheck **Popup New Private Messages**. Now, when other chatters try to send you a private message, it should appear instead on the main chat screen with (PRIVATE) before the message and a **Reply** link after it. If you want to respond to the message, click on the **Reply** link. ▲

< 294 >

## Internet Relay Chat

If you get really serious about chat, the place to go is IRC. There are so many different conversations happening on IRC at any one time that you're bound to find something to interest you. However, IRC is relatively complex. New users probably need to take more care than they would on the web. The first thing you need to do is get your IRC program – mIRC or IRCLE. Next, configure your software. To give you the basic idea, we'll run through what you do with mIRC. The other programs all work in a similar way.

When you first try to open mIRC, a **Setup** dialog box with come up, with the IRC Servers box displayed. If that doesn't happen, click on the **File/Options** menu. To set up mIRC, first you need to specify an IRC server to connect to. As mentioned before, chat servers are hooked up in nets. Whatever chat server you connect to, you'll be able to access the channels being hosted on the particular net that it's a part of. There are all sorts of different nets, each with their own distinctive flavour. Here's a few you could try. Check their web pages for more details on the channels they offer and their rules.

Undernet – **http://www.undernet.org/**
Dalnet – **http://www.dal.net/**
KidLink (an IRC net for kids) – **http://www.kidlink.org/IRC/**

For more information about other nets, try
**http://www.irchhelp.org/irchhelp/networks/**

< 295 >

When you're just starting out, you shouldn't get too hung up about which net you use. mIRC has a good list you can use. So, on the **IRC Servers** dialog box, use the drop-down menu to find a chat server reasonably close to home.

Next you need to enter **Full Name, Email Address, Nickname** (and an alternative choice) in the relevant boxes. You could enter your real name and address, but women in particular might want to put something fake in here. There are various computer commands which let IRC users look at the information you enter – they might discover you are actually a woman, for example. So if you're worried about this, enter a fake name in the **Full Name** box or just a witty one-liner. You could also enter a fake email address. However, it's probably worth only faking the first part of your address – the part before the @ sign, since your program will always tell those who know how to ask what your internet domain really is – so if your address is **janesmith@newisp.net**, you could put **elvispresley@newisp.net**.

Nicknames are fairly straightforward. However, remember not to pick something too provocative if you can't stand the potential heat. In addition, some names won't be acceptable in some IRC channels. If you

---

### Tips - IRC Setup

You can add all sorts of information during mIRC set up. For a more detailed guide and lots of other useful chat/IRC information, try the excellent New IRC Users page **http://www.newircusers.com/** and look for the mIRC section.▲

< 296 >

want to retain a degree of privacy on IRC, you could tick the box next to **Invisible Mode**. That means that people won't be able to find you online unless they know your exact nickname. You don't really need to do much more, though you should click the **Identd** tab and make sure that the **Enable Identd** server box is ticked. Many IRC servers quickly check your user ID when you log on. mIRC, like a lot of other programs, will take care of this automatically (if you tick this box). If you entered a fake email address before, don't worry. It won't matter.

Now you're ready to connect. Either click the **Connect** button (the one with the lightning on it) or select the **File** menu, then **Connect**. You'll then connect with the server you chose when you configured mIRC. When you connect, a screen should come up with some general information about the computer you're connecting to. Often there will also be a message of the day and some details about the person responsible for the server. The **Channels Folder** should then open automatically. If it doesn't, you can call it up via a toolbar button. This lists all the channels available on the server. To join one, just click the **Join** button. When you're just starting out, look for channels like **#newbies**, **#newusers**, **#beginners** or **#ircbeginners**. (Note that all IRC channels start with the # sign.)

mIRC and other new IRC programs feature plenty of user-friendly toolbar buttons. However, you can also use text commands to get things done. You type the command then press **Return**. If you really get into IRC, you'll probably prefer using commands (there are hundreds of them). Anything preceded by a / is interpreted by mIRC as a command. So if you wanted to join a channel, you would write **/join #newbies** in the

< 297 >

**Read about it online - Chat Circuit**

For more IRC speak and lots of, ahem, newz and viewz, see Chat
Circuit **http://chatcircuit.com/webzine/**, which started out as a
webzine but has grown into a kind of chat network. There's lots of
beginner's info here, along with more hardcore IRC stuff and some
web chat rooms. ▲

main text box, then hit **Return** and you would go to that channel. Always
remember the **/** sign. If you miss it out, mIRC assumes what you've typed
is chat and broadcasts it to the channel. Result? Everyone now knows you
are a new user who doesn't know how to work their software.

Once you've joined your channel, you should see a listing of the
people currently on the channel on the right. The main chat window
(which may show a welcome message at first) takes up most of the
room. Below is the text box where you enter your contributions. It's
polite to say hello to everyone. Type 'Hello' in the text box then hit
**Return**. After that, it's a good idea to lurk for a while and see what's
happening. If it seems that this channel really isn't you, you can leave by
typing **/part** and look for another one. Alternatively, just close the
window. If you do want to get involved, just type your thoughts in the
text box and hit **Return**. Remember that smileys and TLAs are big on
IRC channels, as is a fairly distinctive way with spelling. (You often feel
as if you're in a world filled with people who learned to read and write

< 298 >

via the sleeve notes on Prince records; there's lot of 'I would die 4 U' and 'Chat Rulz' business).

If you want to chat privately with someone in an IRC channel, double-click on their nickname in the people list. A query window should open. Alternatively, right-click on a nickname in the list and a mouse menu will appear which will let you open a private query window with that person. If the person you want to talk to privately is not in your channel (and you know their nickname), type **/query**, then their nickname. If you want to find out if they're actually on the system, type **/whois**, then their nickname, which is also a good way of finding out a little bit about the person involved (or rather the information they entered when they configured their chat software). Alternatively, use the **/uwho** command then the nickname. mIRC has a function called DCC Chat which lets you chat more securely with individual users (basically, it connects directly to their IRC program). To use this, click the **DCC Chat** button on the toolbar or select the **DCC** menu, then **Chat**. You can then send a message to someone and, if they accept, you can start chatting and even exchange files.

As you explore IRC, you'll find out that there's all sorts of things you can do in a channel, from sending coloured text and messages when you leave to creating a new channel. Look in the mIRC help files for a good list of commands you can use. Here's a few to be going on with:

**/list** will get you a list of all channels currently running on the computer you're connected to

< 299 >

**/list *subject*** will list all channels devoted to the subject specified between the asterisks, as in **/list *football***

**/part message** leaves a channel with a message which tells everyone else what you're up to as in **/part bye everyone, off to get some lunch**

**/away** tells everyone in a channel that you're temporarily away from your computer

**/away message** will tell everyone why you're away, so if you really want to share you can type **/away off to the loo**

**/nick** can be used to change your nickname

**/msg nickname** then your message can be used to send a private message to the user specified without opening a query window.

You can use commands to set up your own channel on an IRC net. Think of a new name for it, then type **/join**, then the name you came up with, as in **/join #mychannel** (always remember the # sign). That's all it takes. Since it's your channel, you might as well make yourself the channel 'op' (as in 'operator', the person in charge). Type **/op**, then your nickname. Everyone who enters the channel will now know that you're in charge. Of course, power may not be your thing at all, so you can start a channel and make someone else the op using the Mode command. Type **/mode** then your channel name, then **o**, then the nickname, as in **/mode #mychannel o sid.**

You can invite other users to your channel by typing **/invite**, then their nickname and the name of your channel, as in **/invite dave #mychannel.** Of course, people might turn up off their own bat if you

< 300 >

pick an interesting topic for discussion. To set the agenda, type **/topic**, then details of the subject you want to talk about. As channel op, you are in charge, which means that if someone is being disruptive, it's up to you to keep order. If necessary, you can kick troublemakers off the channel. Type **/kick**, then the channel name, then the name of the troublesome user. One of the general principles of IRC netiquette is that you should use power with responsibility. So don't set up a channel and then act like some sort of demented digital dictator.

IRC is mostly made up of ordinary people who want to chat. However, some channels are hacker hangouts. For some bored computer teens, IRC is a wonderful playground. They can create bots or special sets of commands that will do all sorts of things on chat channels. Some hackers seem to like nothing better than trying to take over certain IRC channels. You aren't that likely to run into the more malevolent kind of IRC user if you don't go looking for them. However, there are precautions you can take. First and foremost, if someone asks you to type a

### Tips - Timers

For some people, chat can be remarkably compelling. You can lose track of time quite easily. mIRC has a useful Online Timer function (look for the Clock button on the toolbar) which tots up the hours you've been nattering on about Arsenal's ageing defence or the wondrousness of the cast of 'Dawson's Creek'. ▲

< 301 >

## Read about it online – IRC

It is a world all its own and you could easily write a book about what goes on there (and some people already have). For more information about IRC and what you can do, try the web. IRC Help is good place to start, particularly the IRC prelude – **http://www.irchelp.org**. Alternatively, try the links to more information at the bottom of the Mirc homepage – **http://www.mirc.co.uk/**. ▲

particular computer command, **don't ever do it,** whatever they say. It will do something nasty to your PC and may even let someone else control it.

Don't tell the truth about your name and address. Remember you don't have to accept private messages. If someone hassles you via private messages, raise the problem in the public part of the channel or get help from the channel op. Alternatively, type **/motd** to get the Message of the Day which should feature contact details for the system administrator. You can set your software to ignore certain users. Type **/ignore** then the nickname of the user. (mIRC allows you to be much more specific when it comes to ignoring people and messages, so look in its help files).

When it comes to getting by on IRC you also have to make allowances for the system in general. Lag (delays on the line) can be a problem sometimes; the best way round this is to always connect to a server near you. Sometimes channels can split. Basically, you and the users on a particular server lose contact with the users in the same

< 302 >

channel who were logging on to a different server. Channels stay up but half the users disappear. Splits aren't that much of a problem and usually right themselves fairly quickly.

## Instant Messages

As mentioned before, the most popular chat-like tools on the net at the moment are instant message programs (also sometimes known as buddy lists). These are a bit like intelligent online pagers. You can send messages that are halfway between email and chat. You can carry on conversations using instant message programs or use them to set up proper chat sessions. First you have to register with the company running the software and network, get a password and a screen name or number. You then pass this to friends who use it to send you instant messages.

You can create a 'buddy list' of friends who also use the same software, so that when they come online you're notified, via a small window on your desktop (obviously you have to be online too) and then you can page them to say hello. If you (and your friends or work colleagues) spend a lot of time online, this can be incredibly useful. Obviously, one of the pleasures of being online is that you can't be bothered by other people, so most instant messages have various privacy features which let you block messages (and in effect hang up a virtual Do Not Disturb sign).

AOL users have long been able to track friends and send them quick messages (via a function called the buddy list). In the last two years, instant messaging has spread on to the net in general. The program that's made the biggest splash is ICQ (as in 'I seek you'). In fact ICQ

< 303 >

made such a big splash that AOL bought the company behind it – Mirabilis. You can download a beta/evaluation copy from **http://www.icq.com**. When it comes to the big names, Microsoft recently launched Messenger **http://messenger.msn.com** and Yahoo also has its own pager which is available at **http://pager.yahoo.com/**. AOL has also taken its buddy lists on to the net, with AOL Instant Messenger, which lets you 'page' AOL users, anyone else who has registered the software and ICQ users. AIM is now bundled with Netscape Communicator so you'll probably already have a copy. Obviously with messaging systems (which are incompatible) the number of users you can reach is one of

### Read about it online – Telephony & Instant Messages

Voice messaging is coming to Instant Messages. The idea is that once you've established contact with someone via your Instant Message program, you can, if you're both kitted out with the right add-on programs, switch to a crackly voice chat over the net. Of course, you'll need a microphone for this to work. The programs you need are versions of the net telephony programs/video chat programs that so far have remained geek toys. Instant Messages may finally bring them to a wider public. For more info on the ICQ site go to **http://www.icq.com/telephony/telephony.html#conventional** or on Yahoo go to **http://pager.yahoo.com** and look for the Voice message link. ▲

< 304 >

the key things to look for. ICQ and AIM are the two leading programs and they can talk to each other. So they're the ones to go for really. As mentioned before, the competition is trying to make its software compatible with AOL's progams but so far the company has tried to block these initiatives.

ICQ is probably the best Instant Message program. AOL Instant Messenger does the basics and will let you send friends website URLs. It allows you to block certain users and includes a Warn feature that lets you send a warning to abusive users (and the AOL authorities). However, with ICQ you can also send files via instant messages. You can easily use ICQ to set up chat sessions. If you send an instant message to someone and they're offline, ICQ will hold on to the page and send it when they come online. It also has reasonable privacy controls – your authorisation is required before people can add you to their buddy list and you can block messages from certain users. Mirabilis, the company behind ICQ, add new features fairly regularly. So it's worth going to their website to find out what's new.

## Graphic Chat

A couple of years ago, graphic chat (online conversations in which the speakers were represented onscreen as characters in 2D or 3D space) was supposed to be the future of online chat. It might still be, but at the moment, most users don't have the fast connections or fast machines you really need to make this kind of thing work. In addition, visuals often take something away from the chat proper (which remains a textual

< 305 >

thing and appears in speech bubbles above the characters' heads). People inevitably start talking about each other's avatars. Adding a visual dimension, setting the chat in space station, the bar from Star Wars or a South Park-type environment, often winds up making the whole experience less interesting. Text is such a 'low-bandwidth' thing, it leaves space for imagination, projection and fantasy. Visuals lock you into a particular (often rather corny) space.

If you feel like checking it out, you can try 2D chat spaces, which look like variations on comic books. The best known of these is probably WorldsAway which used to be confined to Compuserve but has now moved on to the net (for info, go to Avaterra's site at **http://www. worldsaway.com/**). The easiest 2D chat to access is Microsoft Chat, which you will get if you download the full version of Internet Explorer. Once you start the program, you can design your own character, connect to Microsoft server, then chat as you would in a normal IRC chat room.

Alternatively, 2D visual chat is available on the web courtesy of The Palace **http://www.thepalace.com**. Go to the website and you'll get a chance to check out the various 'Palaces' that have been set up around the world. (Some are business-oriented, some are just for fun; all are cartoon-y spaces in which you are represented by avatars aka onscreen characters which can be anything from cartoon faces and animals to flowers.) You can download a Palace plug-in but if you have a Java-capable browser, you don't need one and can just drop in to a room to check things out. For the full 3D chat experience, try WorldsChat. Here you can create your own avatar and wander around a giant space

< 306 >

station, chatting as you go. However, you will need to buy special software – go to **http://www.worlds.net** for more information..

## MUDs

Some users may see chat as one of the more trivial of online activities. But for an example of how seriously some people take chat (and what strange places it can take them to), check out a MUD. Multiple User Dungeons (or Dimensions or Dialogues) are chat spaces in which users have collectively talked up a whole world, with its own rules and customs. Relying simply on text, users create an alternative geography (and alternative identities) where they can play out ideas, theories and fantasies.

At a more basic level, MUDs are programs on a remote computer. Users log on and explore them, via their own computerised character.

---

### Read about it online – MUDs

For a form of graphic chat that's coming to the web, try the website put up by Artificial Life Inc **http://www.artificial-life.com**. The company is developing intelligent, natural language chat bots that come with a graphic animated interface – i.e, they look like people and they move when they talk. The idea is to create on screen guides who can help people round the networks of the future. At the moment, you can test this out and have a conversation of sorts wit a couple of bots – Roy, a blue android-y type or Rachel, a kind of identikit young woman at The Gap type. ▲

---

< 307 >

You can wander round the textual spaces other users have created, chat with other users, play games, even create your own rooms and buildings. Typically, when you log on, some text will appear on a screen telling you that you're in, for example, an entrance lobby and that in front of you are three doors, a table and a book. You move around by typing textual commands. So you can choose to go through one of the doors. If you do, some text will come up telling you what's behind it. You can continue like this for hours, and some users do. For those who get into them, MUDs seem to be among the most compelling of online activities.

MUDs don't get as much press as they used to but they remain very popular. They started as a kind of online extension of Dungeons and Dragons role-playing games. As you moved around them, you competed with other users, tried to gain more power, move up the MUD hierarchy and eventually become a wizard or some such. You can now play these sorts of games in MUDs themed around novels (for example, those by Tolkien and Terry Pratchett) and films (Star Wars). Some users didn't really get into this and began to develop MUDs that were more social, in which people kicked around ideas rather than each other. Strictly

## Jargon File – Identity Hacking

As in the creation of alternative identities online. Much as you hack code, you can also apparently hack your own personality and try out different versions of yourself. ▲

< 308 >

### Jargon File – Digerati

Aka the self-styled cyber-elite – a group of software programmers, business people, theorists, gurus, old hippies, rich people and self-publicists who are bravely helping us all out by living the future now – on expenses, naturally. The premier digerati web hangout is Edge **http://www.edge.org** where you can find out who's in with the in-crowd and see what they're currently thinking about. Leaving aside the snide comments, the site does feature some interesting discussions about science and technology. However, if you want an antidote, try ditherati – a regular selection of dumb things the digerati have said – **http://www.ditherati.com/**. ▲

speaking, these often weren't really exactly what you called MUDs. These alternative MUDs were often called TinyMUDs or MUSHes, MOOs, MUSEs or MUCKs (you really don't need to know what all these stand for). In one of the alternative MUDs people pretended to be small, cute, furry animals and spent their time having 'cyber sex' with each other. In others, people explored identity hacking and alternative lifestyles.

These alternative MUDs were almost the online equivalent of the communes of the sixties and early seventies. Unlike chat in general, they were taken very seriously by the digerati, who devoted plenty of academic papers to them. For one example, try Julian Dibbell's A Rape in Cyberspace, a fascinating account of a 'sexual assault' that took place in

< 309 >

## Read about it online – Telnet

For a useful guide to other computers and resources you can access using Telnet, try the HYTELNET site at **http://www.cam.ac.uk/Hytelnet/index.html**. ▲

LambdaMOO, a particular well known, determinedly bohemian MUD; it's available at **http://www.levity.com/julian/bungle.html**.

MUDs are an example of the pre-Web net. To use them, you really need an old piece of software called Telnet. This lets you connect to a remote computer via the net and then use the programs on that computer. You can use Telnet for lots of things (searching library databases, for example) but it's mainly used now by MUDers. You may have been given a Telnet program as part of your ISP's introductory software package, or you may already have a version if you're running a Windows 95/98 PC.

However, it's probably still easier to pick up Telnet from the net. PC users could try CRT (available from **http://www.vandyke.com**). Mac users could try NCSA Telnet (look around for it at **ftp://ftp.amug.org**). Telnet programs all work in roughly the same way. You have to enter the domain name/address of the computer you want to log on to, along with the port number. When you connect, you'll usually see an introductory screen which should give you some useful details on the commands you need to move around the system, For more help, type **help** then hit **Return**.

< 310 >

One of the best places to go for information about MUDs is the web. You could start with a very useful general FAQ at **http://www.lysator. liu.se/mud/faq/faq1.html** (this site is worth exploring – there are some good links to programs designed to make using MUDs more easy.) There's a good list of MUDs at the MUD Resource Collection at **http://www.godlike.com/muds**. For a list of currently active MUDs, try the MUD Connector at **http://www.mudconnect.com**. Usenet newsgroups are also a good place to go for general information about MUDs. Try **rec.games.mud** or **rec.games.mud.announce**.

When it comes to getting into MUDs, the best thing is to take your time. It does take a while to find your way around and master the text commands a particular program requires. Always read the help files. Starting out in a social MUD might be a good idea. Users here aren't going to be trying to wipe you out and accumulate more wizard points (or whatever), so you'll get the time to get used to the whole concept.

---

**Read about it online – Made in the UK**

MUDs are another online British invention. Richard Bartle and Roy Trubshaw, created the first MUD, at the end of the seventies, when both were students at Essex University. The pair are still working in the field. You can see what they're up to at their website **http://www.mud.co.uk**. Their new MUD (it's called MUD2, obviously enough) can be accessed via the web at **http://www.mud2.com**. ▲

< 311 >

## Read about it online – Graphic MUDs

MUDs are a crucial influence on some of the huge multi-player gaming worlds currently being developed on the web. Here, much of the action is MUD-like – there's lot of talk, character creation and troll-bashing, but there are pictures too. Try Ultima Online **http://www.ultimaonline.com/** or Everquest **http://www.everquest.com**. ▲

Finally, one piece of advice about MUDs that is fairly crucial. They're clearly not for everyone. But those who do get into them can end up stuck. It's not unknown for users to spend hours on end in MUDs and to experience real grief if their online persona gets killed. If you do get hooked, fine. But try to keep the whole thing in perspective.

## Where to Next?

By now the net is pretty much your oyster. Next, you could beef up your web browsing – on page 313 there's information on the web and multimedia. However, if you've had more than enough of the web, you could cut to page 379 for some tips on security and survival online.

< 312 >

# 4 TAKING THE WEB TO THE NEXT LEVEL

• • • • • • • • • • • • • • • • • • • • • • • • • • • • • • • • • •

I hope you now feel as if you know your way around the net. You've done the work, slogged your way through the basics. You know your ftp from your http. But of course there is more to learn (there always is with the net). This section looks at web multimedia and the software you need to check it out. It also covers shopping on the internet. By now, we're assuming you're more comfortable with the net and net software (and know how to find a Help file), so there isn't so much detail about how to work individual programs.

## Multimedia on the web

A few years ago a friend came round to my house to check out the net. She'd caught some of the hype and wanted to see what all the fuss was about. I set everything up and left her to it. After a while, she came downstairs looking disappointed. What was it with all the text, she asked. Where was the MTV-style multimedia sound and fury you were supposed to get? The answer was that, despite the impression given by the hype, it wasn't on the net. However, it is now . . . sort of. The net, or rather the web, has gone multimedia in the last few years. You can

< 313 >

now listen to sound and watch video in real time. You can play games or watch animations bounce around web pages.

Whether this is an uncomplicated Good Thing is open to question. Is your browsing experience radically improved by web pages that play Beethoven's 'Ode to Joy' on what sounds like Rolf Harris's old stylophone? Do pages with twirling logos, jumping type and rolling tickers of 'breaking news' really engage and inform you more than simple legible text? Too much web multimedia still feels like something of an indulgence, a programmer's high-tech toy. However, as with lots of things online, it's getting better all the time. It won't be long before multimedia stops being a gimmick and becomes an essential part of the average browsing experience (some would argue that it's there already). As for now, the best thing is not to expect too much and just have some fun.

## Getting Started

To get the best out of web multimedia, you will need a reasonably up-to-date computer. The old PC you bought five years ago won't cut it. The minimum you need is a soundcard, a good graphics/video card with at least 2 Mb of memory (more will make video look better), a reasonably speedy Pentium processor and a fast modem – 28.8 Kbps should just about be OK but 56.6Kbps is preferable. A fairly big hard disk is also useful. You'll need some extra software, most of which you can download for free from the web – which means it's easy to fill up your hard drive without realising. However, browsers are now multimedia devices with built-in programs that can handle video and sound. When you click a link

< 314 >

to most sound files, your browser will usually play them, sometimes in a separate window. The same goes for video files, once downloaded. Don't worry about whether your browser can or cannot handle a particular file. If it has problems, it will tell you that you need more software.

You will be told you need either a plug-in or an ActiveX control. You can also get a separate viewer or helper application to handle some sound/video/image files but we'll get to those later. A plug-in is a kind of booster program that enables your browser to handle a specific sort of web multimedia. You don't need to know how to use a plug-in; you just click a link and it goes to work, playing the multimedia content within your browser window. The plug-in idea was first developed by Netscape. Of course, you can get plug-ins for Internet Explorer, but, just to be helpful, Microsoft has also introduced its own way of handling multimedia within the browser – ActiveX. As a result, if you're using Internet Explorer, sometimes when you go to get a plug-in you'll wind up with an ActiveX control instead. ActiveX controls are a bit like plug-ins in that they are integrated with your browser and enable it to play multimedia within its main window. Navigator can play ActiveX controls so long as you install the NCompass ScriptActive plug-in. You can get it from **http://www.ncompasslabs.com/**. If all this sounds confusing – well, it is, but it really isn't an issue when you're browsing.

## Getting Plug-ins and ActiveX controls

The new versions of Navigator and Internet Explorer both come with lots of the more popular plug-ins and ActiveX controls pre-installed.

< 315 >

### Tips - Plug-ins

Take care if you're downloading plug-ins from sites you haven't heard of before. Stories have circulated online about a porn site that required users to download a special viewer. This turned out to be a bit of software designed to hijack users' telephone lines and run up huge bills. So it pays to look around the site and think a bit before you download. ▲

Navigator, in particular, makes it easy to check what you've got. Select the **Help** menu, then **About Plug-ins** and you'll access a handy list. However, if you're using Navigator and you click a link to a multi-media file it can't handle, a dialog box will appear, directing you to the Netscape plug-in page. Often web sites that use multimedia provide links to the appropriate plug-in. Some plug-ins now install themselves. With others, you may need to close your browser (and any other applications you're running) and start the installation process yourself. Generally plug-ins are self-extracting compressed files with the extension .exe or .sea: just double-click them and the installation process will start up. Sometimes you may come across a plug-in that has been compressed using WinZip or Stuffit – for details on this, go back to page 263.

If you're using Internet Explorer and you come across a page that uses an ActiveX control you haven't got, your browser will start to

< 316 >

download it. It may flash up a **Security Warning** screen to check that it's OK. Some ActiveX controls go to work once you've downloaded them. Others will need to be installed. You can get new ActiveX controls from Microsoft – go to **http://www.microsoft.com/com/** or try the ActiveX site put up by C/Net: **http://www.activex.com/**. If you want to get your plug-ins before you browse, you could start at the software sites mentioned in the chapter on downloading.

| | |
|---|---|
| Download.com | **http://www.download.com** |
| Shareware.com | **http://www.shareware.com** |
| Stroud's | **http://cws.internet.com** |
| Tucows | **http://www.tucows.com** |
| WinFiles | **http://www.winfiles.com** |

Download.com runs a special sub-site for browsers, called Browsers.com at **http://www.browsers.com/** which has a vast list of all available plug-ins. It's worth investigating this list later, but for now, start with the Browsers.com chart of the most popular plug-ins (rated in terms of the number of downloads).

### The Plug-ins You Need

One plug-in you're bound to use is RealPlayer, so let's try getting that one first. RealPlayer started out as RealAudio, which handled streaming audio – the files play as you download them, you don't need to wait until they're completely downloaded. RealPlayer now handles streaming video and

< 317 >

animation as well. Quality isn't always up there with files that you download, then play, but it's getting better all the time. Actually, you'll probably already have a version of Real Player – the current version is the G2 and it comes as standard with both of the big browsers now. But by the time you read this, there may be a new version. And Real Networks are continually introducing new plug-ins and players. Take the company's RealJukebox player, also available for free. A useful, all-purpose tool for online audio, this plays all sorts of music files, in particular MP3s.

Start your browser and go to Real Networks' UK website at **http://uk.real.com/**. There should be a current version of RealPlayer available for free download. Enter various details – your computer's operating system and processor, your connection speed, your name and email address – and then click the **Download Free RealPlayer** button. If you read the chapter on downloading, the rest is straightforward. If not, go back to page 252. So what can you use RealPlayer for? The UK Real Networks have some good links to sites that use their technology at **http://uk.real.com/showcase/index.html**. The US Real Networks site also

---

### Tips – Unused Plug-ins

As you try out various plug-ins, you're bound to download some you don't use much. Don't let them clutter up your disc: get rid of them. And if you want to keep your hard disc in good order, get a decent utilities/uninstall program to take care of this. ▲

< 318 >

points you to sites making the best use of its plug-in via its RealGuide **http://realguide.real.com/**.

Now you know how to download plug-ins, you might as well spend some time beefing up your browser. Two other plug-ins you definitely need are Shockwave Player and Flash Player. Shockwave and Flash were developed by Macromedia, and are the standard tools for interactive multimedia and animated gimmicks on web. Both are available for free. Again, you will probably already have a version of both pre-installed in your browser. If you don't (or you want to update), go to **http://www. macromedia.com/shockwave/**. For links to sites using Shockwave/Flash, try Shockwave.com **http://www.shockwave.com** or Shockrave **http://www. shockrave.com/** for, amongst other things, links to web cartoons (every-thing from 'South Park' to 'Dilbert' and 'Peanuts') created using Shockwave. Shockwave animations and games often take a while to download. Once they have, you don't have to be online to view/play them. Save money and log off for a while.

The latest versions of Internet Explorer should come with something called Windows Media Player, which plays most sorts of audio and video online. However, it won't hurt to also install the latest version of Apple's QuickTime, which comes as standard with Navigator. You can down-load the full version, which includes plug-ins amongst other things and handles sound and 3D visuals as well as video, from **http://www.apple. com/quicktime/**. Read the QuickTime documentation. Once you've installed QuickTime proper, you may need to locate the plug-ins and then put them in the **Plug-in** folder of your browser.

< 319 >

Plug-ins aren't just about interactive multimedia. They can do more boringly useful things too. Try the Adobe Acrobat Reader plug-in which lets you read documents created using Adobe's Acrobat graphics program **http://www.adobe.com/**. Alternatively, there's NetZip, which lets you unzip compressed files via your browser **http://www.netzip.com/**. There are all sorts of new plug-ins you can try. You could also try Get Right **http://www.getright.com**, a plug-in which aims to make down-loading files from the web easier.

## Helper Applications and Browser Companions

There are all sorts of other programs you can use to boost your browser's capabilities. Strictly speaking, these aren't plug-ins, because they are separate programs that aren't completely integrated into your browser. Instead they work alongside. Some people refer to these as helper applications (or helper apps). Other people prefer to talk about browser companions, utilities or add-ons. In the end, the terminology is neither here nor there. All you need to know is that there are some more programs you might find useful.

You can use browser add-ons/helper apps to handle some multimedia files you find on the web. Usually a helper app deals with one sort of file (though not always). If you download a sound file from the net, you can then log off, close your browser, and use the helper app to play it. However, you can also configure your browser so that if you come across the file type your app handles, the browser will start it up and it will then play the file in a separate window. If you do want a helper app to auto-

< 320 >

matically handle a particular kind of file while you're browsing, you need to associate it with that file type. To do this:

▶ If you're using Internet Explorer, you'll need to open Windows Explorer, then select the **View** menu, then **Folder Options**, then the **File Types** tab. Use the **New Type** button to add a new file type.

▶ In Navigator, select the **Edit** menu, then **Preferences**, then **Applications**, then just fill out the relevant boxes. Use the **New Type** button to add a new file type. Aside from the file extension, you'll be asked for the MIME type – something like audio/x-mpeg or video/quicktime. Don't worry too much about this: it's just another way of identifying and organising files on line. If you don't know the MIME type for a file, check in the documentation for the helper app you're using.

▶ In the Mac version of Internet Explorer, select the **Edit** menu, then **Preferences**, then, in the **Receiving Files** section, click on **File Helpers**. Here you can change the various helper apps your browser works with.

This process can be a bit fiddly but you can get a neat free utilities program which does it all for you. WAssociate is available at **http://www.xs4all.nl/~wstudios/Associate/index.html**.

One program you should definitely have a look at is WinAmp (or MacAmp), an excellent audio player which handles most MPEG audio files, specifically MP3s **http://www.winamp.com/**. Alternatively, have a look at some of the browser companions that aim to add more 'community' to the web. Over the last six months, various news programs have been released which let web page visitors interact with each other. The

< 321 >

first example was Third Voice **http://www.thirdvoice.com**, which lets people leave comments and add notes to web pages they visit. Third Voice users visiting pages that have been annotated can see the notes left (via a small 'snap-on' window on the side of their browser). Imagine post-it notes for the net. They can also add their own, in theory developing discussions related to the material on the website in question.

Extending this idea, a new set of programs have appeared which let people visiting a particular website chat to each other (so long as they're using the right program). Think of it as instant messaging adapted to the web, sort of. The best known program here is Gooey **http://www.gooey. com** though you should also have a look at uTok **http://www.utok.com** and Odigo **http://www.odigo.com** (stupid names seem obligatory). These don't just let people chat on web sites. They collect information about web sites and point users in the direction of popular sites. The companies behind these products make big claims for them. Apparently Gooey

---

### Read about it online – TV Graffiti

Lots of web sites seem to view Third Voice with suspicion. Certainly the program has been abused, with people adding links to porn sites or just random abuse. That said, the program has also enabled serious 'inline' discussions on other sites. For a site that argues that the program needs to be reworked, try Say No to Third Voice.com **http://saynotothirdvoice.com/index.html**. ▲

< 322 >

---

**Jargon File - Scripting Language**

A set of programming shortcuts which make it a little easier for programmers to create interactive routines. ▲

---

enables Dynamic Roving Communities (aka DRC – it's apparently a play on IRC – the net chat network). UTok apparently stands for users' Tree of Knowledge. These programs are pretty new so it's not clear how well they work or whether they will catch on, but they're definitely worth a look. For more browser add-ons, visit CNet's Browsers.com **http://www. browsers.com**.

### Java

Java is a programming language developed by Sun Microsystems which, amongst other things, can be used to deliver interactive web content. Programmers use Java to create applets, small programs that are placed directly on web pages. They can also add interactivity to their pages with something called JavaScript, a scripting language. You need a reasonably up-to-date browser for JavaScript and Java applets. Often you probably won't be aware when your browser is running a Java applet. But sometimes you have to wait for an applet to download before you can do anything. Java is mostly used to create little animations on web pages, scrolling news 'tickers' and interactive games/routines – everything from calculators to real-time chat. Most web chat rooms now use Java applets

< 323 >

**Read about it online – Java**

For a slightly dated but still interesting look at the fuss surrounding Sun's much-talked-about programming language/virtual religion, try the special report put together a couple of years ago by Wired News **http://www.wired.com/news/news/java/**. ▲

rather than plug-ins. If you want to see what applets can do, try the mildly diverting demos at **http://www.gamelan.com/** or **http://www.java.co.uk** Alternatively go to Sun's own Java page at **http://java.sun.com** for more applets and updates on Java in general.

Java will undoubtedly continue to develop and become ever more crucial to the all-singing all-dancing web. As it does, worries about its security implications will probably grow too. When you access a Java-boosted web page, you download a small program on to your computer, a program that could in theory contain a virus. So what can you do? Play and pray seems to be about the size of it. Sun insists its security measures are top-notch, but people are always saying that and then being caught out by hackers. Unscrupulous types can also use Javascript to snatch your email address while you browse their site. You can then find your-self on the receiving end of a lot of spam. If you're worried, get your browser to block Java applets and Javascript.

▶ In Internet Explorer, select the **Tools** menu, then **Internet Options**, then click the **Security** tab. Click the box next to the line **Custom** (for expert users), then click the **Settings** button. In the **Security Settings**

< 324 >

---

**Tips - Applets**

Even if you're not worried about security, it can be a good idea to disable Java. Applets can be unstable and crash your browser. They can slow down your time on the web too. And a fair few of them are so trivial or irritating that you're often better off without them. ▲

---

dialog box, look for the Java Permissions section.

▶ In Navigator, select the **Edit** menu, then **Preferences**, then click on **Advanced** and look for the Java section.

▶ In the Mac version of Internet Explorer, select the **Edit** menu, then **Preferences**, then, in the **Web Browser** section, click on **Java**, then make the changes you want in the **Java Options** box.

## Music on the Net

According to Search Terms **http://www.searchterms.com**, a site which tracks what people are searching for on the web, the most used search term on the net is MP3 (it beats things like 'sex', 'warez' and 'pokemon'). This is perhaps the best sign of just how big the online culture around MP3s has become in the last two years or so. The letters are short for MPEG Layer 3, a technique used to compress music or video files stored on a computer to about a tenth of their normal digital size, without a noticeable loss of overall sound quality. Software for playing MP3 files is freely available on the net, as are the programs you need to convert ordinary CDs into computer files and then compress them.

< 325 >

As a result, it's easy to convert tracks from your CD collection into MP3 files and upload them to the net, where they can be downloaded for free by other fans and then played at home on a computer. All this can happen without any money beyond the original CD purchase price going to the record companies. In effect, MP3 files have helped home taping go global. They've re-booted bootlegging for the digital age. Not surprisingly, the record industry are not best pleased about all this. Though their attitude is changing, the big record companies have claimed at various times over the last two years that MP3 files were holding back the development of music shopping online.

Whether or not you believe this, it is true that the MP3 format has spawned a huge scene on the net, one organised mostly around the illegal trading of tracks made by big name artists. It takes in web sites and online chat rooms. Its adherents include new bands looking for a break, old bands looking for pr and online con men looking to make a quick buck. It's mainly dominated by American college students and

## Tips – Don't be a leech

If you do want to help yourself to some illegal MP3 files (and I strongly advise you not to, because if you do, you'll be breaking the law), you may find that you have to give something back in return. The MP3 scene has a definite code of conduct. 'Leeching' – downloading tracks and not giving anything back – is discouraged. ▲

< 326 >

their musical tastes – if you fancy downloading something by the Smashing Pumpkins or Rage Against the Machine, you're fine. If you're after something by Pulp or the latest underground garage tune, you might struggle.

One of the best places to go to catch up with what's going on is Michael Robertson's website MP3.com (**http://www.mp3.com**). The way MP3.com has developed in the last year or so is a sign of how quickly things move on the web. A year ago or so, MP3.com was home to critics of the mainstream record industry. Robertson and others praised the MP3 format and sounded off about clueless record companies. They didn't feature any illegal material on their site – just MP3s willingly uploaded by unsigned bands. But they did have links to MP3 search engines and to the software you needed to convert your CDs to MP3s and to play them on your computer. This summer, however, the site was floated successfully on the stock market (at one point, it was valued at $7 billion) and it now looks very corporate, features ads for well known bands and the odd MP3 willingly made available by a big name (along with lots of files from unsigned bands). It's moved from being a rallying post for a net subculture to being a sort of online record company in the making.

There has been a lot of idealistic talk around MP3s. Some claim that the unsigned bands using the format are beginning to route around the hated record companies and are showing that you won't need them in the future. This is mostly hokum. Most new bands are using MP3s to create a bit of a buzz in the hope that it will eventually lead to a more conventional record company deal. In addition, downloading an MP3

< 327 >

file still takes a sizeable amount of time – up to half an hour sometimes. Most people aren't willing to waste that kind of time on bands they don't know.

For that reason, perhaps the only artists who will be able to use MP3s and the net to liberate themselves from record companies are big names who already have a sizeable fan base. Long term it might make a sort of sense for the likes of David Bowie (who has also started his own service offering internet access to fans) to cut out the record companies and use the net to deal more directly with his fans. Certainly some smarter big name artists are using MP3 as a way of generating PR. The Beastie Boys made a couple of rare tracks available as MP3 files at their website (**http://www.beastieboys.com**). They've been followed by the likes of Public Enemy and Frank Black formerly of the Pixies.

## Read about it online – The Rio

You now don't have to play MP3s on your computer. There's a new generation of digital music players you can also use. The first to come out was Diamond Multimedia's Rio – for more information, go to **http://www.rioport.com/**. Recently it was joined by Creative Labs' Nomad **http://www.nomadworld.com/products/welcome.html** and Samsung's Yepp **http://yepp.co.kr/eng/**. There are undoubtedly lots more of these on the way – to keep track, try **http://www.mp3.com/ hardware/portables/**. ▲

< 328 >

Though more and more well known artists are making selected tracks available online as MP3s, most of the big name material on the net is there illegally. Obviously I can't give you advice here on how to find it, though it can be a lot harder than some claim. Lots of newspaper stories suggest that it's possible to find and download illegal MP3s in half an hour. If you just want something from the current American top ten, that's perhaps true. If you want to find something more palatable, especially something non-American, get ready for a long search and a lengthy download process.

Incidentally, lots of the sites claiming to have illegal MP3s are advertising scams. Visit them and you'll usually be frustrated. Often the link to the track you want will take you to another page, which features yet more supposed links to the MP3s you want. Crucially, they also feature advertising banners, often for porn web sites. What the people behind these sites want to do is rack up 'page views'. The more people they can persuade to visit their sites, the more page views they get and the more money they can then get from the people who advertise on their sites. This kind of thing upsets a lot of MP3 users (and has led to sites like Pure MP3, which only lists sites which don't feature porn site advertising).

Despite record company attempts to portray all MP3 users as criminals, the majority are, in fact, the music business' core customers. They're hard core music fans. If you talk to them, you find that they don't download MP3s instead of buying CDs. They do both. Nevertheless, the record industry has attempted to introduce more secure formats which let them restrict and track copies. Other companies also

< 329 >

**Read about it online - SDMI**

The American record industry's solution to the MP3 problem is something called the Secure Digital Music Initiative aka SDMI, an attempt to create a standard music format for the net which will enable copyright protection. For more information, try **http://www.sdmi.org**. ▲

offer more secure formats for music online – for example Liquid Audio **http://www.liquidaudio.com**. Big companies like Microsoft and IBM have also pushed their own secure music formats. Some pundits argue that such efforts are pointless, that MP3 has established itself as the online music format of choice and the big companies need to work with it. In fact, AOL recently bought Nullsoft, the company behind Winamp, the most popular MP3 player **http://www.winamp.com**. They also bought Spinner.com **http://www.spinner.com**, one of the biggest 'net radio' sites, so clearly the company sees online music as a crucial area in the future. If you visit some of the big online music shops, you can already buy music downloads – try amazon.com **http://www.amazon.com** or CD Now **http://www.cdnow.com**. Alternatively, try Emusic.com **http://www.emusic.com** (which used to be Good Noise, an independent record label that embraced the MP3 format early on).

With more and more big businesses getting involved with music on the net, some theorists now suggest that MP3 won't ever deliver on the

< 330 >

---

**Read about it online – MP3 news**

The MP3 scene is changing all the time, with new developments announced almost every week. One good place to catch up with what's going on – aside from MP3.com **http://www.mp3.com** – is Wired News, which has a special section devoted to the area at **http://www.wired.com/news/news/mpthree/**. ▲

---

dream of artistic independence. They suggest that it is really a transitional technology, caught between a past when music was a product you owned and a future when it will be a service you subscribe to. According to this theory, 'streaming' is the real future of music online. Punters will access real time feeds of the music they want wherever and whenever (thanks to fast wireless networks). Imagine a kind of ubiquitous personal jukebox. I'm not sure if this will really happen. People still want to feel they 'own' something, even if it's only a file on their computer. But clearly, music and the music business are going to change a lot more over the next few years.

## Radio on the Net

In the States, there's been a lot of interest recently in sites and companies that deliver radio to the net. The idea here is that as you surf, you can also tune into a radio station via something like RealPlayer. Though you can access some real world radio stations via the net, it seems peculiarly point-

< 331 >

less. It is quite interesting to be able to listen to stations on the other side of the world and tune into internet only 'pirate' stations. One of the biggest net radio sites is Spinner.com **http://www.spinner.com**. You need to download the site's own player to get the most out of this but there is a great selection of channels here. Alternatively, you could try Imagine Radio **http://www.imagineradio.com**. Lots of more general music sites offers some sort of net radio. Try SonicNet **http://www.sonicnet.com**, which bills itself as a music network and offers something called Flash Radio (which is apparently 'visual radio' – isn't that TV?). In the same vein, Tunes.com **http://www.tunes.com** has MP3s you can download and something called Rolling Stone Radio (it's linked to the magazine, not the band).

Perhaps more interesting are the sites that aim to give people the technology they need to set up their own net radio stations. Try Shoutcast **http://www.shoutcast.com**, which is owned by AOL or Gogaga **http://www.gogaga.com**. Some techno-enthusiasts see a bright future for net radio, but even those working in the business say that the technology has to develop. According to one net radio company, less than one

---

### Tips – Toolbar Tuner

The new version of Internet Explorer (5.x) has been adapted for the age of net radio. You can display a special radio toolbar which lets you pick a station to listen to while you surf. Select the **View** menu, then **Toolbars**, then **Radio**. ▲

< 332 >

**Read about it online – Pirate Radio**

If you want to try a UK-based online net radio station, try interFace at **http://www.pirate-radio.co.uk**, where you can hear various dance genres after six in the evening. This isn't radio, but it's one of my favourite dance sites online – for real audio files of various UK garage tracks, try DJ SL's page at **http://www.mcs.surrey.ac.uk/Personal/Student/cs61ja/docs/garage.html**. ▲

million people can listen to radio via the net at any one time. If too many tune in, they'll 'max out' the net, apparently. Perhaps we should stick to our trannies.

## Video on the Net

There have been stories recently suggesting that shortly the film industry will be facing the same kinds of problems as the music business. Bootleg copies of popular Hollywood films are beginning to appear on the net – two popular choices over the summer were the SF action film 'The Matrix' and 'The Phantom Menace'. Of course, the files involved are massive, so at the moment this kind of thing is restricted to people with access to high speed networks – i.e. people who work in the net business and some students. But as bandwidth increases and as compression technology improves, there's no reason to believe that this kind of thing won't become more widespread.

< 333 >

---

**Read about it online - Wild Feeds**

Lots of web sites now showcase material from the conventional TV
channels that you're not supposed to see (aka wild feeds). This
covers all sorts of things – politicians picking their noses as they
prepare to be interviewed, outtakes from commercials and the rest.
For a taste, try Wild Feed TV **http://www.wildfeedtv.com**.▲

---

In the meantime, you can check out video on the net. It's still scratchy
and very small screen for most of us, but there are some interesting things
if you look. RealNetworks' RealPlayer can handle streaming video and
the company's showcase page **http://realguide.real.com** has links to
different video sites online. Alternatively, try Broadcast.com **http://www.
broadcast.com**. Plenty of film sites will let you view the trailers for big
Hollywood blockbusters. More interesting are the sites that showcase
small films and the kind of quirky videos that never really find their way
into the traditional media. Try the iFilm network **http://www.ifilm.net/**, the
Bit Screen **http://www.thebitscreen.com/**, The Sync **http://www.thesync.com**,
Atom Films **http://www.atomfilms.com/** and the Digital Entertainment
Network **http://www.den.net/coolnew/homepage.content. html**. The
webzine Salon ran an interesting piece on small films online – you
can find it at **http://www.salon.com/tech/feature/1999/07/21/short_films/
index.html**.

< 334 >

## Shopping on the net

Net analysts love to talk about the billions of bucks net shopping will apparently generate over the next few years. Neo-luddites sniff grumpily and go on about how computers won't ever replace the deep sensual pleasures of shopping in the real world. The truth, as ever, lies somewhere in between the two. Net shopping is becoming more and more popular. Some of the leading online retailers (eg amazon.com **http://www. amazon.com**, eBay **http://www.ebay.com** and eToys **http://www. etoys.com**) are amongst the most valuable companies in the States, thanks to their inflated stock prices. Venture capitalists and money men are rushing to find and fund the next big ecommerce idea. And all sorts of big high street names are now setting up on the net, worried that new online upstarts will eat into their customer base if they don't.

With more and more getting online and trying to make an immediate impact, there have been some incredible stunts over the last few months. In the summer, BOL **http://www.uk.bol.com**, an online bookstore attempting to catch up with amazon.com gave away books from its UK site for two hours. More recently, the big net 'department store' Jungle.com **http://www.jungle.com** gave away £10 million worth of products as part of its launch. Aside from these dramatic giveaways, lots of net shops are heavily discounting best selling stock. If you want to get a chart CD or a best selling novel, chances are you'll now find it cheaper on the net.

However, all the publicity stunts and big numbers can't hide the fact that plenty of people still have a bit of a problem trusting online retailers

< 335 >

enough to make a purchase. I think the security problems are overstated. In general, so long as you take the right precautions (more on this later), it is possible to shop safely and securely on the net. Despite all this, it still takes people a while to get used to the idea. Some surveys suggest that most people spend at least a year getting used to the net before they attempt their first purchase. You can see why. Surfing is one thing. But handing over your money is altogether more serious. So it's not surprising that people take their time. That said, more and more are taking the plunge and shopping online. It seems clear that this will be one of the boom areas on the net over the next few years.

That doesn't mean that shopping on the net will replace real shops. People who claim as much are, as usual, talking rubbish. Most of us enjoy shopping in our favourite real world stores – whether they're bookshops or high fashion boutiques. We're not going to give that up. On the other hand, it is possible to overstate the sensual pleasures of the weekly supermarket shop.

Once you give net shopping a try, you'll realise that it isn't the same thing as real-world shopping. It gives retailers the opportunity to sell in a very different way. Some mistakenly attempt to simulate a real-world environment (from supermarket shelves to shopping malls). The smart online retailers know that graphics aren't the best use of computer power. Go to Amazon **http://www.amazon.com/**, the leading online retailer and check out the books department. You get all the top ten recommendations you might expect. But shoppers are invited to post reviews of books they've bought. And Amazon cross-references its records, so that as you check out a

< 336 >

possible buy you'll see a list of titles also purchased by people who bought the book you're contemplating. And when you go back after making a purchase, you see a list of books bought since by people who also bought the same title as you. You can also get email updates about new titles on subjects you're interested in. The main problem with all this is that it is so effective it becomes very hard not to buy something after a while.

The advantages of online shopping are fairly obvious. It's convenient. It gives you access to a wide range of goods. You can buy American products that often never make it over here or have sold out – books by American authors, hiphop CDs, that hard-to-get Christmas toy. At the moment, even with telephone and shipping charges, net shopping is also pretty cheap. As mentioned above, many online retailers use discounts and giveaways to persuade people to give them a try.

Nevertheless some cynics dismiss net shopping as a version of mail order in which the customer (rather than someone at a call centre) searches through a computerised database and fills out an order form. It's true that at the worse net shops, you're often doing little more than scrolling down a dull list of products ticking things off. But the good online retailers know that the net can deliver much more than mail order.

First of all, there's the huge product range. Print catalogues can only be so big – and the bigger they get, the harder they are to search through. Online you can also get more information about individual products. You can find out whether they're still in stock. You can zoom in for a closer look. You can rotate them to see what they look like at the back. Beyond that, the net can create interactive relationships between buyers

< 337 >

and sellers. Sellers can respond to your demands. Via email, they can let you know when things you want arrive, or update you immediately about sales and special offers.

Net shopping also allows for different sorts of retail models to develop, models in which the customer has a little bit more control and, often, a little bit less hassle. For example, at Autobytel UK **http://www. autobytel.co.uk** you can research which new car to buy, using various sources of information on the site. Then once you've decided on the model you want, you tell Autobytel and they go off and get a low, no-haggle price for you from one of their dealers.

Cars might not seem like the most obvious product when it comes to net shopping. It's true that not all products are suited to online retail.

---

### Read about it online – Fashion online

When it comes to developing new online sales techniques, clothes retailers are at the cutting edge. For a glimpse of what can be done (though you need a new-ish browser, with the Java enabled) try the big fashion sportswear shop Boo.com **http://www.boo.com**, where you can rotate products so that you can see what they look like at the back. Alternatively, try Bras Direct **http://www.brasdirect.com**, where you can preview lingerie on different models, change the colours and zoom in for a better look. (That said, it's unclear whether the latter isn't really aimed at geeky/laddish windows shoppers). ▲

< 338 >

You probably wouldn't want to buy a made to measure designer suit online. But books, CDs, videos and video games another thing entirely. They're portable and you don't need to touch them to know roughly what you're getting. The latter are among the growth areas for net shopping, along with computer hardware and software, travel, financial services and, yes, pornography. Porn doesn't completely dominate net shopping, despite what you may have heard. And other types of product are becoming available all the time – electronic gadgets, clothes and food and drink are all becoming popular.

Once they solve the logistical problems involved, the big supermarkets will become major online players. Both Sainsburys **http://www.sainsburys.co.uk** and Tesco **http://www.tesco.co.uk** are running net shopping trials. Go to the sites and enter your postcode to see if you can get involved. Waitrose is also running a scheme that lets people at work shop online and have their goods delivered to the office before they go home

---

### Tips - Surf and Save Money Offline

You can use to net to save money in the real world. Try Buy.co.uk **http://www.buy.co.uk** where you'll find a set of useful tools which can help you find the cheapest rates for gas, electricity and water in your area. Alternatively, try Price Offers **http://www.priceoffers.co.uk**, where you can find information about current sales and offers at supermarkets and elsewhere. ▲

< 339 >

– for more information, go to **http://www.waitrose.co.uk** and look for the section on Waitrose@Work.

Even if you don't actually buy, the net is great for researching purchases and prices. For example, you can now read some of Which? Magazine's product tests at their website **http://www.which.net**. In addition, classified ads are also coming online. On the net, it's much easier to find an ad for something you want. Then you go ahead and telephone the seller in the usual way. In the UK, many of the major classified ad outlets are online, from the general: Loot **http://www.loot.com** and Exchange and Mart **http://www.exchangeandmart.co.uk**, to the specialist: Autotrader **http://www.autotrader.co.uk**.

---

### Read about it online – The Future of Shopping

Some critics have pointed out that the discounts that come with net shopping are another example of tax breaks for the rich. Whether you worry about social inequality as you play with the half-price laptop you got online is down to you. But clearly, if it takes off on a large scale, net shopping will have massive social effects. For thoughtful speculation on what these might be and some interesting ideas on how the net (with the government's help) might let ordinary people buy and sell, try the Guaranteed Electronic Markets site put up by TV presenter/cyber-pundit Wingham Rowan **http://www.gems.org.uk**. ▲

< 340 >

## Making an Online Purchase

This tends to work in the same way at most online shops. You browse for the product you want, then press a 'Buy' button, which adds the item to your online 'shopping cart'. Once you're ready to pay, you press the 'checkout' button. You go to a page where you enter your details – name, address, credit card number. You also choose a shipping method. The total cost is totted up and you're given an opportunity to confirm the purchase or change your mind. Then it's just a question of waiting for your goods to arrive. Some online retailers mail you to confirm the purchase and will also send an update about your order's progress.

Obviously, security is a worry when shopping on the net. However, as mentioned before, this has more to do with the novelty of the online world and less to do with real risks. Giving your credit card number to someone over the telephone is potentially risky, but most of us do it without thinking. To protect yourself online, first make sure that personal information and credit card details are sent to a secure server. Both Navigator and Internet Explorer are set up for secure transactions (they use something called Secure Sockets Layer (SSL) technology to make sure that important information is encrypted when it is sent over the net).

If you're connected to a secure server, you should see a little graphic of a locked padlock in the bottom left of your browser screen. Some earlier browsers use the image of a key. If it's broken, you aren't on a secure site. You can also check by looking at the address in the browser location bar. If you're on a secure server, the URL should start with **https://**. When you enter, your browser may also flash a dialog box telling

< 341 >

you as much (you'll see another one when you leave). You can also check a site's security status by looking at its security certificate.

▶ In Internet Explorer, select the **File** menu, then **Properties**, then click the **Certificates** button.

▶ In Navigator, press the **Security** button on the toolbar, then click on **Open Page Info** if you want to find out more.

If you are worried about sending details over the net, good online retailers always give you the option of telephoning them in. Don't shop on a site that isn't secure. Don't send personal/credit details by unprotected email. And don't give out any more information than you would with a standard credit-card purchase via the telephone. Incidentally, if you use a credit card, you are protected in various ways against fraud. Many online retailers also offer protection (money-back guarantees and the like), if you can prove that you were the victim of online fraud.

### Tips - Online Retailers

It's worth checking how quickly online retailers process your credit card purchase. Ideally, you want them to do it as soon as possible, the way it happens in most real-world shops. Some online retailers save up their credit card purchases and process them all in one go. This is not ideal. The longer your details are sitting around on someone's computer (or desk), the more vulnerable they are to misuse. ▲

< 342 >

**Tips - Which? Webtrader**

Which? Magazine has recently attempted to boost consumer
confidence in net shopping with its Web Trader scheme, which
offers full legal support and refunds if you have trouble with one of
its approved net traders. You can get more information about the
scheme and a list of approved traders at **http://www.which.net/
webtrader**. ▲

There are a few general precautions you can take when shopping
online. First, check out the retailer. Make sure they have a real-world
address and telephone number. Don't buy from an organisation with just
an email address. Check the refund and return policies before you buy
anything. Ask for confirmation of your order. At the very least, save and
print the order screen when you make your purchase. Use your common
sense. Be suspicious of incredible offers or discounts. It's worth visiting
the pages on online shopping put up by The Office of Fair Trading
**http://www.oft.gov.uk/html/shopping/**. There's some good basic advice,
along with details on your legal rights when you buy on the net from a
UK-based company and what to do if things go wrong.

## Net Shopping in the UK and the US

Britain lags behind America when it comes to shopping on the net. Many
more Americans have made an online purchase. There are many more
US-based sites for them to visit. Of course, American net shops are just

< 343 >

## Tips - Shopping and Privacy

Obviously shopping on the net raises certain privacy issues. An online retailer like Amazon can remember who you are and what you've previously purchased because it creates a little identifying file on your browser – called a cookie. There are benefits to this. Net shops can tell you about special offers in an area you've shown an interest in. But there are problems too. What will they do with your data? Will they sell it to junk emailers? Can you stop them? For more about net shopping and privacy, go to page 405.▲

as accessible to UK surfers. There are lots of reasons to try them out, aside from the greater variety of what's on offer. Many products – books, CDs and computer software and hardware – are a lot cheaper in the States. And often online they're discounted as well. Even when you pay the shipping costs (and the duty – more on this shortly), they are still cheaper than buying at home. That said, not all US sites will sell to overseas visitors. So it's as well to check their policy on this before you start browsing. Look in the customer service/help section for their policies on international shipping.

Shopping overseas requires a little thought. You need to check how much shipping will cost and how long it will take. Some shops attach conditions to international orders (e.g. you have to spend over a certain amount). You need to check whether guarantees apply. You need to check on formats

< 344 >

(US videos use the NTSC format, whereas here we use the PAL format) and sizes (American clothes sizes are different to ours). To keep track of how much you're spending, you could use the Universal Currency Converter **http://www.xe.net/ucc**. Remember that what you pay at the net shop isn't the end of it. You will pay more when your goods enter the country.

There are three basic charges you pay on goods imported into the UK – customs duty, excise duty and VAT. However, there's a whole series of exemptions. You don't pay duty or VAT on books. You don't pay VAT on kid's clothes. You don't pay duty on computers or computer parts. You don't pay duty or VAT if the total value of the goods bought on the net, including shipping costs, is less than £18 (so you might just squeeze in 2 cheap CDs sent rather slowly). But this exemption doesn't apply to tobacco products, alcohol or perfume.

You don't have to pay customs duty on stuff you buy on the net anywhere within the European Union. But you do pay VAT. And if you've

---

### Read about it online – Europe Online

Shopping online overseas doesn't just mean shopping in the States. For a glimpse of net shopping across the channel, try the French shopping directory Achetenligne **http://www.achetenligne.com** – apparently an English translation is on the way. Alternatively, try Europages **http://www.europages.com**, an online directory of European businesses. ▲

< 345 >

bought booze or tobacco products you pay excise duty as well. Incidentally, items that exist in purely digital form that you buy and download on the net are considered as 'services' and hence are exempt from duty. However, they are liable to VAT. But given that the duty/VAT liable on physical goods sometimes goes uncollected, it's hard to see how the law on VAT on electronic goods will be enforced properly for the moment.

VAT is charged at 17.5%. Duty rates vary from product to product. They can go up to 15% of purchase price. There's a useful guide to the rates at the HM Customs & Excise website **http://www.hmce.gove.uk/bus/regions/dutyrates.htm**. It doesn't cover everything – just the most popular products. If something isn't covered on the HM C&E web page, you need to call the Tariff Classification Service on 01702 366077 to get the commodity code for the product you're interested in. Then you have to call HM C&E on 0171 202 4227. You can find detailed information about the whole duty system in Notice 143 – **http://www.hmce.gov.uk/notices/143.htm**. Duty and VAT is supposed to be collected by the Post Office on delivery. They may charge you 'a clearance fee' for this. The Royal Mail charges £1.20, and Parcel Force charges £5.10. However, it does seem that they often don't get round to collecting any of these various charges. If you get something sent by one of the big international courier firms, they may collect the duty/VAT instead (and may charge even more than the Post Office).

When it comes to finding places to shop online in the States, you could try the big American portal web sites. Many offer shopping areas and directories that are worth a look. Try Yahoo **http://shopping.yahoo.**

< 346 >

com or Excite's Shopping Channel **http://www.excite.com/shopping**. Alta Vista has Shopping.com at **http://www.shopping.com**. There are plenty of specialist shopping search sites – try Shopfind **http://www. shopfind.com**, Buyer's Index **http://www.buyersindex.com**, ShopNow **http://www.shopnow.com** and ShopGuide (US) **http://www.shopguide.com**. For a more offbeat directory, try Cool Shopping **http://www. coolshopping.com**. Alternatively, for a more manageable selection of the better known sites, go to Top Ten Links **http://www.toptenlinks.com** and look for the shopping section.

## Shopping online in the UK

The US may be leading the way, but more and more online shops are opening up for business in the UK. Perhaps the easiest way to see what's on offer is to use one of the shopping directories. Or you could try Shop Guide **http://www.shopguide.co.uk**, Enterprise City **http://www. enterprisecity.co.uk**, Shops on the Net **http://www.shopsonthenet.co.uk**, the Shopping area on UK Plus **http:// www.ukplus.co.uk**, My Taxi **http://www. mytaxi.co.uk** or UK Shopping **http://www.ukshopping.com**. Alternatively,

---

### Read about it online – Buying from American Sites

Obviously if you do choose to buy from an American site and experience problems, it will be difficult to sort them out. There are US organisations that monitor commerce on and offline. Try the Better Business Bureau at **http://www.bbb.org/**. ▲

< 347 >

try the shopping areas on some of the big UK portal sites – Zoom is quite good here – **http://www.zoom. co.uk**. However, remember that the sites you see here are the ones who have signed deals with the portals. You're not seeing everything the net has to offer. You could also give some of the UK online shopping malls a look. Try Shoppers Universe **http://www.shoppersuniverse.com**, Home Town **http://www.hometown. co.uk**, ShoppingCentre.net **http://www.shoppingcentre.net**, Barclay Square **http://www.barclaysquare.com** or eDirectory **http://www.edirectory.co.uk**.

Here's a quick list of some of the leading contenders in the most popular online sales categories.

### BOOKS
Amazon.co.uk **http://www.amazon.co.uk**
BOL.Com **http://www.uk.bol.com**
Alphabet Street **http://www.alphabetstreet.co.uk**
Internet Bookshop **http://www.bookshop.co.uk**

### CDS AND VIDEOS
101CD **http://www.101cd.com/**
Yalplay **http://www.yalplay.com**
CD Paradise **http://www.cdparadise.com/**
Audio Street **http://www.audiostreet.co.uk/**
Blackstar **http://www.blackstar.co.uk/**
Film World **http://www.filmworld.co.uk/**

< 348 >

## COMPUTER SOFTWARE AND GAMES

Software Warehouse **http://www.software-warehouse.co.uk**
Special Reserve **http://www.reserve.co.uk**
URWired **http://www.urwired.com**
Software Paradise **http://www.softwareparadise.co.uk**
Gameplay **http://www.gameplay.com**
Games Street **http://www.gamesstreet.com**

## COMPUTER HARDWARE

Dell **http://www.dell.co.uk**
Gateway 2000 **http://uk.gw2k.com**
Apple **http://www.apple.com/ukstore**
Technomatic **http://www.technomatic.co.uk**
Dabs Direct **http://www.dabs.com/**
21 Store **http://www.21store.com/**

---

### Tips - Read the book, visit the site

This is only a small fragment of what's available online. For lots more tips on shopping on the net and an extensive directory of sites and shops, have a look at my other net guide, 'The Guardian Guide to Shopping on the Internet', which is also published by Fourth Estate. Or visit its companion website **http://www.shoppingunlimited.co.uk**. ▲

< 349 >

**TRAVEL**
A2B Travel **http://www.a2btravel.com**
Bargain Holidays **http://www.bargainholidays.com**
Last Minute **http://www.lastminute.com**
Expedia **http://www.expedia.msn.co.uk**
Travelocity **http://www.travelocity.co.uk**

## Shopping Bots

There are various search tools – usually referred to as shopping bots – which you can use online to do price comparisons so that you can find the lowest price for a particular item. Techno-gurus see a bright future for shopping bots. They think that in the future they will go online, interact with the bots run by shops, buy items and arrange shipping all by themselves, leaving us free to get on with our lives. That's a long way off yet. However, price comparison is available now and is worth looking into. Shop Guide **http://www.shopguide.co.uk** has a bot called Bargain Finder, which will research prices on books, videos and CDs. Alternatively, try Best Deals, on My Taxi **http://www.mytaxi.com** (the technology is actually provided by Bottom Dollar, a well known US shop bot). Also worth a look is Acses **http://www.acses.com**, which searches a larger range of shops for prices on videos.

There are a couple of things to look out for with shopping bots. First, check on the number of shops they search. Sometimes, the sites behind the bots have deals with certain retailers and only search those pages, missing out competitors that are a lot cheaper. Second, check whether the

< 350 >

### Tips – Price isn't everything

Shop around for a good price but don't spend too much time on it
An evening spent staring at a computer trying to save a couple of
pounds here and there is probably an evening that could have been
spent doing something more interesting. ▲

price served up by the bot includes shipping. If it doesn't then the results
may be misleading – lots of sites are currently offering free delivery.
Sometimes, it pays to hunt around on your own after you've done a price
search with a shopping bot, just to see what else is out there. If you want
to try some American shopping bots, which search a lot more sites, try
MySimon **http://www.mysimon.com**, Price Scan **http://www.pricescan.com**,
Deal Time **http://www.dealtime.com**, Bottom Dollar **http://www.
bottomdollar.com** or RoboShopper **http://www.roboshopper.com**.

## Online Auctions

In the last year or so, buying (and selling) at online auctions has become
one of the most popular activities on the net. For proof, log on to eBay
**http://www.ebay.com**, the place where it all got started (the UK end is at
**http://www.ebay.co.uk**). You'll see millions of auctions in progress – individuals selling everything from remaindered computer parts and their old
record collections to modern day collectibles like 'Star Wars' and Beanie
Babies to other individuals all round the world. Imagine a global car

< 351 >

boot sale and you come close to understanding what's going on here.

Where once journalists used to write about the net, they now write about eBay. There are plenty of confessions of auction addiction. There are tales of the crazy things for sale on eBay – guns, drugs, companies and people. There are warnings about the scams and cons at eBay and other online auctions. There are interviews with people who run businesses via the site, selling collectibles round the world. Indeed, now eBay is so big, when it has a technical problem and goes offline, it's news. Perhaps the biggest eBay story – it even made the press here – concerned the 13 year old who managed to spend several million dollars on his mother's credit card whilst on a eBay spree. On the way he bought an antique bed used by the first governor of Canada and bid on a medical centre and a Viking long boat.

Unsurprisingly, eBay's success has brought competition from big net names. Both Yahoo and Amazon.com now run their own auctions. The best known online auction site here is QXL **http://www.qxl.com** who

---

### Read about it online - The eBay underground FAQ

eBay does a good job of providing information for beginners, but if you want to get the inside dope on how things really work, try this collection of 'the things eBay doesn't tell you'. There's also some good links to other eBay fan sites – find it all at **http://www.frii.com/ ~afs/ebay/**. ▲

< 352 >

started out selling refurbished computers and now take in travel, holidays, sports gear and much else, as well as running an eBay style operation called QXL Exchange. They've been joined by other companies – try Auction Hunter **http://www.auctionhunter.co.uk** or eBid **http://www.ebid.co.uk.** Even Loot now has its own auctions at **http://www.loot.com.**

It's easy to see why net auctions have become so popular. They do the thing the net was always supposed to do – they allow people with similar interests to pursue those interests together. At their best, they do create genuine communities. More than all this, though, online auctions are fun. Seeing the incredible prices at the start of auctions, you can't help but be drawn in. And because online auctions are time-limited, you hang around to see what happens, to see if that laptop is still going for £200. You can't help it. And you want to join in.

In online auctions, you can either buy direct from the site hosting the sale or from another individual. Bids are sent in via the net and auctions are time-limited, In other words, products go the person who gets the

---

### Read about it online – Auction search sites

Bidfind **http://www.bidfind.com** is an auction search engine that covers around 300 different auctions worldwide. You enter the name of something you want to buy and it finds auctions that have that thing currently up for sale. I wouldn't try a search on Beanie babies though. ▲

< 353 >

**Tips - Escrow services**

If you're buying from an individual on an auction site, think about using an escrow service. QXL Exchange **http://exchange.qxl.com** has set one up. Here the buyer pays by credit card into a special 'escrow account'. QXL tells the seller that the money is there. It stays there until the buyer gets the goods. Once the buyer confirms that the goods have arrived, the money is released to the seller. ▲

highest bid in before the deadline. Often people try to wait until the last minute and things can get a bit hectic. There are other more complicated auctions – for instance the Dutch auction. This is a way of selling multiple identical items – 15 videos, say. The seller sets a minimum price and the number of items available. Bidders bid at or above that minimum for the quantity they are interested in purchasing. At the close of the auction, the highest bidders purchase the items at the lowest successful bid.

You should take a few precautions when buying at an auction site. Check on exactly what you're buying. That super-cheap computer is more than likely refurbished (i.e. second hand) or end of the line stock. If you're buying from an individual, check on their past performance. EBay and QXL post reports on sellers from previous buyers, so you can see how they behaved, whether the goods were sent on time and much else. Find out what the item you're bidding on is actually worth in the real world. Of course, auctions specialise in items that are hard to price

< 354 >

exactly. So you'll need to do some hard thinking about what the thing is actually worth to you. Then set a price you're willing to pay and stick to it. It's very easy to get carried away at online auctions and end up paying way over the odds (that's why sellers like them, despite those apparently low prices).

## Future Shop

In America, lots of new online retail ideas are being tried out and they're sure to find their way over here soon. So look out for the reverse auction idea pioneered by Priceline **http://www.priceline.com**. Here, customers say what they want to pay for a certain item, and retailers see if they can cope with that price. Respond.com **http://www.respond.com** offers something similar. You tell them what you want, and they get in touch with various retailers who then get in touch with you with offers and deals. The sellers don't know who they're sending offers to i.e. they don't know your email address or other contact details, until you choose to respond to an offer.

A more basic form of retail is available at 'zero margin' shops. These sell items at cost and hope to make money via advertising. The best known is Buy.com **http://www.buy.com**, which does have some incredible prices. At the moment it doesn't sell to overseas users. But it is apparently planning to come over here. Good prices are also on offer at so-called 'we commerce' sites. Here people club together to buy things. The more people sign up to buy a particular item, the more the price falls. Two American sites attempting this are Accompany **http://www.accompany.**

< 355 >

**com** and Mercata **http://www.mercata.com**. The Swedish site Let's Buy It **http://www.letsbuyit.com** is apparently going to bring the idea over here.

Affiliate marketing is very big on the net. This turns everyone into a potential online shopkeeper. Say you put up a site that reviews books. You can put a link on your site to the page on Amazon where people can buy a book you've reviewed. If someone does, you get a small cut from the sale. Now sites are appearing in the States which set out to get those commissions and give them back to the customer – for more try Ebates **http://www.ebates.com**. Another popular idea in the States is inviting ordinary people to review shops – one site trying this is Epinions **http://www.epinions.com**.

One thing that still hasn't really taken off is electronic currency. Early enthusiasts for net shopping claimed that soon we would be doing it with special electronic currencies that would protect our privacy and enable all sorts of micro payments which would eventually build up into a thriving info-economy. E-cash and micro payments have yet to take the world by storm, for various reasons. First, it's a difficult thing to pull off technically, before you tackle the real problem of building trust in it. Second, we already have a kind of secure electronic currency we trust – our credit cards. Third, people can't be bothered with such small purchases. As one net theorist put it, do you want to be nickel-and-dimed to death?

However, some loyalty points schemes (which are currently very big in online retail) sell themselves as electronic currencies in the making. Have a look at Beenz **http://www.beenz.com** and try to decide whether or

< 356 >

---

**Tips – Take it slow**

One crucial tip as far as net shopping is concerned – slow down. Net shops remove a lot of the barriers that often slow us down in the real world. Fine, you say. Isn't that the point? Yes, but sometimes, time spent in a queue, time spent hauling your purchase to the checkout, allows time for reflection and you decide not to buy. The net allows a new kind of hair-trigger impulse buying. See it, want it, buy it. Point. Click. Shop – as someone's net shopping ad campaign says. Sometimes it pays to wait, hang back a bit and think whether you really want something. ▲

---

not they're a prototype form of electronic cash or just the Green Shield stamps of the net. E-cash may not have happened yet, but more conventional banks are now online and will let you manage your real world money via the net. Try Barclays **http://www.barclays.co.uk** for an idea of what you can do. Many of the big high street banks now offer a similar service. The insurance business is also moving online. For a glimpse of what's on offer, try Screentrade **http://www.screentrade.com**, which lets you compare quotes and buy travel, home and car policies online.

## Next Step

It may bring lots of benefits, but online shopping does raise concerns over privacy online. If you want to find out more, go to the next section.

< 357 >

## The Essential Clicks

Net guides and manuals usually find space for long directories of interesting places to go. These can be pretty useful, but they're not without problems. By the time you sit down to read the book, more than a few of the links can be out of date. Sure, general guides tell you what's out there. But they can never really be a match for online directories. And I'm not sure how much people really use them. Perhaps they pick out a few categories and try the links. But pretty soon, if there's something they're interested in, if they've got any sense they'll get online and search for sites themselves.

This book takes a slightly different approach. The following isn't supposed to be a comprehensive listing. It features one hundred sites and there are millions online. The idea behind this book has been to give you the skills you need to find the information you want on the net. We've now got to a stage where everything that happens in the real world is represented in some way online. If you're interested in something – gardening, sailing, fashion – it's there on the net. Just go and look. That said, there are some things online, a net culture, that you wouldn't know about unless somebody told you. And there are some sites that are so useful or entertaining, you can't afford to miss them.

So it seems useful to put these into a list. The resulting Essential Clicks are strongly tilted towards net culture. There are a few sites here that I particularly like but which may leave you cold. However, there are also plenty of sites you'll find yourself returning to on a regular basis. Think of this as a kind of Favourites/Bookmarks starter pack. As ever with the net, feel free to edit and add your own.

< 358 >

## Guardian Unlimited

Before I start plugging other people's sites, allow me a moment to talk about The Guardian's own pages on the web. Launched earlier this year, Guardian Unlimited has been designed as a diverse but linked network of sites – News Unlimited, Film Unlimited, Football Unlimited, Cricket Unlimited, Jobs Unlimited, Work Unlimited, Shopping Unlimited and Education Unlimited. The various projects build on and extend specific sections of the paper. But they also can stand on their own, as destinations in their own right, something you might find useful and entertaining even if you don't read The Guardian.

I think this is a clever idea and seems part of the general aim to give people more than just a newspaper online. Techno-types often insist that old media organisations don't get the net. They accuse them of 'shovelware' – simply dumping the material that works in print onto the net and expecting it to work just as well. Actually, I think the problems of 'shovelware' can be overstated. Sometimes it can be just what you want. If I've been away for a few days, it's rather nice to get online and check out what's been in the paper and catch up with favourite columnists (something the News Unlimited site makes very easy).

That said, The Guardian sites do supplement what's in the print edition very well. On News Unlimited, stories come with extra material and links to other sources and documents online. Online you also get Guardian Eye, a smartly written take on the day's top story from Derek Brown, which also comes with lots of useful links. The sports sites are packed with statistics and extra material from partners like Wisden and

< 359 >

When Saturday Comes. The award-winning Film Unlimited pulls together all the film stories from The Guardian and The Observer, but it also pulls down material from film sites on the rest of the web and has a useful search tool that lets you find out what's showing near you.

Along with its tales from the office frontline, Work Unlimited has some fun games – for example an IQ test that lets you see if you're earning a salary commensurate with your brainpower. Education Unlimited has a terrific set of links to resources online that parents and teachers will find useful. Jobs Unlimited lets you set up tailored searches that track only the kinds of job ads you're interested. OK, I'm biased. I read The Guardian and I do the odd bit of work for them too. But I think all the sites have something going for them (though I particularly like Film, Work and Education). Plus they look good too (they've picked up awards for their design). Some people still seem to think that isn't important. But once you've spent some time online, especially at other newspaper sites, you'll appreciate how important a clear user-friendly net-wise look and feel really is.

The Guardian Unlimited **http://www.guardianunlimited.co.uk**
News Unlimited **http://www.newsunlimited.co.uk**
Football Unlimited **http://www.footballunlimited.co.uk**
Cricket Unlimited **http://www.cricketunlimited.co.uk**
Film Unlimited **http://www.filmunlimited.co.uk**
Education Unlimited **http://www.educationunlimited.co.uk**
Jobs Unlimited **http://www.jobsunlimited.co.uk**

< 360 >

Work Unlimited **http://www.workunlimited.co.uk**
Shopping Unlimited **http://www.shoppingunlimited.co.uk**

## THE ESSENTIAL CLICKS
## SEARCH

Yahoo – **http://www.yahoo.com** Now packed with all sorts of add-on services (from chat and free mail to shopping) but still the leading general net directory.

AltaVista – **http://altavista.com** An excellent search engine, which seemed to be falling behind last year but has come back strong and is still one of the best.

Google – **http://www.google.com** One of the new contenders in the search site business – by using the descriptions of sites created by people who link to those sites, this search engine aims to deliver more relevant results and is pretty good.

Deja News – **http://www.dejanews.com** This used to be a brilliant Usenet archive site. It's been revamped as a more business friendly 'community' resource and the new design makes it hard to use the archives that originally made it worthwhile. But it's still worth persevering with, just.

Liszt – **http://www.liszt.com** Looking for a mailing list on a particular subject? This is the site you need. It was recently bought by Topica, one of the companies that have taken mailing lists on to the web, so it may start looking a little slicker fairly soon.

The WebCrawler Search Ticker – **http://webcrawler.com/SearchTicker.html**

< 361 >

Voyeurism reconfigured for the net. Lots of search sites now give you the chance to see what other people are searching. This was one of the first. Harmless fun, sort of.

About.com – **http://www.about.com** Formerly The Mining Company, this search site continues its policy of supplementing technology with various human 'guides' who cover a variety of subjects and point you in all sorts of interesting directions.

## RESEARCH

Scoot – **http://www.scoot.co.uk** Brilliant research tool that lets you track businesses, people, products and films. Results are served up quickly and in a very legible form. Essential.

Research-It – **http://www.itools.com/research-it/research-it.html** A research and reference tool that lets you search all sorts of dictionaries, use currency converters, delve into map databases and much else, all on the one page.

Learn2com – **http://www.learn2.com** Don't know how to carve a turkey, make a compost heap or tie your bow tie? Come here for useful tutorials (2Torials as they put it) on just about everything.

## SOFTWARE

Download.com – **http://www.download.com** Huge software warehouse site maintained by the computer information network CNet. Along with links to software, this has reviews, recommendations, news and charts showing what's currently being downloaded.

< 362 >

Stroud's Consummate Winsock Applications – **http://cws.internet.com**
Yet another software warehouse. If Download.com feels too overwhelming, try the more focused selections at Stroud's.

## CULTURE

Irational – **http://www.irational.org**  For some British net art/wind-ups, try
this site maintained by techno-artist/provocateur/prankster Heath
Bunting with links to his various online art escapades, from the
Internet Beggar and online graffiti to net pirate radio and biotech
hobbyism.

Po Bronson – **http://www.pobronson.com**  Most print world writers leave
the net to their publishers' press department. Po Bronson (author of
high-finance satire Bombadiers and Silicon Valley comedy The First
$20 Million is Always the Hardest) just gets on with things himself.
Lots of bits and pieces relating to 'The Nudist on the Late Shift', his
recent non-fiction book about Silicon Valley, along with links to
interviews, his journalism and other bits and pieces.

Levity – **http://www.levity.com**  Excellent selection of links to post-sixties
boho literature, which means everything from the official avant-
garde of Burroughs and Acker to psychedelic rambling from the likes
of Terence McKenna. Luckily, there's space in between for cyberpunk
authors like William Gibson and technocult critics like Mark Dery
and Erik Davis.

Arts And Literature Daily – **http://www.cybereditions.com/aldaily/**  A useful
collection of links to the more cultured pieces of writing on art, liter-

< 363 >

ature and politics on the web. Updated every day, so it's worth checking in regularly.

The 24 Hour Museum – **http://www.24hourmuseums.org.uk** A listings page for over 2000 of the UK's museums and galleries. Check in here for news and the latest information on exhibitions.

## FILM

Dark Horizons – **http://www.darkhorizons.com** Yet another excellent film gossip/news site – this one has the edge on the much praised Ain't It Cool News, if only because it's less messy and better written.

Popcorn – **http://www.popcorn.co.uk** Carlton Online's film site has everything you need – news and gossip, links to new trailers you can watch on the net and a searchable film listings for the whole country.

Jeeem's Cinepad – **http://www.cinepad.com** Billed as a 'cyber hangout for passionate movie lover', this mixes fannish intensity with buff-ish learning as it ponders Frank Sinatra, film noir, recent releases and even Microsoft.

The Blair Witch Project – **http://www.blairwitch.com** The scariest horror film of recent times was a sensation online before it came out – thanks to this site, which spread all sorts of material relating to the central film and set off a 'Phantom Menace'-style movement of fans sites that did the film's marketing for it.

Internet Movie Database – **http://uk.imdb.com** One of the great net resources – put together and consulted by the film fans of the world. Obsessively detailed databases about any film you might care to wonder about.

< 364 >

Mr Showbiz – **http://www.mrshowbiz.com** Celebrity gossip. All the usual tabloid fare. Lots of fun.

The Astounding B Monster – **http://www.bmonster.com** Less fanzine, more research tool, Marty Baumann's site is the place to come to tap into B movie culture and history.

## MUSIC

Spinner.com – **http://www.spinner.com** An internet music service, no less. Recently acquired by AOL, this is a great place to check out streaming audio online – everything from drum and bass and R&B to classical and bluegrass.

Ultimate Band List – **http://www.ubl.com** Though a bit biased towards American artists and tastes, this is still a great place to find out more about your favourite bands online – the search service is good at finding fan web sites.

MP3.com – **http://www.mp3.com** The place to come to download music uploaded by unknown hopefuls or just catch the latest news on MP3s.

## GAMES

Gamespot – **http://www.gamespot.co.uk** British version of an excellent computer/video games site, with news, reviews, demo downloads, tips and much else.

Yahoo Games – **http://play.yahoo.com** There are now plenty of sites using Java apps to let you play trad games (poker, backgammon, chess and the like) with punters from around the world. Typically, Yahoo's

< 365 >

effort makes it all very easy and accessible. For a similar British game site, try Jamba **http://www.jamba.co.uk**.

Classic Gaming – **http://www.classicgaming.com** Retro games, as in old video games, are very big online with fans trading ideas and emulators that let you play old faves on your new PC. This is a good way into the scene.

## NEWS AND WEATHER

BBC News Online – **http://news.bbc.co.uk** One part of the Beeb's online operation. An excellent news site.

Press Association – **http://www.pa.press.net** Go to the place where the hacks go to get their stories. Another impressive news site.

Out There News – **http://www.megastories.com** An interesting, award winning site which tries to broaden the conventional focus of the conventional news media, covering global stories in more depth that usual. Check out the excerpts from the North Korean news agency while you're here.

Institute of War and Peace Reporting – **http://www.iwpr.net/** An excellent site that provided a ground level view of the Kosovo crisis and continues to reflect the experiences of ordinary people caught up in the turmoil in the Balkans.

Met Office – **http://www.meto.govt.uk/** Get your forecasts from the people who are supposed to know, along with features on how they do it and lots of links.

< 366 >

## COMPUTERS AND TECHNOLOGY

C/Net – **http://www.cnet.com**  A monster site which can tell you just about everything you need to know about computers. News.com is the place to catch breaking technology news, but elsewhere you'll find information on getting started online, software reviews and much else. Indispensable.

Wired News – **http://www.wired.com**  An excellent technology news site, updated daily, featuring sections on culture, technology, business and politics. Less bogged down by press-release details and with more analysis than the competition.

Tasty Bits from the Technology Front – **http://www.tbtf.com**  Highly digestible alternative to big tech/net news sites – a quirky selection of technology news culled from a variety of online sources.

Need To Know – **http://www.ntk.net**  A sarcastic British digest of the week's technology/net news, plus updates on geek culture, brilliant tips on web pages to check out, a rundown on the week's media for geeks and a fair few laughs. Sign up to get this in your mailing box every Friday. Otherwise, drop in at the website every week.

## WEBZINES

Salon – **http://www.salon.com**  The most dependable of the attempts to bring a New Yorker-style, intelligent, general-interest mag to the net. Updated daily, this has great news and media coverage, good travel writing and much else. The technology section is excellent.

Urban 75 – **http://www.urban75.com**  British webzine covering all strands of alternative culture, from direct action and road protesting to

< 367 >

outdoor raves. It used to featur the infamous Slap a Spice game, where you could interactively take it out on Scary, Sporty and the rest. For more of the same, try Schnews **http://www.schnews.org.uk**.

The Drudge Report – **http://www.drudgereport.com** This daily dose of Washington gossip and planted 'scoops' has had more impact on mainstream culture than most web sites (it broke the Zippergate story, sort of). And parasitic, right-wing info-junkie Drudge himself is some sort of symbol of the age.

The Drudge Retort – **http://www.drudge.com** An answer site to Matt Drudge's rants. Niftily using an address close to its target, this site parodies the Drudge Report's daily shots of gossip and has a brilliant list of links to left-leaning sites online.

McSweeneys – **http://www.mcsweeneys.net** The super smart, deliberately low tech online presence of the offbeat satirical zine from David Eggers, former editor of much loved twentynothing magazine Might.

The Onion – **http://www.theonion.com** One of the most reliably funny comedy sites. Takes a favourite net joke genre – the spoof press release – to another level with its selection of news stories that sound as if they ought to be true. Much ripped off but rarely bettered.

The Obscure Store – **http://www.obscurestore.com** Jim Romanesko's 'daily news zine' puts together links to all sorts of interesting stories from the US media and showcases some of his own writing. There are also useful links to US media sites and an online shop packed with excellent zines as well. A truly wonderful site. Look out for his Media Gossip site too **http://www.mediagossip.com**.

< 368 >

The Obvious – **http://www.theobvious.com** Michael Sippey's zine specialises in thoughtful speculation on digital tech. It went a bit quiet last year but has come back with a new design and all sorts of interesting discussion forums.

Feed – **http://www.feedmag.com** Yet another excellent American webzine, covering pop culture and techno-culture. This one retains a commitment to words and links rather than flashy animations. Look out for the special issues, in which one theme gets picked over in great detail – the recent special on Computer Games was excellent.

Suck – **http://www.suck.com** Almost an institution now and, like all comic institutions, deemed to be not quite as funny as it used to be. Suck fires a daily blast of vitriolic analysis and wordy spleen at the big, soft target that is the net. Still funny.

## SPORT

Football365 – **http://www.football365.co.uk** Probably the best football site on the web at the moment – certainly the one that aims to stay closest to ordinary fans – look out for the email forum where you can read the thoughts of Man U haters from all round the world.

Cric Info – **http://www-uk.cricket.org** This is a great site. News, scores and opinion from all round the world.

Scrum.com – **http://www.scrum.com** The place to come for all your rugby news online – everything from club and international games to women's rugby.

< 369 >

Sneaker Nation – **http://www.sneaker-nation.com** OK – so this isn't exactly a sports site –more sport related, sort of. A great place to come to catch up with the latest on sneaker, trainers and the rest – look out for some good shopping links. For something similar try Sneaker Central **http://www.sneakercentral.com**.

## TRAVEL

A2B Travel – **http://www.a2btravel.com** A sizeable, UK-slanted travel resource from Emap Online. You'll find everything you need here, details cheap flights and holidays, guides to airports, information on ferry times and prices, maps and currency converters and much else. Very useful.

Railtrack – **http://www.railtrack.co.uk** Access the train information you need in a fraction of the time it takes to call the telephone timetable. Look out for The Train Line **http://www. thetrainline.co.uk** where you can book train tickets too.

Expedia – **http://www.expedia.co.uk** Microsoft's monster travel site is another excellent place to come to research and book journeys and holidays. Look out for the comparison tools that let you compare flights.

UpMyStreet.com – **http://www.upmystreet.com** Enter your post code here and get the latest data on property prices, crime rates, schools and much else. Weirdly compelling.

Multimap.com – **http://www.multimap.com** Enter the name of the British town you're going to, or the street and get a map of the area you can print out. Look out for the feature which calls up related web sites.

< 370 >

AA – Where to Stay, Where to Eat – **http://www.theaa.co.uk/hotels/index.asp**
Useful site which lets you search the AA's reviews database for details
on UK hotels and restaurants in the region you're travelling to.

## SHOPPING

Shop Guide – **http://www.shopguide.co.uk** Useful UK online shopping
directory, which has links to UK net shops and helpful reviews and
recently introduced Bargain Finder, which lets you search for the best
price on books, videos and CDs. For something similar and just as
good, try Enterprise City **http://www.enterprisecity.co.uk**.

Bull Electrical – **http://www.bull-electrical.com** Online heaven for those
who like to build their own radios/computers. Get your components
here along with some very odd end-of-the-line techno-toys. Fancy
some solar panels or a tank laser? Check in here.

The MoMA Store – **http://store.moma.org** New York's Museum of Modern
Art very own online shop – get furniture, lighting, kids toys, clocks and
much else here, all done by big name designers – Le Corbusier, Philippe
Starck, Tibor Kalman and numerous others.

Archie McPhee – **http://www.mcphee.com** A wonderful online store
packed with joke shop junk, kitsch and all round good stuff. Choose
from Martian Popping Things, potato guns, Pez dispensers, the
Bolshevik Vertical Snackbox and much else.

Last Minute – **http://www.lastminute.com** An excellent British site that
started out offering last minute bargains on hotels and flights but has
now expanded its central concept – buy stuff at the last minute, give

< 371 >

yourself a break etc – into other areas and now also offers tickets for nights out, gifts, auctions and services.

Toysmart – **http://www.toysmart.net** Excellent US toy site specialising in more educational toys. Delivery can be expensive but there are some great toys here.

Ebay – **http://www.ebay.com** The open access online auction/global car boot sale where you can buy everything and anything, from computers and CDs to rare 'Star Wars' toys. Worth a visit, even if you aren't in a buying mood, just to see what people are trying to sell.

The Teddington Cheese – **http://www.teddingtoncheese.co.uk** A strangely wonderful online cheese shop. Get your Camembert and Cheddar here, along with crackers and chutneys and, if you're really, join the cheese lovers club.

## NET CULTURE

Urban Legends Archive – **http://www.urbanlegends.com** The web archive of the newsgroup devoted to logging and debunking urban legends. The place for all those stories about strange things in your burgers, ghostly hitchhikers and the extra apparently shown hanging himself in The Wizard of Oz.

The Smoking Gun – **http://www.thesmokinggun.com** The web is packed with conspiracy sites which claim to have the truth. This offers something both odder and more 'real'. You can view actual documents relating to celebrity crimes and cover-ups – i.e. the police reports on Janet Jackson's stalker, Neve Campbell's divorce documents – it's all here. For more true crime online, try APB Online **http://www. apbonline.com**.

< 372 >

Disinformation – **http://www.disinfo.com/** The website of choice for people looking for the 'hidden information' that 'falls through the cracks of the corporate-owned media conglomerates'. Come here to find out about apocalypse culture, conspiracy theories, weird science and much else.

Driveways of the Rich and Famous – **http://www.driveways.com** The website of a public access cable TV show which does what it says in the title and hangs around outside the homes of B list celebs and talks to their gardeners and next door neighbours.

Top Secret Recipes – **http://www.topsecretrecipes.com/** Ever wanted to cook up some Kentucky Fried Chicken at home, or whip up your very own Mickey D milkshake. Come to Todd Wilbur's website – the online companion to his recipe books for tips and advice.

The Darwin Awards – **http://www.officialdarwinawards.com/** Something of a net landmark now – this site hands out awards for those who have managed to end their lives in the stupidest way possible. It also dispels some of the urban myths around the subject too.

Memepool – **http://www.memepool.com** A regularly updated page of links to interesting stories and sites on the net, complete with little reviews. Very useful.

JenniCam – **http://www.jennicam.org** A camera placed in Jenny's bedroom and hooked up to the net so that everyone can see what she gets up to, twenty-four hours a day. Yes, she sometimes takes her clothes off. Net voyeurism or online happening/ performance art? For yet more webcams, try The Webcam Resource **http://www.webcamresource.com/**

< 373 >

Carl Steadman – **http://www.freedonia.com** The homepage maintained by the net celeb who co-founded the webzine Suck. This has links to his multiple online projects, wind-ups, parodies and an ongoing diary.

Ghost Sites of the Web – **http://www.disobey.com/ghostsites/** Steve Baldwin's excellent listings site tracks ghost web sites, sites that are online but show no signs of life, haven't been updated in months or years and are hence like time capsules from an earlier era. Web history on the hoof.

The Useless Pages – **http://www.go2net.com/internet/useless/** This collection of links to incredibly stupid or pointless web pages has been given a corporate redesign, which makes its sniggering at silly pages put up by ordinary idiots feel a little queasy. Still strangely compelling.

The Fray – **http://www.fray.com** As in the real world, personal confessional is thriving online, in various forms. Your own homepage is the perfect place to vent your feelings. Take this much-praised site, which has great design and personal pieces by creator Derek Powazek and his friends on everything from work to drugs.

The Bot Spot – **http://www.botspot.com** The net is packed with lots of small automated programs beavering away doing searches for us. This site delves into the world of bots, covering search bots, shopping bots, chatterbots, auction bots, update bots and much else.

Edge – **http://www.edge.org** Site hosted by power agent John Brockman, who scores techno-gurus and celeb scientists their big book deals. In return, they turn up here to ponder all sorts of interesting questions. Always interesting.

< 374 >

## WOMEN

iVillage – **http://www.ivillage.com** Vast portal site aimed at thirtysomething
women online. A mix of different women's resources (from parenting
info and financial tips to links to software to help you work from
home), plus message boards, chat rooms and an unpatronising tone.
For something similar, try Women.com **http://www.women.com**.

WWWomen – **http://www.wwwomen.com/** Useful search site that
specialises in women's resources online. Aside from the search engine
and directory, there are discussion forums here too.

## KIDS

Yahooligans – **http://www.yahooligans.com** Typically dependable set of
links to kid-centred sites, along with advice and all the usual commu-
nity-building extras.

Bonus – **http://www.bonus.com** Enjoyable site packed with kids' games,
some educational, some just for fun. Very bright and very American.
You need to register and you also need a reasonably speedy computer.

Disney.com **http://disney.go.com** If you're a parent, you know that resis-
tance if futile. Typically bright and busy site packed with activities
built around the films, videos and TV shows.

BBC Schools Online – **http://www.bbc.co.uk/education/schools/index.shtml**
Excellent site from the Beeb which has various learning resources for
primary and secondary school kids and also has a useful home
learning section for parents who want to help out with homework.

GCSE Answers – **http://www.gcse.com** Parents may be a little worried

< 375 >

about sites where kids can do their homework by buying ready-made school essays and papers. This is an altogether more responsible operation, offering revision tips and tutorials for English and Maths GCSEs. For a more general homework aid, try the Homework Lizard **http://www.chilias.sunderland.ac.uk/homework/reference.htm**.

Babyworld – **http://www.babyworld.co.uk** Useful site packed with information on pregnancy and babies. There's a useful online shop too, with links to product reviews and buying guides.

## POLITICS/NET POLITICS

McSpotlight – **http://www.mcspotlight.org** Direct action online – sort of. Set up during the McLibel trial, this is still arguing the case against McDonald's and multinationals in general.

Cyber Rights and Cyber Liberties – **http://www.cyber-rights.org** Yaman Akdeniz's excellent site points you towards everything you need to know about privacy and censorship on the net in the UK.

Junkbusters – **http://www.junkbusters.com** Exhaustive, slightly exhausting but still brilliantly useful site aimed at helping you rid your life of all forms of unwanted junk communication, from spam and junk snail mail to web ads and those late-evening telephone sales calls.

Consumer Project on Technology – **http://www.cptech.org** Imagine a highbrow Watchdog for the digital age and you get the gist of this site put up by James Love and Ralph Nader – information on anti-trust actions against Microsoft, biotechnology, pharmaceutical companies and intellectual property, amongst other things.

< 376 >

Lawrence Lessig – **http://cyber.law.harvard.edu/lessig.html** A lawyer who has taken a special interest in the net, Lessig writes columns for webzines and longer more academic essays on privacy, spam and censorship online – all of which you can find here.

## WORK/MONEY/LIFE

Top Jobs on the Net – **http://www.topjobs.co.uk** Fancy changing that nine to five grind – check one of the better job ad sites on the net.

Guru – **http://www.guru.com** If you're working for yourself, come here for lots of advice on how to manage your own career – from making the most of your time to hacking the media and much else. For more of the same try Free Agent Nation **http://www.freeagentnation.com/**.

Disgruntled – **http://www.disgruntled.com** If the previous sites seem a tad upbeat, check in here. A webzine for all those who want to sound off about work or find out about their rights. For more of the same, try Net Slaves **http://www.disobey.com/netslaves/**.

Buy.co.uk – **http://www.buy.co.uk** Come here to use the simple calculators to find out if you're being overcharged for your gas, electric and water. There's also a useful reminder service which sends email when birthdays and the like are looming.

Money Extra – **http://www.moneyextra.com** Very slick financial advice site which helps you search for the best rates on mortgages, credit cars, personal loans or get quotes for various types of insurance. There's also lots of basic advice and guides to different financial products.

Health A to Z – **http://www.healthatoz.com/** Vast American site that

< 377 >

covers sickness and health, has various news stories, lets you test your health IQ and ask various experts about your particular problem/illness. For more of the same, try Health Central **http://www.healthcentral.com**.

< 378 >

# 5 LOOKING AFTER YOURSELF ON THE NET

●●●●●●●●●●●●●●●●●●●●●●●●●●●●●●●●●●●●●●●

Despite the claims of moral guardians, the net is not an alien hostile space. It's not a dangerous place. But you do need to take care. Like the real world, there are people online who do not have your best interests at heart. And, unlike the real world, the net is such a novel space that sometimes you might not realise you're getting into trouble. So here are a few . . . no, not survival tips, just bits of advice on how to make your time online as painless as it is enjoyable. ▲

## Pornography, free speech and protecting your kids online

It's a shame that a book like this inevitably has to devote more space to the 'threats' the net poses to children than to the benefits it offers. However, hysterical reporting has set the agenda and, in a way, become self-fulfilling prophecy. If they hear often enough that the net is awash with pornography, what do you think children are going to think about when they do get online? The net is not a risk-free environment. Parents

< 379 >

should not let children use it without advice, guidance, boundaries and some form of supervision any more than they would let them play out in the street without the same. The best thing parents can do when it comes to their children and the net is learn about it, be realistic, balanced and sensible. Then they might have a chance of communicating the right attitude to their children.

Now, pornography. Yes, there is indeed a lot of it on the net. It doesn't generally jump out at you when you log on, despite what alarmists say. That said, junk email advertising porn sites can be a problem – not the sort of thing you really want turning up unannounced in your mailbox, especially if you share it with the kids. On some search sites it's possible that running a search on something like 'little women' might either turn up sites that are a long way from Louisa May Alcott or cause the various programs running the site to think that you're looking for something pornographic and hence load a series of ads for X rated

---

### Read about it online – Children's Sites

For a quick way of tracking down child-friendly material online, try Yahooligans – basically a directory of children's sites put together by Yahoo **http://www.yahooligans.com**. Alternatively, try Kid's Space **http://www.kids-space.org**, a nice collaborative site where children can post artwork and exchange ideas, or Bonus **http://www. bonus.com**, a vast compendium of interactive games. ▲

< 380 >

pages. (Of course, the thing to do here is make your search more focused – for more information, go back to page 152). Some irresponsible webmasters do try to con people into coming to their porn sites – by using misleading meta tags which trick the search engines. (Their aim here is usually to make money from advertising other porn sites. The more people who turn up on their sites – whether or not they wanted to go there – the more money they can get for their advertising).

Obviously, if a set of links to porn sites turn up on the results screen of your search site of choice, you will ignore them, refine your search and get on with your work. However, your twelve year-old son might find it difficult to resist clicking the odd link. Parents should also be aware that some porn sites have web addresses that are very close to the addresses of popular sites. A favourite trick is to use a familiar domain name but change the top level domain. For example, the web address of the Whitehouse is **http://www.whitehouse.gov**. However, there is also a very popular porn site at **http://www.whitehouse.com**. Typos of well known web addresses (Netscape, Yahoo etc) are also sometimes taken up by porn sites.

So, it is possible for unwanted pornographic material to find its way onto your computer screen. But usually you have to look for it. If you're a consenting adult who likes that sort of thing, there's plenty online for you. If you're an adult who doesn't like that sort of thing, don't go looking for it. Of course, adults aren't the problem here. The problem is hormonal teens and curious children accessing this material. However, many sites are pay-per-view commercial operations. To get in, you have

< 381 >

to enter credit-card details and sign up with a service to verify that you are an adult. That said, all sites offer free samples as a come-on. And there are plenty of completely free porn sites online. The more responsible use some sort of adult check service. But plenty don't. Pornographic images are also freely available in some Usenet newsgroups – usually the **alt.binaries** groups. These tend to be ads for web sites, complete with embedded links. However, some people just swap images for fun.

In addition, there are indeed newsgroups covering the more bizarre sexual practices. There are some groups devoted to paedophilia and child porn. It's likely that your internet service provider is already blocking access to these, though they are accessible via remote news servers outside the UK. There are plenty of other things for parents to worry about apart from sexual material. There are racist web sites put up by Nazi-sympathisers and White Power types, sites denying that the Holocaust took place, sites that feature information on making bombs, sites that feature autopsy and accident scene photographs. There's also plenty of uncontroversial, non-visual material that just isn't suitable for children – discussion about recovering from sexual abuse, for example.

The web and newsgroups aren't the only things parents should be aware of. Recently, stories have also emerged about paedophiles emailing schools and attempting to strike up relationships with children. Though they're mainly a text thing, chat rooms are often filled with talk about sex. It's also clear that some paedophiles do hang out in chat rooms frequented by children. Online, visual cues that might alert you to potential problems are absent. So it's harder to spot dodgy characters. That said, it can be

< 382 >

pretty difficult in the real world. According to those who work with them, many paedophiles are capable of great superficial charm in the real world. They know how to get people to drop their defences.

So there's material and people online you want to keep away from your children. The first thing to do is to get this into perspective. The net is not packed with pornography, paedophiles and perverts. It's mostly used by ordinary people like you. So don't believe the moral panic-mongers. They're not that concerned about your kids. They're more interested in selling their book or TV series. Second, the presence of pornography and dodgy characters online is no reason to keep your kids offline. Most children use the net happily without ever coming into harm's way. You kids will enjoy the net and learn from it. Don't deprive them out of ill-informed fear.

I once heard a net user point out that certain city streets are used at night by prostitutes but that doesn't stop families using the road system in general. I know what he was getting at, and I'm generally sympathetic, but the analogy doesn't hold. Red-light districts in cyberspace run 24 hours a day. Plus, your children aren't likely to wander into a real red-

---

**Tips – IRC for Kids**

Chat can be a risky area for kids. However, there are areas of the IRC network that are specifically for kids which might be worth a look. Try KidLink (an IRC net for kids) **http://www.kidlink.org/IRC/**. ▲

< 383 >

light district in the middle of the night. But it's easy for them to find their way to porn sites on the net. The barriers we find in the real world – physical, legal, social – aren't yet there in cyberspace. In the real world there's a top shelf. Sure, there's bomb-making information around, but it's often under the counter at independent bookshops or hidden away in the less accessible parts of a library. Eventually a set of similar barriers will develop in cyberspace.

For example, a top-level domain for pornography has been suggested – X-rated sites would end in **.porn** for example – and it would then be easier to block children from that area of the net. It might work, though it wouldn't be without problems. But many pornographers would be happy to go along with it. Despite what alarmists say, the majority don't want children on their sites. They're not out to corrupt anyone. They just want to make money. Hence they generally want to avoid anything that might lead the police to stop them making money.

Some people think governments should set up legal barriers online to protect children. Some American politicians have a particular fondness for drafting legislation in this area, though it often comes to nothing. Oddly enough, the right wing senators who have pushed hardest to create new laws aimed at controling sexual content online might have fallen foul of their own legislation during the whole Zippergate fiasco. The same right wingers wanted to release that windy combination of pornographic rumbling and legalistic prose, The Starr Report, on to the net in order to cause Bill Clinton the maximum embarrassment. However, Kenneth Starr's document would probably have fallen foul of

< 384 >

laws designed to censor the net, if they had been passed. As it was, the Starr Report – one of the biggest events online in recent years – was blocked by some filterware programs (more on these shortly). That said, in the aftermath of the Littleton school shootings, it seems like that some sort of net censorship law will be attempted again. Actually, it isn't just Americans who are fond of attempting new legislation in this area. The British government is working on an E Commerce bill, which ranges far and wide beyond simple net shopping, in particular proposing new powers of net surveillance.

Certainly the powers that be got into a real state about the net earlier this year when it was claimed that the ex-spook Richard Tomlinson had posted sensitive information about MI6 agents online. Though they claimed they wanted to stop the spread of the information (and prevented the old media from reporting in detail on the affair), the authorities' actions ended up drawing attention to the apparent breach in security. In the end, the supposedly sensitive information about MI6 turned out to be rather dubious and some net conspiracy types suggested that the fuss had been drummed up on purpose to create a general sense amongst the public that the 'net was dangerous and needed to be controlled'. For a typically snappy column on the subject, and much else, try Observer writer John Naughton's page at **http://molly.open.ac.uk/ Personal-pages/citations.htm**.

There are areas where everyone seems to be in agreement (banning child porn, for example). But the law concerning things like hard-core porn and hate speech is different, country to country. And so far, the

< 385 >

attempts of individual countries at drafting legislation have been so vague that, if put into practice, they would cover much more than pornographic material, would treat adults as children and ruin much that's good about the net (the fact that it connects everything and that it makes it so easy for information to move freely).

Some free-speech activists argue that, aside from being undesirable, censorship on the net is also impossible. Hang out online for a while and you'll come across the claim that 'the net interprets censorship as damage and routes around it'. There is something glib about the way free-speech fundamentalists repeat this as if it closed the argument, as if the technology was going to decide things for us. But without taking draconian measures, national governments have found it difficult to block access to a site in another country that contains political or pornographic material they don't like. There always seems

---

### Read about it online – Censorship on the Net

Net users campaigned successfully against the Communications Decency Act – an ill-conceived attempt to censor obscene material on the net – and they continue to keep a close watch on worldwide attempts at online censorship. For details on campaigns past and present, try the Electronic Frontier Foundation site **http://www.eff.org**. For a British site, try Liberty's Campaign against the Censorship of the Internet in Britain **http://www.liberty.org.uk/cacib/**. ▲

< 386 >

**Read about it online – Ratings**

The leading ratings organisation online is the Retail Software Advisory Council **http://www.rsac.org** which started out rating video games but moved on to the net with its RSACi ratings. For the arguments against ratings, read the interview in the Internet Legal Practice newsletter with the American law professor Lawrence Lessig (who was briefly involved in the Microsoft anti-trust case) – **http://www.collegehill.com/ilp-news/lessig.html**. ▲

to be a way for smart people to get to the forbidden information. And the job of would-be censors is made harder by activists who delight in putting up mirror sites of banned web pages. Hence the rather bizarre spectacle of right-on activists hosting pages put up by scumbag Holocaust revisionists.

In the UK, the police have argued that plenty of existing laws do apply to the net and they have put pressure on UK ISPs to block access to newsgroups that carry illegal or obscene material or face prosecution themselves. Critics argue that the police are setting themselves up as censors and are disregarding a complex set of legal issues. Put simply, the police claim the ISPs are 'publishers' of this material and are legally responsible. ISPs argue that they are merely carriers of this stuff and hence are not responsible. You don't prosecute the telephone companies if people use their lines to conspire to commit crimes, they suggest. The

< 387 >

---

**Read about it online – Resources for parents**

Mums and dads who want to keep up with their kids could try The
Parent's Guide to the Information Superhighway, a guide put up by
The Children's Partnership **http://www.childrenspartnership.org/bbar/
pbpg.html**. Despite the outdated I-way talk, it's pretty useful. For
some more general advice that takes in computers and CD ROMs,
try the Parents Information Network **http://www.pin-parents.com**. ▲

---

whole thing's a bit more complex than this, but you get the gist. In practice, though this isn't completely resolved, many UK ISPs have blocked
access to newsgroups used by paedophiles.

The UK net industry has argued that it can regulate itself and has set
up the Internet Watch Foundation **http://www.iwf.org.uk**, which collects
reports about child porn online – amongst other things – and alerts ISPs.
The net industry in general is anti-legislation. It would prefer a system of
ratings used in combination with blocking software. The idea here is that
sites are rated according to their content. Then parents can install and
configure special software that blocks access to certain categories of sites.
This was deemed to be the perfect solution by many techno-gurus, since
it seemed to put control in the hands of individual users but didn't affect
the general space of the net.

Unfortunately, it's not that simple. Critics say the ratings system
currently being implemented – PICS, aka Platform for Internet Content

< 388 >

Selection – actually brings an unacceptably high level of regulation to the net as a whole. Again, this is fairly complex, but the problem is that PICS allows for control beyond the level of individual. ISPs and even countries can use it to block access to certain sites. And once a site is rated and filtered, it will disappear completely. You won't know it exists. Worried by PICS, some net users have now come round to the opinion that carefully framed legislation might in the end be the best way to protect children online and preserve the freedoms made possible by the net. Unfortunately, the net has become caught up in the larger, ongoing moral panic about children. So it's highly unlikely that people will take the time to develop sensible ideas about how to make legislation work. But you can do your bit, simply by taking a sensible and realistic attitude to the net and your children.

## Setting guidelines and boundaries for children online

If you have a family computer, think about where you put it. Don't allow your child to keep it in his or her bedroom. Set it up in a communal space where they will at least feel you're keeping an eye on them. Don't let them password-protect areas of the computer. Use the computer yourself and keep an eye on any new bits of software or new files that appear on it. You may want to give older children their own computer (and net connection) but recognise the implications of that decision. Recognise that you will (a) have to talk to them more about what they do online (not something teenagers will relish) and (b) have to trust them more. You can make the choice not to let your kids use the net on their own.

< 389 >

---

### Read about it online – Larry Magid

He has established himself as an authority on child and teen safety online. Check his sites **http://www.safekids.com** and **http://www.safeteens.com** for advice, tips and some good links to kids/teens sites. ▲

---

Certainly with younger children this is the best bet. With children over ten, it's not going to work.

So set some basic guidelines. Set time limits on their net use and the places they can and cannot go. Tell them they can and should talk to you if they find material that makes them uncomfortable, if they get nasty email messages and the like. Tell them to never give out personal information (everything from name, address, telephone number and the location of their school to personal photographs) without your permission. Incidentally, they may be at risk here not from dodgy individuals but from dodgy companies who often try to con kids – with the offer of prizes – into handing over information about their parents. It's always worth checking the privacy policy on sites your kids use a lot. Finally, make sure your kids know that they must never meet online friends without checking with you first. If you do agree to meet someone, go with your children and make sure the meeting is in a public place.

If you don't trust your children to resist temptation, you can set up a few technological barriers. First, AOL and a few ISPs sell themselves as

< 390 >

family operations and provide ways for you to block access to 'unacceptable' material. If you want uncensored access to the net for yourself, sign up with a more liberal ISP and install blocking software. Several programs are on offer. The best known are probably Cyber Sitter **http://www.cybersitter.com**, Cyber Patrol **http://www.cyberpatrol.com**, Net Nanny **http://www.netnanny.com** and Surf Watch **http://www.surfwatch. com,** but plenty more are coming on the market. These do the same sorts of things but all work in slightly different ways, so visit the web pages for more information. Filterware blocks access to certain sorts of sites and let you set times during which the net can (or cannot) be used. They all use some sort of list of unsuitable sites, which they compile in various ways. Some let you unblock certain sites if you think they're fine for your kids. Some let you choose more sites to be blocked. Most record attempts to access restricted web sites. Some let you restrict access to certain areas of your computer as well.

These programs are fine if you want to let younger children use the net unsupervised. If you've got teenage children, it's more complicated. For one thing, computer-literate teens might find a way round blocking software. Filterware also needs maintenance. The list of banned sites is constantly changing. New sites appear. Old ones disappear. So you'll need to download a new list of censored sites fairly frequently. More importantly, many of these programs come with a built-in political agenda. As part of their right-wing family-values approach, they block access to non-pornographic sites promoting gay/feminist politics. Unfortunately, it's often unclear what some programs are blocking. Not

< 391 >

## Read about it online – Filterware critics

One of the most determined filterware critics is Bennett Haselton, founder of Peace Fire, the Youth Alliance Against Internet Censorship. His site – **http://www.peacefire.org** – has extensive reports on the problems of each individual piece of software along with revealing reports of his rather rancorous dealings with Solid Oak, the makers of Cyber Sitter. ▲

surprisingly, some of the companies who make these programs won't reveal what's on their banned list. They work hard on compiling it and see it as their crucial piece of intellectual property.

It's obviously up to individuals whether they use these programs. However, the increasing use of filterware programs by public libraries is more contentious. Some libraries seem unaware of the hidden agendas of many of these programs. Beyond that, a real problem with many of these programs is that they often just don't work that well. They can't keep up with the web. Recently the Censorware Project **http://www.censorware.org** released a report on Bess, a popular filter program, which revealed that whilst it didn't block some porn sites, it did block a host of other sites. Some were the kinds of activist/left leaning sites these programs often block. But others were completely harmless. For example, Bess stopped users accessing a site that featured a selection of Biblical passages compiled by Thomas Jefferson. In general, if I were going to use one of these

< 392 >

programs, I'd want to know what they blocked. I'd also want to be able to add sites to the blocked list and to take off others that I thought were fine. Some filterware programs do now give users a measure of control. It's your choice. You don't necessarily need to install software to begin blocking sites. Both the browsers allow some web filtering. If you want to try it out:

▶ In Internet Explorer select the **Tools** menu, then **Internet Options**, then click the **Content** tab. Click the **Enable** button in the **Content Advisor** section. You'll go to a **Content Advisor** dialog box. Once you set a password, you can use a little slider control to set acceptable levels as far as Language, Nudity, Sex and Violence are concerned. You can also set up a list of approved sites and create passwords that allow access to restricted material.

▶ In the Mac version of Internet Explorer, select the **Edit** menu, then **Preferences**, then in the **Web Browser** section, click on **Ratings**.

▶ In Netscape, get online, then select the **Help** menu, then **NetWatch**. Then click the **NetWatch Set Up** link, then click the **New User** button. You then have to specify the levels of nudity and language that you'll tolerate and choose a password.

Both browsers use the RSACi ratings and the Safe Surf ratings. Both are PICs-compliant ratings systems. You can either pick one or use both at the same time. For more information on how each system works, go the RSAC page **http://www.rsac.org** or try the Safe Surf page **http://www.safesurf.com**. Both pages have information on how to set up content filters in the two big browsers, just in case you're confused.

< 393 >

Blocking access isn't the only option. You can also snoop on your children's use of the net. Filterware programs allow a measure of this. But there are now specially dedicated surveillance programs that will tell you everything your child gets up to online and will even mail you at work if they click on something naughty. Basically these are home versions of the programs that are now used in many offices. One of the best known products in this area is Prudence **http://www.bluewolfnet. com/pru.htm**. It was launched in 1998 and doesn't really seem to have caught on.

Certainly, using surveillance technology on your kids does seem rather drastic. If you install something like Prudence, you can either tell them you're using it or keep it secret. The latter seems a particularly unhealthy option. Parents might find out more than they bargained for about their children (and what they think of their mum and dad). Are you ready for outing by software, for example? On the other hand, if you do tell your kids you're using surveillance software, you can see how it might be incorporated into adolescent rites of passage. When they seem old enough to look after themselves, you can make a big deal of turning the thing off.

Of course, your browser is already a surveillance tool. It keeps a record of where you've been (in the **History** file), stores pages you've visited in the cache, retains addresses entered in its location bar and has a file filled with cookies – special identifying files placed by some sites on your hard disk (more about these later). So if you do want to keep a less invasive check on what Junior has been up to, look in these.

▶ In Internet Explorer, your cookies will be in a **Cookies** folder in the general Windows directory.

< 394 >

### Tips – Clearing Your Machine

If you choose to check out porn on the net using the same software as your kids, that is, of course, your business. However, your browser can easily make it your kids' business. The URLs will be in the **History** file, the pages in the cache and the addresses in the location bar (if that's where you entered them) unless you clear them out. Some sites may also put cookies in your browser which identify whoever happens to be using the browser as a porn consumer. Some sites will then target what they see as appropriate advertising at whoever is using your browser. So, if you want to protect your kids (and keep your late-night surfing to yourself), you'll need to clear **History**, the cache, the location bar and your cookies. ▲

▶ In Navigator, the cookies will be in **cookies.txt** in the **Users** folder. You'll find it under Netscape in your computer's general file directory

Of course, smart kids will know about all this. But a completely clear **History** file and an empty cache after a couple of hours' surfing is suspicious. Note that Messenger and Outlook Express also save details of newsgroups that have been subscribed to, then unsubscribed. Just spend some time looking around in the files and folders. If you're really obsessive, a good utilities program will also enable you to recover deleted files. So you can tell if your child has downloaded images, transferred them to

< 395 >

a floppy disc, then deleted them. Of course, if you're that obsessive, especially without grounds for suspicion, it may be you, and not your kids, who needs help.

Finally, when people talk about protecting kids online, it always seems to be in the context of dangerous material or people. In fact, plain vanilla chat can end up being harmful. Some children find it incredibly compelling. Even if all they're doing is nattering about Robbie Williams or the new Chelsea away strip, it can be a problem if done to excess. So keep a tactful eye on them and make sure that chat (and the net in general) doesn't stop them from enjoying other things. You could always try one of those pieces of software that tots up the time spent online (also useful when it comes to keeping your own net use under control). Try Net Meter **http://www.cracker.u-net.com/**.

## Privacy on the net

The fact that the net allows ordinary people to communicate anonymously has been much discussed. The online porn business clearly benefits because its customers feel that they are acting (if that's the word) in private, that there's no one watching them download those dirty pictures the way there might be if they reached up to the top shelf in their local newsagents. In chat rooms and MUDs people continue to play fast and loose with the truth about themselves, because they feel that other users only know the personal details they choose to reveal. However, it's become clear that there are people taking note when you download porn. And some chat-room users know how to sniff around

< 396 >

your software and retrieve the email address you may have entered during configuration (an email address that might reveal your real name). The net may allow a superficial kind of anonymity. But at a more fundamental level, much of what you do online is accessible to all sorts of people who know how to look. The web, in particular, now looks almost purpose-built to collect and process personal data about ordinary users. As privacy activists have pointed out, the net is redefining the nature of privacy, is allowing governments and corporations greater and greater access to the lives of ordinary people. So first, be aware of the lack of real privacy online. Don't assume that anything you do or say online is private. Take precautions and get involved in the ongoing debate about privacy online.

## Privacy Online at Work

This should really be the shortest section in this book. Put simply, there is no online privacy at work. Assume that your boss is using software to track your use of the net. Assume that he or she owns whatever you say online. The law has tended to back this up so far. Don't use the net at work for serious personal communications. Don't use email for anything that might get you into trouble. It will be impossible to delete it easily, since it will be stored in all sorts of places. And simply deleting sensitive email is never enough. People will be able to retrieve it, if they feel the need. To really get rid of email you need a file wiping utility. Also, don't use the web for non-work related activities. It's likely the boss will know exactly what you're up to. Download porn on company time and you

< 397 >

## Read about it online – EPIC

For information on privacy online, try the Electronic Privacy
Information Centre at http://epic.org. For more general information
on privacy, try Privacy International **http://www.privacy.org/pi/**. For
British information about net politics, including privacy online, try
Yaman Akdeniz's excellent Cyber Rights and Cyber Liberties site
**http://www.cyber-rights.org**. ▲

may end up fired. You can keep personal communications at work
private by using web mail but your boss will still know if you spend a lot
of time at a web mail site. The only thing you can really do at work is
find out what the privacy policy is and whether surveillance software is
being used.

## Read about it online – Sacked for net shopping

Getting the sack for downloading porn in the office is nothing new.
But last summer, it was reported that a woman had been fired for
researching her holiday online during company time. The facts of
the case were disputed. The BBC Online report about it is at
**http://194.130.56.40/hi/english/business/the_company_file/newsid_
370000/370497.stm**. ▲

< 398 >

## Internet Service Providers and Privacy

When you're thinking of signing up with an ISP, check their privacy policy. Make sure they're not going to sell your personal details to junk mailers, on or offline. Check whether they include any personal/sensitive information in their member directories. Remember that it's possible for them to track what you do online, if they want to. Be careful with the password to your net account. Obviously, if someone gets your password, they will be able to read your mail and use your account to cause mischief in your name. Don't ever give it out to anyone online, even if they identify themselves as working for your ISP. Your ISP will never ask for your password online. Never email your net account password to anyone. Change it frequently and choose a random combination of letters and numbers.

## Email and Privacy

The first thing to realise about standard email is that it is not private. On its way to and from your computer it will sit around unprotected on various computers. Even after you download it, read it and delete it, it will still be accessible to someone with a good utilities program. Just ask Monica Lewinsky. Again, the only way to completely remove it is with a file-wiping program. And the only way to ensure email privacy is to use encryption. An encryption program scrambles your messages so that they look like random gobbledegook. The most popular form of encryption online is public key cryptography. The idea here is that a net user has two 'keys', one public, one private. The public one is distributed to friends and

< 399 >

colleagues. Often people tack it on the end of their emails. The private key is kept secret and secure. If you want to encrypt a message to someone, you use their public key. When they get your message, they need their private key to decrypt it. Without access to the private key, communications encrypted in this way are very difficult – if not impossible – to unscramble. Encryption software also allows you to create digital signatures so that you know for certain who sent a particular piece of email.

Sounds simple, doesn't it? Unfortunately, it isn't. Though the business world is more than a little keen, the government and the police remain unhappy about the spread of so-called strong encryption software. They argue that it will be used by terrorists, drug dealers and other criminals to frustrate law enforcement. So they've tried to introduce encryption programs which, in various ways, allow the police access to encrypted communications. The net community is campaigning vigorously against this and some have resorted to direct action. In 1991, a programmer called Phil Zimmerman finished a public key encryption program called Pretty Good Privacy. He sent it to friends who then made it freely available on the net. Zimmerman was then taken to court by the US government on a charge of illegally exporting munitions. The case collapsed a couple of years ago and Zimmerman has since gone into the encryption business proper, selling commercial versions of PGP. It remains the most popular encryption program online, thanks to its rebel history.

However, the US government still prohibits the export of strong encryption technology. If you want to use PGP, you need to get it from a European site. The UK government has gone back and forth on the

< 400 >

subject of strong encryption. It has said that it wants ordinary people to be able use programs like PGP. But for a while it was also pushing a scheme in which all the encryption keys used by ordinary people would be held by an 'independent' organisation that would hand them over to the police and the powers that be with the minimum of fuss.

It's now dropped that idea but has introduced some rather dodgy ideas into the proposed Electronic Commerce bill. Along with measures that seem designed to increase the government's ability to spy on ordinary net users, the bill would also give the authorities the power to demand your decryption key. They wouldn't need a warrant or a court order. Instead, a police office who came into possession of material encrypted by you could just demand the key. If you refused, you might face a jail term. To keep up with developments here, try the Liberty and Cyber Rights pages mentioned previously. For more general information about cryptography, try the page maintained by UK crypto activist Ross Anderson **http://www.cl.cam.ac.uk/~rja14/** or Sam Simpson's page **http://www.scramdisk.clara.net/**, which has some excellent links and some interesting software to download too.

Incidentally, both browser mail programs allow you to encrypt and sign your mail. They're not as good as PGP, but still worth a look.

▶ If you use Outlook Express, you first need to get a digital identity from Verisign, Microsoft's chosen commercial certifying authority. Select the **Tools** menu, then **Options**, then click the **Security** tab, then click the **Get Digital ID** button. After that you can choose to digitally sign your email and encrypt it by ticking the boxes in the **Secure Mail** section.

< 401 >

---

**Read about it online – PGP**

Phil Zimmerman's PGP Inc is now part of Network Associates. Go to **http://www.nai.com** for more details and look for links to info on his past, PGP and the trial. Alternatively, try the EFF site and look for the archive **http://www.eff.org**. To download a version of PGP, go to the International PGP homepage **http://zone.pspt.fi/pgp/**. ▲

---

▶ In Navigator, get online, then click the **Security** toolbar button. Click the **Messenger** tab and you're given the option of encrypting or signing your mail. You need a personal security certificate. To get one, click the **Yours** tab then click on the **Get a Certificate** button.

Of course, email privacy isn't just about stopping nosey people from reading what you say. Sometimes you want people to read what you say. You just don't want them to know it was you that said it. For example, you might want to post personal messages to a public mailing list about depression or alcoholism. You might want to send anonymous email blowing the whistle on malpractice where you work. You can, if you use an anonymous remailer. You send your mail to one of these, it strips away identifying details then sends it on. Some remailers also permit replies to anonymous messages.

Remailers remain controversial with police and journalists, who in the past claimed they were primarily used to send abusive mail and circu-

< 402 >

---

**Tips - Encrypted web mail**

There are now all sorts of free web-based email services around, all offering pretty much the same sort of thing. One that has distinguished itself from the pack is Hush Mail, which will let you send secure encrypted mail via the web **http://www.hushmail**. ▲

---

late child porn. The most famous anonymous remailer – **anon.penet.fi** – closed after coming under fire from hysterical hacks and the Church of Scientology. There are still a few anonymous remailers up and running. There's a list at **http://www.cs.berkeley.edu/~raph/remailer-list.html**. Alternatively, try the Nymserver, which you have to pay for – **http://www.nymserver.com**. Incidentally, you can also achieve a superficial anonymity by entering a false name and address when you configure your email software. Of course, it means people won't be able to reply to your mail, though. You can use a non-gender specific nickname rather than your real name in your email address. You can also set up multiple web mail accounts and use them for specific things – keeping your ISP mail account for select recipients.

## Newsgroups, Mailing Lists and Privacy

In theory, you should attach your email address to newsgroup postings. That way, people can respond privately if they wish. In practice, if you reveal your email address in newsgroups it may be collected by the

< 403 >

---

## Read about it online - Anonymity

For more information about anonymity online, with links to
software, academic research and other resources, try the site put up
by the American Association for the Advancement of Science at
**http://www.aaas.org/spp/anon**. ▲

---

programs used by direct marketing monsters and you may soon find
yourself deluged with spam. So when you configure your newsreader,
you may want to enter a bogus name and email address. You could also
use an anonymous remailer when participating in newsgroups. There's
another reason why false names or anonymous remailers are also useful
with newsgroups and mailing lists. Many sites now archive newsgroups
and mailing lists (for example, Deja.com **http://www.deja.com**) and some
suggest that these databases are being used for something beyond simple

---

## Tips - Avoiding Spam

When you put a return email address on your newsgroup postings,
try something that will confuse the automated programs used by
spammers but will be easily decoded by human readers. One
popular choice used to be **yourname@nospam.yourisp.net** –
though the spam kings are wise to that one now. Try
**yourname@stripthisbitouttoreply.yourisp.net** or something similar. ▲

---

< 404 >

research. It's claimed that some employers run searches on potential employees to see what they've said in the newsgroups/mailing lists. Contributing anonymously might avoid any potential problems. Some search sites allow you to add details to your postings which prevent them from being archived and searched. Check in their help files.

## The Web and Privacy

By now it may have dawned on you that your browser collects all sorts of information about what you do on the web. The information stored in the cache and the **History** files is only the half of it. The real problem as far as the web and privacy is concerned is cookies. These are little identifying text files which some sites place on your computer when you visit them. When you go back to a particular site, it will be able to read the cookie to tell what you did there before. It will also be able to add more information. There are obviously benefits to this. Many sites use cookies to log your personal preferences. Shopping sites use cookies so that they can remember what you bought before and direct you to other things you might like. Whilst this sounds fine, you might feel less comfortable about companies surreptitiously snooping around your cookies, building a database on you and then sharing it with others who use the information to target advertising at you. As mentioned before, you can check on which sites have put cookies on your computer.

▶ If you use Internet Explorer, look for the **Cookies** folder in the general **Windows** directory.

▶ In Navigator, look in the **User** folder.

< 405 >

You can instruct your browser to refuse cookies.

▶ In Internet Explorer, select the **Tools** menu then **Internet Options**, then click the **Advanced** tab, then scroll down to the section on **Cookies**. Disable both options.

▶ In the Mac version of Internet Explorer, select the **Edit** menu, then **Preferences**, then in the **Receiving Files** section, click on **Cookies**, then select **Never Accept** via the drop down menu.

▶ In Navigator, select the **Edit** menu, then **Preferences**, then **Advanced**. In the **Cookies** section you can choose to block all cookies or **Accept only cookies that get sent back to the originating server**, which in theory ought to offer more privacy, if you trust the originating server. If you want to see how often cookies are used on the web, tick the option which sets Navigator to warn you every time it's offered a bite.

For more information about cookies, try Cookie Central **http://www. cookiecentral.com**. One of the neatest ways to deal with cookies is to use Luckman Interactive's free Anonymous Cookie program. This disables all the cookies on your browser while you surf, so no one can sneak a look. But when you get to a site that has put a cookie on your file and you want to take advantage of it, you can immediately re-enable them, then turn them off again when you leave. Download it from **http://www.luckman.com/**. There are lots of good cookie-control programs you can try out. Kookaburra's Cookie Pal automatically accepts and rejects cookies, according to a list you specify. The Limit Software's Cookie Crusher does something similar. To download either

< 406 >

of these or have a look at some other privacy protection programs, look in the Privacy and Access Control section on the general software site Softseek **http://www.softseek.com/Internet/Web_Browsers_Utilities/Privacy_ and_Access_Control/**.

Cookies aren't the only threat to privacy on the web. Some sites use JavaScript to copy your email address while you're browsing. One way to stop this is not to enter your email address into the relevant sections of your browser. Of course, that means you won't be able to use it for email. Alternatively, change the settings on your browser to block Java and JavaScript.

▶ In Internet Explorer, select the **Tools** menu, then **Internet Options**, then click the **Advanced** tab, then scroll down to the **Java** section.

▶ In the Mac version of Internet Explorer, select the **Edit** menu, then **Preferences**, then in the **Web Browser** section, click on **Java**, then make the changes you want in the **Java Options** box.

▶ In Navigator, select the **Edit** menu, then **Preferences**, then **Advanced** and look for the **Java** section.

You can achieve complete anonymity on the web via an anonymiser, which sets up a protective barrier between you and the sites you surf. Try Anonymiser.com, a commercial service that also offers anonymous email **http://www.anonymiser.com**. There's some good general privacy information here too. Recently, Anonymiser.com was in the news because people suggested that it wasn't as private as claimed, thanks to a couple of bugs. I imagine that's been fixed now, so give it a look if you're worried. But it

< 407 >

### Tips – Anti Junk Mail

You can run a quick check to see if your browser is giving away your identity – i.e. your email address – to sites you visit. Go to the Junkbusters site **http://www.junkbusters.com**, a terrific general anti-junk mail resource. Specifically go to **http://www.junkbusters.com/cgi-bin/privacy** and look for the privacy test link. ▲

can slow down your surfing. Another site offering something similar is Zero-Knowledge Systems' Freedom **http://www.zeroknowledge.net**. Perhaps a better all round solution would be to try a new program called Proxymate **http://www.lpwa.com**, which offers anonymous browsing and a junk mail filter. The neat thing about it is that when you have to enter personal details to access a particular site, it comes up with false information but remembers it next time you visit. In other words, you can enjoy the benefits of customising/personalising certain pages without giving away anything really personal.

Giving away personal data without realising is one thing. What about information you choose to hand over, when you register with a site or buy something? The first thing you should do here is consider who's asking for the information. Do they have a real-world address? Do they have a privacy/security policy? Do they tell you what they're going to do with your information? It's become clear recently that, after insisting it be allowed to regulate itself in this area, the net industry is still doing a

< 408 >

**Read about it online – Children's privacy**

Privacy campaigners in the States are particularly worried about sites aimed at children. These concerns seem likely to grow as kids are targeted as potential net consumers by sites like I Can Buy **http://www.icanbuy.com**. The US Government is attempting to bring in something called the Children's Online Privacy Protection Act – for more information, read the Federal Trade Commission's report on online privacy at **http://www.ftc.gov/reports/privacy3/toc.htm.**▲

very bad job of protecting consumer privacy. Information collected when users register at sites or buy something is being sold on and swapped without their knowledge or consent.

Sometimes on the web, it can be difficult figuring out who you're actually giving information too. Fortune magazine recently ran a story about a pregnant woman who visited a baby-themed website, noticed a free subscription offer for a magazine advising women on how to stay fit during pregnancy and decided to give it a go. Though the site she was visiting had a proper privacy policy in place, the magazine offer had been put on the site by a company that didn't. They sold her address around and soon the junk mail, spam and telephone calls started coming. Worse, the woman in question had a miscarriage. Though she tried to take action to get off some of the commercial mailing lists, she wound up being bombarded with offers and calls around the time she would have

< 409 >

### Read about it online – Privacy protectors

Lots of companies now offer to give users some control over their personal information. Described as infomediaries, because they're essentially a new sort of middleman, they include Privaseek **http://www.privaseek.com**, YourCommand **http://www.yourcommand.com**, Lumeria **http://www.lumeria.com**, and Privacy Bank **http://www.privacybank.com**. These companies don't offer complete anonymity online. It's more about control – you give them information that then gets passed on to approved net retailers. You know what you've passed on and who it goes to – in return, when you shop, you get discounts and frequent flier miles. ▲

been due to give birth. It's a sad example. Most of the time, junk mail and sales calls are irritating rather than upsetting. But that doesn't mean you should have to put up with them.

In the UK and Europe, we have more legal protection, when it comes to keeping our personal information private. Things are much looser legally in the States, something it's as well to consider when you use American web sites (especially online shops). Recently, the US Government proposed various guidelines for safeguarding people's private information online. They suggested that web sites should disclose when they are collecting information about users and say clearly what they will do with it, that visitors should be allowed to decide how that information will be

< 410 >

used and that companies should be accountable if privacy policies are violated. There is a Federal Trade Commission website **http://www. consumer.gov** that features the US Government's suggestions on how to preserver your privacy online and off, among other things.

In an attempt to show willing, some web sites are beginning to sign up with an organisation called TRUSTe, which is attempting to set certain standards regarding privacy and commercial web sites. If a site has signed up, you should see a little TRUSTe logo somewhere. For more information, go to **http://www.truste.org**. Aware that they are losing the PR battle over online privacy, various big corporations (Disney, Apple, Microsoft, Dell and others) have set up something called the Online Privacy Alliance, which will apparently attempt to set down standards to protect net users – for more information go to **http://www.privacyalliance.org**.

## Harassment on the net

Some techno-gurus used to talk about how the net would help people escape old prejudices and work together productively. It's now clear that, like everything else, this technology can be abused and some people deliberately use it to make mischief and cause problems. This can encompass everything from sabotaging mailing lists and newsgroups with wind-ups and spoof messages to making someone's life a misery with abusive and unwanted email. The press love to refer to the latter as cyberstalking, which may seem somewhat overstated to some. However, email is such an intimate form that a continual unwanted presence in your mail box does feel like some sort of invasion of your personal space.

< 411 >

## Read about it online – Harassment

For advice about tackling online harassment, lists of safe chat rooms and MUDs and much else, try the excellent Women Halting Online Abuse at **http://whoa.femail.com**. ▲

And if someone is technologically literate, it's clear that the net can help them obtain information that would enable real-world stalking.

This obviously isn't a problem that only afflicts women but clearly women in particular need to take precautions. Problems often start in chat rooms. So, as mentioned in the section on chat, configure your software so it doesn't reveal anything important or real about you. Pick a non-gender-specific nickname. If someone gets on your nerves, use the Ignore function on your chat software to make them disappear. If problems persist, report them to the people running the chat room. If someone gets hold of your email address and sends you abusive mail, use mail filters to block it. But not before saving some of it and sending it to your tormentor's ISP to complain (try mailing **postmaster@ispname.com**). If their mail gives a false name and address, look at the header for more information about them and their messages. Get help from your ISP. Ultimately, if you're worried, save the mail and get the police involved.

### Email and Harassment

Abusive or obscene messages are something that could come by ordinary mail. However, the net makes new forms of mail abuse possible. A tech-

< 412 >

nologically literate net user who wants to give you a hard time can mail bomb you – in other words, flood your mailbox with thousands of messages, thus rendering your mail account useless. There's not a lot you can do about this apart from wait until the dust clears. You can attempt to see if the bulk mail reveals details of where it came from. If it does, contact the ISP responsible. But if someone is smart enough to send you thousands of messages, they're usually smart enough to cover their tracks. Sometimes, people attempt to crash your mail by signing you up to lots of high-volume mailing lists. Here the only thing you can do is to sit down and unsubscribe from all the lists. If you have multiple web mail accounts, you will be able to continue emailing people while your mailbox proper is cleared. However, it is a hassle. But you're unlikely to receive a mail bomb, unless you're nasty enough to send out junk email and foolish enough to include your real return address. Mail bombs are sometimes used against spammers (and supportive ISPs) by activists – punishment in kind.

## Spam

People who have never been online get incredibly het up about pornography on the net. People who are online don't worry that much about it. The thing they get really uptight about is spam – unwanted junk email sent to hundreds of thousands of users at once. It's fair to say that, for the net community, spam and spammers have now replaced the government and clueless journalists as the number-one hate objects. Now, don't get me wrong. Spam is a major pain. But it's interesting to speculate on why the net hardcore despise spam with such intensity. Perhaps it's

< 413 >

**Read about it online – Spam**

The web is packed with sites about spam, how to deal with it and what to do about spammers. For legal angles and links, try the Coalition Against Unsolicited Commercial Email **http://www.cauce.org/** or the new EuroCauce site **http://www.euro.cauce.org**. For news, history, links and practical information, try Junkbusters **http://www. junkbusters.com**. Alternatively, try Fight Spam on the Internet **http://spam.abuse.net/** for information and links to useful tools. ▲

because it's a daily refutation of their misplaced idealism about the net. Every day there's more in their mailboxes. And whatever it actually says, the basic message is always the same: the net is not automatically a force for good. Perhaps it's also that much spam – with its idiotic get-rich-quick schemes – feels like a cruel parody of some netheads' early fantasies about making their first million on the net.

Leaving aside pseudo-intellectual speculation, it's pretty obvious why net users don't like spam. It costs time and money. Deleting the stuff every morning can be a lengthy process. And in contrast to real world junk mail, the recipient actually pays for the privilege of getting spam. There's also no disincentive to spammers to stop spamming. In contrast to the real world, there's not much difference, cost-wise, between sending one piece of mail and several hundred thousand copies. Spam has also destroyed certain online communities – some newsgroups for example. There are further problems if you actually take the time to read the stuff.

< 414 >

Some spam is offensive. Most of it consists of fraudulent get-rich-quick offers, fake charity appeals, pyramid schemes and other cons, all designed to trick the gullible into handing over money.

So the first piece of advice for net newcomers concerning spam is: don't read it. Don't even open the mail when it turns up in your mailbox. I have heard stories about messages that come with Javascript commands that open your browser and load a particular page if you do – another advertising scam. If you do read your spam, don't believe it. Sick kiddies collecting email addresses/ business cards/money for charity? A can't-fail chance to get in early on the next hot stock? A killer scheme in which if you send money and addresses of friends now you will, in just a few weeks, receive thousands of pounds? All rubbish. The second tip is: get angry by all means, but don't let it take over your life. Spam has become a fact of life online. You can do certain things to minimise the problems it causes. But you can't make it go away completely. So do what you can and get on with your online life.

Many junk emailers assemble their mailing lists with email addresses they get from newsgroups and web pages. So you could simply never contribute to the newsgroups and avoid putting up a web page. Of course, if you did this, there'd be little point in being online. A better alternative might be to use false email addresses when posting to Usenet. In addition, don't post your email address publicly on the web. Don't use your browser for mail and remove your email address from the relevant sections. It will probably have been entered there during installation/ configuration when you signed up with your ISP. If you do this, people

< 415 >

**Tips - Spam Lists**

Treat with a degree of suspicion any sites that say they will remove you from mailing lists. In the past some of these have actually been set up by spammers looking for more email addresses. ▲

can't sneakily snatch your address while you're browsing. If you do give personal details to web sites, check their policy on this. Setting up several email accounts (and keeping one for dealings in the newsgroups) might be one way to keep one mailbox spam free.

You can also use filters and blockers either to automatically send anything that looks like spam into the trash folder or to stop your mail program from downloading the stuff in the first place. None of these will block everything but they're still worth trying. There's some good advice on how to set up spam filters in Eudora at **http://wso.williams.edu/ ~eudora/ eudora-3-0-spam-filter.html**. Even if you use Outlook Express or Messenger, it's worth checking this out, since it will help you attempt something similar with your software. You can get extra bits of software to deal with spam. Try Spam Killer **http://www.spamkiller.com**, Spamicide **http://www.cix.co.uk/~net-services/library/** and Email Chomper **http:// www.sarum.com/echomp.html**. The best of these programs let you identify spam before you download it. They also provide safeguards so you can avoid deleting mail you actually want.

Another program worth looking at is Cyber-Info's Email Notify **http://www.cyber-info.com**, which lets you check multiple mailboxes and

< 416 >

web mail accounts for new mail and delete spam at the same time. Also worthwhile is POP3 Scan Mailbox **http://www.netcomuk.co.uk/~kempston/smb/index.html**, another general mail utility which can also scan for spam on your ISP's mail server. Your ISP should also be taking anti-spam action. Some of the best spam blockers work at the server level. So if you are having problems, call your ISP and find out what they're doing. If they're not doing much, you might want to change to someone else. However, many are trying their best to deal with spam and (in the States) some are even taking legal action against persistent spammers.

If spam does get through, don't try sending an email bomb back. More than likely, the spammer won't have given a real return email address, so there won't be any point. But it's not a good idea anyway. If the spammer has been using a legitimate ISP, you will only succeed in

### Read about it online – Net Myths

The net is a great place for spreading urban legends and myths. If people hear an interesting story, it's so easy to pass it on. That said, there are sights online devoted to tracking down urban myths. Try the Urban Legends archive **http://www.urbanlegends.com**. They were quick to point out that the story that appeared on the amusing revenge site Bitter Waitress **http://www.bitterwaitress.com** about R&B star Lauryn Hill insisting that she be served by an African American waitress was a new variant on a common urban legend about black celebrities. ▲

< 417 >

annoying them and they will thus be less likely to help you. Often at the end of spam, you'll see a return address you're invited to use if you want to get off the list and stop receiving mail. Often this is a trick. Spammers want to find out if a particular account is still live. If you reply you'll just get even more spam. Some people suggest you send mail saying that you're happy to receive spam but charge £10 per piece of mail. Apparently, if the spamming persists this will help you sue the spammer, if you take things to court. Of course, this will confirm that the account is live, so you might want to think twice about this. Most spammers don't supply a working email address. In that case, try protesting to the spammer's ISP (for example, send email to **postmaster@ispname.com**.

If all the addresses on the spam are faked, look at the header to see if you can figure out where it came from. You can find information on how to do this at **http://www.mcs.com/~jcr/junkemaildeal.html**. The Junkbusters site also has information on how to understand headers. Get That Spammer **http://kryten.eng.monash.edu.au/gspam.html** has more information on tracking down spammers. You can also get software which helps you decode headers, track down spammers and draft legal threats to send them – try Spam Hater, **http://www.compulink.co.uk/~net-services/library/**. The newsgroups are a good source of information about spam. Try **news.admin.net-abuse.email**. Alternatively check at **news.admin.net-abuse.sightings** to see if the spam you're getting has been encountered by others. If not, report it to the group. For information about spam in newsgroups, try **news.admin.net-abuse.usenet**.

< 418 >

## Trust and security

A few years ago, Pierre Salinger, JFK's spin doctor, went public with 'proof' that the much discussed TWA Flight 800 plane crash had in fact been caused by a US Navy missile. In fact, the crucial piece of evidence was a document Salinger had found online, a document which looked official but which had already been widely discredited. Result – he looked pretty dumb and the online media and net culture in general had a field day. They shouldn't be so smug. Every now and then, everyone online gets taken in by something that seems on the level but turns out to be bogus.

This summer's novelty pop hit, 'Sunscreen' by the Australian film director Baz Luhrman had its origins in a speech circulated on the net that was widely thought to be by American writer Kurt Vonnegut. It wasn't. It turned out to be a newspaper column by a journalist. She

### Tips - Fake Fans

You may have noticed the massive buzz generated online about 'The Phantom Menace' by sites that revealed details of the script/plot long before the film actually appeared. Don't think that film marketing people weren't watching. Expect more film fan sites that claim to have got their hands on footage/script details of a hot new film, footage that the studio doesn't want you to see. Take the claims with a pinch of salt. ▲

< 419 >

hadn't intended to fool anyone. Someone had put her column online. It got passed on. The authorial credits got lost. Imagination filled in a few gaps that weren't there in the first place. However, all the fuss did bring the column to Luhrman's attention and he then set the words to a vaguely plodding dance track.

It's pretty easy to fool people if all they've got is words (and their willingness to believe). This kind of thing is generally harmless, though Pierre Salinger might not agree. If you don't want to make the same mistake, don't automatically believe everything (or everyone) you read online. There's plenty of useful and reliable information online. There's also tons of rubbish. And there's lots of information that is tricked up to look official and reliable, but isn't. Some people are similarly tricked up. In the early days, a certain amount of playing with identities was seen as part of the net experience. It can still be fun, but as the net has become more commercial, there's a little more at stake. Put simply, there are conmen and women online looking to part you from your money. They might do this with spam – with chain letters and 'unmissable opportunities' to make money fast. They might do it with official-sounding email that seems to have come from your ISP and requests you send in your personal information and credit card details again. As a rule, remember that ISPs never ask you to send important information in emails. If you get mail like this, at the very least ring your ISP up to check it out.

Faking mail which seems to have come from someone else, aka mail spoofing, is very easy to do and much used by net pranksters. So if you get mail from **tony.blair@newlabour.org**, don't start planning the outfit

< 420 >

you'll wear to Number 10. Instead think hard about which of your friends might play that kind of trick. If you get mail from a friend that seems completely out of character, don't immediately assume they sent it. Similarly, on mailing lists and newsgroups, if postings turn up from someone that don't seem to fit their previous image, it's likely they're spoofs. If you want email that you and your friends can definitely trust, you can start using the encryption software mentioned above which lets you create digital signatures which prove you sent a particular piece of mail. In general, be sceptical when you're on the web. Remember it doesn't cost that much to make a website look good or official. So think about who put the site up and why they're telling you what they're telling you. Always look for a real-world address/contact number before you hand over information to a site. Be sceptical about 'guaranteed money-making stock offers' and the like. For more information on net cons, try Internet Fraud Watch **http://www.fraud.org/** or Internet Scambusters **http://www.scambusters.com** or Net Watch **http://www.internetfraudwatch.com**.

## Viruses and Hackers

A common and hugely pointless net scam is the fake virus warning – a message warning of an email virus which will infect and crash your computer if you download and read it. These messages are viruses of a sort: mental viruses which infect your brain cells and cause you to waste valuable time worrying about whether they're true. Ignore them. Don't pass them on. However, do take precautions about viruses. You're mainly at risk from software you download from the net. Get a good

< 421 >

anti-virus program and always virus-check programs before you install them. (There are three big anti-virus programs: Doctor Solomon's Home Guard – **http://www.drsolomon.com/**; Norton AntiVirus – **http://www.symantec.com**; and McAfee's VirusScan – **http://www.nai.com**).

Similarly, be wary of documents created using Word which are attached to email. These may contain macro viruses and should be checked before you open them. This was how the much-talked about Melissa virus spread. In general, be cautious with Word attachments. If they arrive from someone you don't know, dump them in the bin. If they come unexpectedly from people you know, why not get in touch to find out if they're bona fide, before you open the attachment

People worry an awful lot about viruses online, more than is strictly necessary. You could say the same thing about hackers. Some people seem convinced that once you get online, these info-age folk devils will seek you out and make your life a misery. The truth is, most hackers

---

### Read about it online – Virus myths

For a very useful guide to online hoaxes, try the About.com Urban Legends page **http://urbanlegends.about.com** and look for the Net Hoaxes and Virus Hoaxes links. Alternatively, try the Computer Virus Myths homepage **http://kumite.com/myths**. For news about real viruses (and lots of stuff about information war in general), try The Crypt **http://sun.soci.niu.edu/~crypt/**. ▲

< 422 >

**Read about it online – Viral humour**

The webzine Salon ran a jokey competition to come up with the best
letter to circulate with a Melissa type virus, i.e. something that would
persuade most people to open up the attached file and hence infect
their computer. The winner was a message purporting to be from
your computer-illiterate 'Mom' (no names, see), who claimed to be
having trouble with a cooking program and wanted help. For a look
at some of the other winning entries (including one from Mathew
Clayton, the editor of this book), go to **http://www.salon.com/
tech/chal/1999/07/31/24_results/index.html**. ▲

spend their time either trying to make other hackers' lives a misery (and
hence prove how hardcore they are) or trying to break into govern-
ment/military computers (and hence prove how hardcore they are).
Generally, they won't bug you if you don't bother them. That said, there
are a few digital-era grifters out there, trying to use their net skills to turn
a buck or score some free telephone calls at your expense. So take care,
especially on IRC. If you're in a chat room and someone tells you to type
a particular command, don't do it. It may let them take over your
computer. Be careful about the software you download from sites that
seem less than reputable. Note that both big browsers warn you about
software you download and information you send. Both let you 'turn up'
the security features. However, if you want to do something more, you

< 423 >

can always install so-called anti-vandal software – something like Guard Dog, which you'll now find at **http://www.mcafee.com/cybermedia/ default.asp** or eSafe Protect **http://www.esafe.co.uk**. These programs will watch over you while you are online, track cookies and tell you if someone tries anything dodgy (for example, accessing private files on your computer).

## Copyright and libel on the net

Digital technology makes it easy to make copies of things. The net makes it easy to share those copies with other people. As a result, according to some net theorists, old intellectual property laws shouldn't really apply online and we need to work out a new way of compensating people for the content they create. Unsurprisingly, many old-school lawyers (and their mainstream clients) don't see things in quite the same way. They're perfectly happy to hang on to the old laws and see if they can make them stick in cyberspace. Hence a regular net news story in which artists on their own or creative industries as a whole take action against web sites they claim are illegally using copyrighted material. Everyone from Oasis to Rag Doll (the people behind the Teletubbies) have attempted to crack down on fan sites which, they claim, are abusing their material.

There are obvious problems with this. The web is what it is today thanks to fan sites. They're often great resources and brilliant adverts for the objects of their devotion. So hardline crackdowns seem somewhat perverse. On the other hand, what if a fan site is making lots of money using someone else's material? There are other problems which seem more

< 424 >

### Read about it online – Domain names

The BBC recently paid a fair amount of money to Boston Business Computing so it could get its hands on the bbc.com domain. The other BBC hadn't set out to get its hands on the Beeb's intellectual property. It was just one of those things. Less innocuous is the case of amazon.gr – an Greek online retail site which has cheekily helped itself to amazon's domain name and its old marketing lines. It describes itself as 'Greece's biggest bookshop'. For a story on amazon.com's reaction to this (they're not best pleased) go to **http://www.wired.com/news/news/business/story/21321.html**. While you're there, check out the story about the man who owns a series of domain names like china.com and russia.com and aims to make millions from them – **http://www.wired.com/news/news/business/story/20818.html**. ▲

clear cut. The net takes home taping to another level. People can record tracks from their favourite CDs, create MP3 files, upload them to the net and swap them with other users. This is illegal, obviously, though not without benefit to the artists being copied, according to some. If you download a track by a band you've never heard before and you like it, you might just go out and buy the CD since downloading a whole album is still a time-consuming process. However, technology is getting better all the time and soon it won't take so long, which is why the music industry

< 425 >

is making a fuss about net bootlegging and attempting to introduce new technologies and formats that block easy copying. They're only following the lead of the computer software industry, which has long been attempting to do something about the spread of pirated programs online.

Bootlegging is a fairly familiar crime. The net makes possible all sorts of novel abuses of copyright and infringements of trademarks. Take domain squatting, in which smart net users buy up the right to use familiar corporate names online (as in mcdonalds.com) in the hope of getting money from selling them back to the real world businesses involved. In general, where it's clear that this has been done with some sort of intent to make money, the courts tend to find in favour of those

## Read about it online – Intellectual Property

Some activists argue that, under cover of responding to the challenge posed by the net (and digital technology), various corporations are trying to extend the intellectual property laws in a way that would drastically curtail free public discussion. For more information, look at the Intellectual Property section on the Consumer Project on Technology **http://www.cptech.org**. For some utopian but interesting thoughts on intellectual property, try John Perry Barlow's essay on 'The Economy of the Mind on the Global Net' – **http://www.eff.org/pub/Intellectual_property/idea_ economy.article**. ▲

< 426 >

who own the trademark in the real world. But things aren't always simple. A couple of years ago in America a toy company attempted to get heavy with a child whose nickname was the same as one of their products. They claimed, to general derision, that his personal website **http://www.pokey.org** infringed their intellectual property rights.

Some businesses have gone to court to argue that links made by one site to stories on their site were an attempt to benefit illegally from their intellectual property. In the States, Universal Studios called in its lawyers to deal with a site called Movie Lists **http://www.movie-lists.com**, which was 'deep linking' to trailers on the Universal site. The big ticket agency Ticketmaster **http://www.ticketmaster.com** has also taken legal action against several sites that 'deep link' to pages on its site. The problem seems to be that by doing so, the linking sites let users bypass the ads on Ticketmaster's front page. You could argue that the whole point of the net is linking, but Ticketmaster don't seem to see it that way.

In another 'only on the net case', Playboy attempted to take action against a former Playmate whose site used the word 'Playboy' as one of its meta-tags – the things web designers use to indicate what's on the site to roaming search engines. They claimed the meta-tag constituted copyright infringement and was an attempt to steal their traffic. The Playmate argued that since she talked about her experiences with the magazine, it was legitimate. Celebrities are also beginning to take action against web sites that circulate pictures of them in the nude – many of which are deliberately faked.

It will be interesting watching all these problems get sorted out over the next few years. In the meantime, what you really need to know is

< 427 >

how you can avoid getting a letter from a lawyer about something you've done online. First, think about the copyright status of material you use online. If you put pictures on your web page that you've scanned in from magazines, it's likely that, legally, they belong to someone else, so try to get permission or give credits and indicate who owns the copyright. If you re-post material to a newsgroup – an interesting newspaper story, say – make sure you say where it came from and put in the appropriate credits. Check with people before you re-post something they sent to one newsgroup to another group or mailing list. It will probably be fine, but since they will own the copyright, you should check anyway.

Incidentally, you own the copyright on any original material that you put online. So you might want to put a little copyright sign on it. That way, if someone decides to put it in a print collection of the wit and wisdom of the net, you have a chance of getting some sort of credit (and possibly even payment). The thing to remember about material you put online is that if it's any good, it will be passed around. Be flattered. Don't immediately call a lawyer. (A few of the features I've written have turned up without my permission on various web sites. So long as my name is still on the copy, it's fine by me. It means more people get to read my work.)

Finally, with regard to your own creations, written or otherwise, remember that the libel laws do seem to apply on the net. People have been successful in suing for libel over things that were said online. In the past, it had been unclear whether ISPs were considered to be legally responsible for libellous remarks that circulate via the services they

< 428 >

provide –for example, postings or articles that appear in newsgroups that they make available. Earlier this year, a case involving Demon Internet and the physicist Laurence Godfrey seemed to set some kind of precedent.

Godfrey brought a defamation case against Demon because of messages that had been posted to newsgroups that it made available to its users. Demon did try to claim 'innocent distribution of libellous material' but the judge in the case ruled against it because Godfrey had warned them about the defamatory messages. Demon were planning an appeal but dropped that in the summer. You can read the court report on the original case at **http://www.courtservice.gov.uk/godfrey2.htm**. Demon are apparently waiting for new legislation on this subject, apparently on the way as part of the E Commerce bill. In the meantime, if you want to avoid hassle, think before you sound off on the web, in a newsgroup, in mailing lists or in chat rooms. People are reading and taking notes. Make sure you cover yourself.

## Next Step

There is only one place to go next. You know pretty much all you need to know when it comes to getting round the net. What you can do now is, learn how to do it yourself online. ▲

< 429 >

# 6
# DO IT YOURSELF

● ● ● ● ● ● ● ● ● ● ● ● ● ● ● ● ● ● ● ● ● ● ● ● ● ● ● ● ● ● ● ● ● ● ● ● ●

Once you've spent a while sampling the delights of the online world, you may get the itch to have a go yourself. Looking at some web pages, it's hard not to come away with the idea that you could do something better. You probably could. But can you keep it up every week, week in, week out? Are you willing to spend the time learning how to add all the new multimedia features your web page is supposed to have to compete with everyone else's? Are you ready to spend some serious money on web-publishing software? Are you ready to spend all your free time working on your homepage? However, you shouldn't assume that taking a more active role online is best left to those who want to spend every waking hour in front of their computer screens. Web gurus say that you need to update your homepage constantly to keep it fresh. But if all you want to do is have a bit of fun putting up something your friends can check out, you can safely ignore them. And the beauty of the web is that, if you're prepared to forgo the high-tech tricknology, it's pretty easy to put up a simple page and then forget about it. It's also relatively easy to set up

< 431 >

mailing lists and create alt newsgroups. However, turning these into
thriving enterprises will take a lot of effort.

## Starting your own mailing list

If you're a frustrated writer, zine publisher or small businessman, a one-
way mailing list is a good alternative to the web for getting your thoughts
(or product information) out to the rest of the world. The idea is to get
a list of (willing) subscribers and send regular updates to their mailboxes;
sending your email newsletter to people you merely think might be interested shifts you into the territory of the spammer. You'll need software
to automate subscriptions and the like. Getting that to work is relatively
easy. The hard thing is publicising your list so that people know it exists
and want to subscribe. Then you have to keep up the flow of regular

---

### Tips – Do it on the web

In the last year, several companies have set up on the web offering
to help ordinary users set up mailing lists for friends and family for
free. You do have to put up with a few ads but the lists are so much
easier to use than the old Listservs. Archiving is easy too. Try
eGroups **http://www.egroups.com**, Topica **http://www.topica.com**, or
One List **http://www.onelist.com**. The one thing to watch out for is
copyright, as in who owns the words on your list. You might want
to read the fine print on some of the sites. ▲

< 432 >

bulletins, which is probably harder still. A one-way mailing list as part of a general web page can be a great way for businesses to build customer interest and loyalty – as long as it steers clear of spam. Two-way mailing lists (in which subscribers can contribute) are a bit more complicated. You don't just need to know how to work a mailing list program; you need people skills. You need to manage disputes, steer discussions without appearing to censor and generally keep things on track. If your list becomes popular, you'll need to provide digests for people who don't want the full thing. It can take up a lot of time.

If you do want to start a mailing list, first figure out what sort you want to do. Check with your ISP to see if they can host it for you. Then you'll need some software. Listserv is available at **http://www.lsoft.com**; there's an excellent manual here which, aside from technical details, gives you a good idea of the problems you might encounter running a mailing list. The other big mailing list program, Majordomo, is available from **http://www.greatcircle.com/majordomo/**. Check out the Majordomo FAQ for technical help.

## Starting a usenet newsgroup

If you really do want to start a newsgroup, there's an easy and a hard way to do it. You can start an alt group. That's the easy way. Alternatively, you can start an official Usenet group, with one of the officially sanctioned hierarchies (**soc**, **rec** and the like). That's the hard way. Trawling through the newsgroups trying to make some sense of it all may be hard work but it's nothing compared to the hassle involved in setting

< 433 >

### Read about it online – Big Step

People seem to be queuing up to help you take advantage of the net/web these days – and for the moment, they don't seem to want any money. Take Big Step **http://www.bigstep.com**, which will help you take your business online. It will help you set up and design a web page and will host it, all for no money. For something a little lower tech, try Pitas.com **http://www.pitas.com**, which gives you the tools and space to run your own weblog. ▲

up a 'proper' newsgroup. At least, that's what some people say. Usenet may seem like lawless chaos, but it actually has very rigid rules and people who (perhaps because they can't find much to read in the news-groups) spend all their time arguing over how to interpret them. Perhaps that's a bit unfair, but it is a lengthy process. You will need to get together enough would-be subscribers to prove that there is interest in your group. You'll need to get the name right and put it in the right hierarchy. Then it has to be approved, announced and voted on. For more on how to do it, go to the UK Usenet homepage at **http://www.usenet.org.uk**. As previously noted, the alt hierarchy was set up in protest at attempts by the Usenet powers-that-be to block newsgroups devoted to sex and drugs. As a result, creating an alt group is pretty easy. To find out how to do it, try So You Want to Create an Alt Newsgroup at **http://www.cis. ohio-state.edu/~barr/alt-creation-guide.html**.

< 434 >

## Creating your own web page

It's a safe bet that most people who get on the net won't try their hand at starting their own mailing list or newsgroup. That isn't the case with web sites. More and more net users are taking the time to set up their own homepages. It's becoming a pretty easy thing to do. HTML – the language used to format web pages – isn't that hard to learn, but now there are plenty of web publishing software packages which make the whole process as easy as creating word-processor documents. It's easy to get free space for your page – either on your ISP's site or on one of the web communities like Geocities. These places will also give you plenty of help with page design and will supply templates and the like. If you want to put lots of pictures up, you will need a scanner of some sort. And if you want to do some sort of cutting-edge multimedia extravaganza, you will have to learn some more complex programming (or buy some fairly expensive software). But if you just want to share your thoughts on The X Files with the world, you probably have the software you need already

### Tips – FTP software

If you do get serious about doing your own web page, you'll need a decent FTP client. The browsers are OK for downloads but if you're going to be uploading your own pages, you need something more flexible. Try Cute FTP **http://www.cuteftp.com** or Get Right **http://www.getright.com** or Gozilla **http://www.gozilla.com**. ▲

< 435 >

and won't need to do that much swotting. Most of the information you need is online. Rather than get into detailed description and advice, the next few sections aim to point you to the information you need.

## HTML Basics

As mentioned above, HTML is the language used to create web pages. Basically, it's a set of text commands – known as tags – which determine the way a document is laid out, the line spacing, placement of images, links to other documents and much else. When a document written in HTML is viewed by a browser, you just see the content the way the designer intended. If you were to open the same document in a text editor, you would see all the tags around the basic content. Actually, you can view the HTML code for any web page you're browsing. In Internet Explorer, select the **View** menu, then **Source**. In Navigator, select the **View** menu then **Page Source**. As you'll see, tags are enclosed by < and >. You may also notice that they generally come in pairs – an opening and closing tag. The closing tag usually features a forward slash, as in </BOLD>.

Looking at the source code of web pages can give you a few clues about how to use HTML. However, there are several useful interactive tutorials online which let you mess around with tags and see what they do. HotWired does a good introductory tutorial on its web developer site WebMonkey – go to **http://www.hotwired.com/webmonkey/teachingtool/**. You could also try HTML for the Rest of Us **http://www.geocities.com/ SiliconValley/Lakes/3933/frame.htm**. Once you feel like you're getting the

< 436 >

basics, go to the NCSA's Beginner's Guide to HTML for some more in depth information **http://www.ncsa.uiuc.edu/General/Internet/WWW/HTMLPrimerP1.html**. For a good general introduction to web page design, try Jonny's HTML Headquarters **http://webhelp.org**.

### HTML Editors

Some would argue that beginners don't need to bother with learning HTML at all. There are plenty of WYSIWYG programs (as in 'what you see is what you get') which will let you design web pages without ever having to expose yourself to any kind of techno gobbledegook. Professional designers argue that you shouldn't rely on these editors because they don't create 'clean' HTML and you will in the end have to go in and sort out the mistakes they introduce. However, this isn't really going to be an issue for ordinary users: they could get by with the latest version of Word, Microsoft's word processing package, which features web page

---

**Read about it online - Web Designers**

There are plenty of sites that specialise in advice for professional web designers. Even if you aren't that serious, they can be good places to go to find out what's new and pick up tips. Try HotWired's WebMonkey **http://www.hotwired.com/webmonkey/**, CNet's Builder.com **http://www.builder.com** or Website Garage **http://www.websitegarage.netscape.com**. ▲

---

< 437 >

templates you can adapt to your own purposes. It will also let you create documents the way you would normally, then save them as HTML. If you don't have a new version of Word, you should have received something you can use when you downloaded your browser. Internet Explorer comes with Front Page Express. Netscape's Communicator suite features a program called Composer. Both are fine if you're just starting out.

There are plenty of other HTML editors/web publishing packages you could try out – Hot Dog Pro **http://www.sausage.com**; Hot Metal Pro **http://www.softquad.co.uk**; Arachnophilia **http://www.arachnoid.com**; HTML Express **http://www.coffeecup.com**. Mac users could try BBEdit **http://www.barebones.com**. When it comes to creating and formatting the visual content of your page (the graphics should be saved as gifs and any photos as jpegs), you could do a lot worse than Paint Shop Pro **http://www.jasc.com**. If you want to see what the professionals use for their flashy sites, go to **http://www.macromedia.com** and look for the links to their web creation package, Dreamweaver or go to the Adobe site **http://www.adobe.com** and look for their Go Live package

## Some General Advice

Mastering the technology isn't the only problem you'll face when creating your own page. Even if you're just doing something for fun, you do need to think about design. After all, you want people to enjoy your page. And good web design isn't just about aesthetics. You also need to think about how people are going to be viewing your page. That big graphic file may look like the perfect way to open your site, but if it takes

< 438 >

several minutes to download no one's going to hang around to see the rest of your site. So think about design, who your page is for and how they'll be accessing it. You can get some advice on web style at **http://www.highfive.com**. Alternatively, just look at the source of pages you particularly like. Some people suggest you help yourself to HTML that you particularly like the look of. In theory, this isn't that big a deal for amateurs. However, there have been cases recently in which professional designers plundered huge chunks of code from others without crediting them. Even if you aren't in it for the money, there is something a bit cheesy about just helping yourself to someone else's hard work. Look and learn by all means. But try to adapt what you find. Some people even suggest that a good way to learn about web design is to look at bad web pages, although what constitutes a badly designed web page is still open to argument. Decide for yourself and try a site like Web Pages That Suck at **http://www.webpagesthatsuck.com**.

Another 'design' issue you need to give some though to is your domain name. If you put your page on your ISP's site (or on a site like Geocities), you'll be lumbered with a long, slightly clumsy web address – something like **http://www.yourisp.net/freespace/yourname/**. Your pages have more impact (and will be easier to find) if you have your own snappy domain name. Your ISP will probably be able to help you register something appropriate. Alternatively try Net Names **http://www. netnames.co.uk**. You could try using V3 Redirect Services **http://come.to/**. They will help you set up a more interesting name and then will redirect the traffic to your site.

< 439 >

## Tips - Free Web Tricks

There are lots of sites that are prepared to give you useful features to use on your page, provided you credit them and feature an ad/link to their page. For a guide to what's available, try The Free Site **http://www.thefreesite.com**. For more information and not quite so much free stuff, try Big Nose Bird **http://www.bignosebird.com/**. Alternatively try the toolbox at the site run by design company Elated **http://www.elated.com/toolbox/** for some advice and some free graphics and the like. Visit Free Find **http://www.freefind.com** and you might come away with a free search engine you can put on your site. Finally, if you start to get more serious, have a look at Link Exchange **http://www.linkexchange.com**, a banner ad swap scheme for smaller web sites. You show a couple of ads for a page, another site shows an ad for yours. ▲

If you're doing your page as part of a business, you need to devote some serious thought to the project. You can't just put up a page and expect it to start boosting your profits. You need to figure what you want a site to do: is it going to be marketing/pr-based or a transactional site where you'll actually sell things. You'll need to make sure it's integrated with the rest of your business literature/communications. You'll need to keep it well maintained and updated. You'll need to publicise it. In the end, you may decide that you need to get a professional in to do it for

< 440 >

you. However, it's always worth learning a bit about HTML and design: at least you'll have a bit more of an idea about what you're paying for.

### Publishing and Publicising Your Page

Once you've laid out your masterwork, you need to upload it to your ISP's server or to the site that will be hosting your page. Get in touch with your ISP to find out exactly how to do this. In fact, it's worth talking to them about your page in general. Though all the ISPs now offer free space for web pages, they have lots of little rules that may come into effect if, for example, your page turns out to be either controversial or incredibly popular. Once your page is up, you'll need to make sure the world knows about it. You can visit the sites of the major search engines

---

#### Tips - Affiliate Schemes

If you want to try to make a little money from your site, why not join one of the numerous affiliate marketing schemes on the net. The idea here is that if you review a book on your site, you can also include a link to a page on one of the big online retail sites where you can buy the book in question. If someone does click the link on your site and buy the book, you get a small percentage of the sale. Amazon pioneered this idea but now everyone is doing it. For a directory of all the different affiliate marketing schemes you could sign up to, go to SimpleSite UK **http://www.simplesite.co.uk**. ▲

< 441 >

and submit the details of your page. This can be time-consuming. There are sites which will let you submit the details to all the engines at once – try Submit It **http://www.submit-it.com** or try the Submission Wizard at Exploit **http://www.exploit.com**. You can also send details to newsgroups or mailing lists if the site is particularly relevant. But be wary of sending anything that resembles spam. You don't want your site to be taken down by anti-spam activists in its first week.

If your site is about a popular topic, you could try joining the web ring devoted to that subject – for more on web rings, go back to the section on search engines on page 152. If you create links on your page to your favourite sites, you can always get in touch with them and see if they'll put in a link to your page. If they do, it might drive a bit of traffic your way. You can also add design touches to your page so that it can be easily identified by search engines – the meta tags discussed in the section on search engines. Remember that abusing meta tags for a few extra visits is bad netiquette. People are unlikely to enjoy your page if they're conned into visiting it. Of course, the easiest way to get traffic is to do something controversial then alert the newspapers so they can run one of their Internuts stories, but if you don't agree that all publicity is good publicity, you might prefer to rely on gradually building word of mouth.

## Next Step

You should now know how the net works. It's up to you what you do with it. Have fun. Here's one last tip to be going on with. There's a lot of rubbish talked about net addiction. However, there's so much infor-

< 442 >

mation online, it's easy to get into a 'wood for the trees' situation, visit loads of web sites without actually paying any real attention to any of them, do a vast amount of research and never get round to your actual project, and confuse a vast amount of apparently relevant information with knowledge and wisdom. So take it easy: more information isn't always better. And remember – there is a real world out there. Sometimes the best thing you can do with the net is log off. ▲

< 443 >

# INTERNET SERVICE PROVIDERS AND ONLINE SERVICES

• • • • • • • • • • • • • • • • • • • • • • • • • • • • • • • • • • •

There are now hundreds of Internet Service Providers in the UK alone. Some are free, some charge. Here's the contact details of a few of the bigger players. For a complete rundown of all UK ISPs, try the specialist monthly magazines on the net – Internet magazine is particularly good here. Numbers starting 0906 are premium rate.

## Online Services

AOL – 0800 279 1234 – **http://www.uk.aol.com**
Compuserve – 0990 000200 – **http://www.compuserve.co.uk**
MSN – 0345 002000 – **http://www.uk.msn.com**
Which Online – 0645 830240 – **http://www.which.net**

## Free Internet Service Providers

BT Click 0800 731 7887 – **http://www.btclick.com**
BT Line One 0906 302 0100 **http://www.lineone.net**

< 444 >

Cable and Wireless Lite 0800 092 3001 **http://www.cwcom.net**
Currant Bun 0845 306 3636 **http://www.currantbun.com**
EidosNet 0906 326 3366 **http://www.eidosnet.co.uk**
Freeserve 0845 079 6699 **http://www.freeserve.net**
Global Nomad 0906 960 0061 **http://www.globalnomad.co.uk**
IC24 09067 444 222 **http://www.ic24.net**
Madasafish 01851 777 727 **http://www.madasafish.co.uk**
MSN Free Web 0345 002 000 **http://wwwuk.msn.com**
Screaming Net 0800 376 5262 **http://www.screaming.net**
TescoNet 0906 3020 1110 **http://www.tesco.co.uk**
UK Online 0845 333 4567 **http://www.ukonline.net**
Virgin Net 0500 558 800 **http://www.virgin.net**
Wireplay Internet 0845 757 7577 **http://www.wireplay.co.uk**
WH Smith **http://www.whsmith.co.uk**
X Stream 0870 730 6466 **http://www.x-stream.com**

Free ISPs are starting up all the time. For a complete list, why not look
in the Internet Section on one of the big search sites – Yahoo
**http://www.yahoo.co.uk** or Excite **http://www.excite.co.uk**. Yahoo is also in
the Free ISP game. Check the site for details. The company has also
joined up with Waterstones to help with their free ISP – go to
**http://waterstones.yahoo.co.uk** for details. Alternatively, you can pick up
one of the discs from your local Waterstones. Similarly, WH Smith now
do their own free ISP (in conjunction with BT Click and MSN) – go to
**http://www.whsmith.co.uk** for details or get a disc from one of their shops.

< 445 >

The big computer manufacturers are now going into the ISP business, bundling accounts with their machines. Gateway was the first with Gateway.net **http://www.gateway2000.co.uk** but now Dell has joined in with Dell Net **http://www.dellnet.co.uk**. Finally, there are two new free ISPs due to launch in the autumn that might be worth looking out for – FreeBeeb is the BBC's effort – **http://www.freebeeb.net** and Netscape Online is AOL UK's attempt to enter the market **http://www.netscape online.co.uk**.

## Subscription-based Internet Service Providers

BT Internet – 0800 800 001 – **http://www.btinternet.com**
Cable and Wireless Internet – 0800 092 3013 – **http://www.cwcom.net**
CIX – 0181 255 5151 – **http://www.cix.co.uk**
ClaraNET – 0800 358 2828 – **http://www.clara.net**
Demon Internet – 0181 371 1234 – **http://www.demon.net**
Direct Connection – 0800 072 0000 – **http://www.dircon.net**
EasyNet – 0171 681 4444 – **http://www.easynet.co.uk**
Global Internet – 0870 909 8041 – **http://www.global.net.uk**
NetDirect Internet – 0800 731 3311 – **http://www.netdirect.net.uk**
Netkonect – 0171 345 7777 – **http://www.netkonect.co.uk**
Onyx – 0345 715715 – **http://www.onyxnet.co.uk**
Poptel – 0171 923 9465 – **http://www.poptel.org.uk**
Prestel Online – 0990 223300 – **http://www.prestel.co.uk**
Sonnet Internet – 0171 891 2000 – **http://www.sonnet.co.uk**
UUNET Pipex Dial – 0500 567000 – **http://www.uk.uu.net**

< 446 >

# INDEX

● ● ● ● ● ● ● ● ● ● ● ● ● ● ● ● ● ● ● ● ● ● ● ● ● ● ● ● ● ● ● ● ● ●

< 447 >

< 448 >